WHO'S DRIVING YOUR BUS?

WHO'S DRIVING YOUR BUS?

Discover Your Flow, Recharge,
And Live Your Best Life!

GILLIAN GORRIE

First published in 2023 by Dean Publishing
PO Box 119
Mt. Macedon, Victoria, 3441
Australia
deanpublishing.com

Copyright © Gillian Gorrie

All rights reserved. No part of this publication may be reproduced, stored in a retrieval system or transmitted in any way or by any means, electronic, mechanical, photocopying, recording or otherwise, without the prior written permission of the author.

Cataloguing-in-Publication Data
National Library of Australia
Title: Who's Driving Your Bus?
Edition: 1st edn
ISBN: 978-1-92545-247-1
Category: Self-help/Self-development

All rights reserved. No part of this publication may be reproduced, stored in a retrieval system or transmitted in any way or by any means, electronic, mechanical, photocopying, recording or otherwise, without the prior written permission of the author.
The information provided in this book is designed to provide helpful information on the subjects discussed. This book is not meant to be used, nor should it be used, to diagnose or treat any physical, emotional or psychological medical condition. For diagnosis or treatment of any medical problem, consult your own physician. The publisher and author are not responsible for any specific health or psychological needs that may require medical supervision and are not liable for any damages or negative consequences from any treatment, action, application or preparation, to any person reading or following the information in this book. References are provided for informational purposes only and do not constitute endorsement of any websites or other sources. Neither the publisher nor the individual author(s) shall be liable for any physical, psychological, emotional, financial, or commercial damages, including, but not limited to, special, incidental, consequential or other damages. Our views and rights are the same: You are responsible for your own choices, actions, and results.

Dedication

For my husband Douglas, I would never have been able to do this without your patience.

For my sons Brad and Stuart – I love you to the moon and back. Hopefully one day you will read my book and understand that 'where there is a will, there is a way' and living a life you love is totally within your control.

For my dad and his ongoing support for whatever I do.

For all my clients past, present and future who, deep down, know there is more to life and realise when enough is enough. You are my inspiration and the reason why I do what I do.

To all those who have struggled in some way or another, this book is for you to help you find your way home.

WELCOME TO THE JOURNEY OF YOUR LIFE!

THE JOURNEY HANDBOOK

THE ROAD MAP

ROADBLOCKS

YOUR GUIDE TO ACTION AND EMPOWERMENT

MAINTENANCE

THE TOOLBOX

CONTENTS

Introduction 1
You have taken the first step 2

Part One: Welcome to the Journey of Your Life!

My wakeup call 7
My journey from childhood 8
Understanding your journey
from here... 11
Where are you sitting
on the bus right now?................................. 15
Your Life Circle 16
Your Life Circle map 20
Make a commitment 24

Part Two: The Journey Handbook

Introduction 29
Your journey to success 30
1. What you need to understand 31
2. Health check 37
3. What you need to know 51
4. The connection to the solution.......... 62
5. The rules to guide you 69
6. The road to success................................ 81
Your Success Circle Map 84

Part Three: The Road Map

The reality of life 92
Dare to dream 93
The road map to your destination 94
Release the handbrake 108

Part Four: Roadblocks

Diversions and distractions
are part of the journey.............................116
How do roadblocks show up?................120
Understanding your roadblocks.............121
Discovering your roadblocks 141
Roadblock awareness...............................149

Part Five: Your Guide to Action and Empowerment

Introduction to navigating your roadblocks 153

The secrets to success 154

Feeling stuck? Start the process........... 160

The process.. 160

Your guide to action and empowerment 169

The four keys 171

1. Good health..172

2. Stuck awareness 180

3. Honesty...................................... 187

4. Good communication 190

Communication tools 196

So, what's next? 197

State 198

Behaviour.. 231

Feelings.. 274

Negative emotions................................. 300

Thoughts... 325

Part Six: Maintenance: The Journey Continues

Maintenance 350

My journey continues 351

Your journey continues..........................354

The four pillars to empowerment and driving your bus 356

The Toolbox

1. Affirmations...381

2. Attitude of gratitude 384

3. Active imagination visualisation exercise 387

4. The power of observation: A different perspective 392

5. Breathe 394

6. Communication reality check/ relationship triangle 396

7. Communication sandwich: A handy tool for communication 397

8. Monthly habit tracker.......................398

9. Journal it out: It's good for your health 399

10. Stop, Think and Flick the Switch .. 403

11. The power of intention 407

12. Asking the right questions............. 408

13. Lists (A - E) 413

About the author.................................... 423

Acknowledgements 424

Testimonials... 425

Suggested reading 426

Endnotes.. 428

Self-love

Self-care, self-love, and self-awareness
often can be thought of as being something simple
like just listening to our bodies, taking breaks
from work or just eating more healthily.

Self-love is a state of appreciation for oneself that
grows from actions that support our physical,
psychological and spiritual growth.

Self-love means having a high regard for
your own wellbeing and happiness.

Self-love means taking care of your own needs
and not sacrificing your wellbeing to please others.

Self-love means not settling for less than you deserve.

Self-love is not selfish.

> This is the new year, the new you. You can pass through another year, coasting on cruise control. Or you can step out of your comfort zone, trying things you have never done before ... elevate from where you are and soar high. Make it happen!
>
> **Pablo**

The New Year's Eve party went well, it was so good to catch up with friends and family over the Christmas period. Now it's time to get back to work.

You are sitting at your desk reviewing the year gone past. There are no excuses or reasons for you to be feeling the way do right now. Work is busy and life has been good to you but something just doesn't feel quite right and you just can't put your finger on it. You seem to be making the same mistakes over and over again and you don't know why.

What is it that's stopping you from getting back into flow and creating those good feelings that have inspired you in the past?

What is it you need to change? So you can be the person you want to be, follow your dreams and just be happy.

Somehow you manage to get through the day and as you are walking up to your front door the postie catches up to you and hands you a package.

Even though you weren't expecting anything, you realise it must be yours because it had your name and address on the front and curiously no return address.

What is it? Where did it come from?

As you walk inside curiosity soon gets the better of you and you open it.

It's a book! It's called **WHO'S DRIVING YOUR BUS?** Discover your Flow, Recharge and Live your Best Life.

It seems to be just what you need right now. You make a cuppa and move over to your comfy chair, sit down and start to read.

INTRODUCTION

No matter where you are or what you are thinking, you are in control of your life. We must be the authors of our own destiny because when we don't write our own scripts, someone else will. To live a life totally on someone else's terms can lead to regrets, bitterness, unhappiness, stress and even disease. We only get one chance at life, so why waste it? It's better to make the most of the life that you have, right? This book was born from my journey of self-discovery. When I was encouraged to write it, I was stuck for a title that represented how far I had come and the philosophy I had developed along the way, then the epiphany struck. When I am presenting my workshops, I frequently use the phrase, "Who's driving your bus?" I use the bus as a metaphor for life. It was my light bulb moment!

Have you ever thought of a vehicle as a metaphor for your journey through life? The roadblocks we may encounter and the different buses that go to different destinations? So many of us just hop on a bus and sit quietly at the back. We silently wait until it's our turn to get on or off at the stops, we don't question who is driving the bus. It took me a long time to realise that I could drive the bus, take control of the roadblocks in my life and so I made a decision to take the wheel.

Once I started to make small steps towards the front of the bus, and eventually grasped the steering wheel of my life, I began to experience a major

INTRODUCTION

transformation. I became the master of my own journey and the captain of my own crusade. And you can too.

"Faith is taking the first step even when you don't see the whole staircase."
Martin Luther King, Jr.

This book is a road map of self-discovery so you can live your best life, a life you can love with you in the driver's seat. Are you ready to take the adventure of your life? Buckle up. It's going to be a great ride. It was for me and still is.

So here it is: *Who's Driving Your Bus?*

Gillian is sharing more in her BONUS CONTENT.
See exclusive downloads, videos, and more.
DOWNLOAD it now at
www.deanpublishing.com/gilliangorrie

You have taken the first step

By picking up this book, it shows you that you are a little curious and that on some level you are ready to change something in your life and get back on track to living your best life.

Deep reflection and self-awareness are a good start when taking the first step away from what you **DON'T** want, when enough is enough and you realise you have a choice.

My book might seem like a challenge at first because of its size. Please note that it is a self-help personal development program, and each part can be read independently from the others.

I am a big believer in the power of small steps, so just follow the steps one step at a time. Parts two and five are in the form of handbooks, resources to support you to move through your roadblocks. The Toolbox is full of lists and exercises that you can use to help you find clarity around your journey challenges.

You see, it's all about asking the right questions and going within to find the answers.

Where are you now? Who are you?

What specifically do you want? Your purpose.

What is stopping you from getting what you want? Your roadblocks.

How do you break through your life challenges and keep moving forward in a positive way? Gratitude.

Have you ever felt that feeling of peace and calm when everything is aligned with where you are right in that particular moment? When we are aligned with who we are, there are no judgements, no analysis, no excuses. It's just pure allowance: allowing ourselves to be who we are, to revel in our own uniqueness and let our light shine.

Believe you can, because you can if you want it badly enough. My book will show you how to get back on track and love the life you live.

Throughout the book I will ask you to actively engage with questions, write lists or complete little tasks that will strengthen your self-knowledge and self-worth. Just look out for the relevant icons so you know what to do at a glance.

Bonus Content | Journal Questions | Tips | Meditation/Breathe

PART ONE

WELCOME TO THE JOURNEY OF YOUR LIFE!

> *The first step towards getting somewhere is to decide that you are not going to stay where you are.*
> **J. P. Morgan**

HERE TO LIVE AND LOVE

We aren't here to hide and shrivel
we are here to live our lives,
to be whatever sees us growing
into love without disguise,
to take the steps and do the things
that make the soul sing loud and true,
we're not here to suffer through
smother joy or split in two.

Anything less than being the best
that we can be is not enough,
unless we tell ourselves it is
or we see life as just too tough,
and sometimes tough is how it is
but human beings rise above,
they meet reserves and hold their nerve
to find the courage in their blood.

It's true the mind can find excuses
and can be programmed into doing
what it's told, as it can drift
into places made for stewing,
but not the heart, the heart's a trooper
born to love, take to the reins,
to couple up, to feel what's real…
to close the heart off, that's insane!

Closed off hearts are worlds apart
From happiness, they tend to stoop,
to fend off, and defends their aim
While "I'll get hurt" is on a loop,
but hearts are bound to break in half
should they be kept from what they need,
and hearts denied don't ever fly
they limp through life, churn up and bleed.

To live is what we came here for
to live without the shackles and chains,
and to love, we're here to love
not to drown in fear and pain,
or hide behind another, a mask
or anything else that kills the beat,
otherwise we leave this plane
as lost remains incomplete.

And incomplete is not much fun
it isn't laced with thrills and spills,
we didn't come to choke the sun
to gorge ourselves on loads of pills,
neither are we here to wallow
in the mire or in the mud,
we're here to flourish, here to bloom
to open up the spiritual bud.[1]

Poem by Andrew Hobbs, 11.08.2021
Published on Andrew's Facebook page and used with permission from the author.

WELCOME TO THE JOURNEY OF YOUR LIFE!

My wakeup call

One Saturday afternoon quite a few years ago now, I was sitting on the couch, musing over the last few years that had passed. I had just come back from seeing my doctor, who wanted to increase my antidepressant medication. I had been feeling dreadful. I was tired, run-down and couldn't think straight. It felt like the whole world was falling down around me, and all I wanted to do was curl up on the couch and go to sleep. What difference was a higher dose going to make? Was it possible that I could start feeling like my old self again?

The questions swirled in my head as my body stayed limp on the couch. I loved my kids and my husband and the home in which we lived. Really, I did. But something inside of me felt wrong, off, like something wasn't in alignment. I felt defeated. How long could I bear this? Was this all life had to offer me? Was this all there was? Was this it?

Later that same day, I was still vegging out in front of the TV, when an ad came on for a health and wellbeing event in the city: The Mind Body Spirit Show. I had always wanted to go but never made the effort. That afternoon I made a decision to go. I had to do something different.

I bought a ticket and little did I know that the experience I had that day would change my life.

Making the decision was the first step. The second step was being honest with myself, which meant taking responsibility for the choices I had made. It was a bitter pill to swallow. Although a friend had told me this some years prior to my depression, as my life evolved I had somehow lost myself. I was living my life on everyone else's terms.

I had chosen not to steer my own life. I had made every decision that led me to where I was. Not recognising the roadblocks, I had to accept that I hadn't actively pursued my best life. I had been an amicable passenger, playing along with whatever others wanted me to do or be. It wasn't pretty to look at but it was honest and I had to own it. All of it! I just wanted to be happy and successful, no regrets. How was I going to do that?

Once I accepted the part I had played, my life really started to change. I was able to identify what I needed to mend and how I was going to do it.

PART ONE

I can assure you that it was not easy but it was worth it! Life-changing in fact. Now, when I look back on my life, I can see that those experiences were the stepping-stones that created who I am today. Taking an honest, hard look at my role within my life's direction was paramount to being able to change it.

> REMEMBER OUR STEPPING STONES ARE NOT EXCUSES, JUST THE REALITY OF OUR JOURNEY TO NOW.

My journey from childhood
Where my roadblocks started to appear

I grew up as an only child on a farm, isolated from other children. When I was six, Mum decided to throw me a birthday party and invited all the kids from school. When it was time for the event, she couldn't find me. I was hiding under the bed and refused to come out. I don't blame Mum; it's just how it was. I was bullied right through my school years, and I felt uneasy in social settings. Instead, I spent a lot of time doing things for other people to gain their attention and acknowledgement. I had never learnt how to stand up for myself and lacked that essential skill.

Unsurprisingly, my people pleasing ways didn't work. I fell further into my rabbit hole of misery, lacking confidence and self-worth. My school years were all about survival. Socially, I was a complete flop. I kept to myself, but this allowed me to develop skills outside of school, often working with my hands and getting creative.

In Form 5 (Year 11), my English teacher took long service leave. The principal took over the class and was appalled at the standard of my work. I had had the same English teacher all through high school, and she had never mentioned any issues with my work before. When the English teacher returned, my mum confronted her about it. Apparently, because I was 'destined' to marry a farmer, she had not thought my standard of English mattered. It made me feel like I wasn't worth investing in. That my teacher figured I wasn't worth the effort of being highly educated and had decided to drive my destiny without my consent.

I'm glad I didn't accept this journey, and worked hard to obtain a standard that would allow me to pass, and I did. I ended up passing Form 5 and took 12 months off. I had no idea what I wanted to do. I landed a job at the post office, and then the local supermarket. Around this time, my mum started working early mornings and late nights at a local school camp. This was good for her and provided her extra income. But for me, it was a nightmare. I was expected to do everything at home before I left for work: cooking, cleaning and looking after my dad. What I did was never good enough. I was often criticised and told that I never cooked well enough, cleaned well enough or contributed enough. The overwhelming attitude felt like, "Gillian, you're not good enough."

Eventually (and unsurprisingly) I collapsed from overwhelming exhaustion. It was decided that I would stay home and leave my job at the supermarket. I started making clothes and decorating wedding cakes to earn some money and fulfil my creative side. By the end of the year, I realised I was longing for more. The technical school in Warragul in southern Victoria offered an art course equivalent to VCE that included eight art subjects, as well as English and maths. It caught my interest as something I would like and successfully applied. By the end of the first semester, I had topped the class. At the end of that year, I received a teaching studentship and attended Teachers' College. I achieved my Diploma of Education and Diploma of Visual Arts, majoring in ceramics (pottery). It was a whirlwind! I was still very naive, but off into the big bad world I went armed with an education and innocence! My first teaching job was in a technical school in Doveton, Victoria.

At the time, this was a fairly disadvantaged part of Victoria. I was the homeroom teacher of a Form 2 group and I discovered (to my horror) that most of the class could only read and write at the level of an eight-year-old. I desperately wanted to teach them these skills, but my curriculum only covered how to make pots out of clay. I did some pretty innovative things with my class. At Teachers' College, I was placed in an experimental group

PART ONE

that consisted of English, maths and arts majors. Together, this group brainstormed how we could combine our subjects to create amazing content for students across the board. I implemented some of our ideas and they were very successful. I regularly spent my time outside of teaching hours – at lunch times, before and after school – supporting those students who wanted to do better. I loved what I did.

I continued on this path for some time and began spending a few nights a week at the pub with my colleagues. They had been teaching much longer than I had and cared immensely for their students. However, they seemed strained and burnt out. I didn't want to end up like them, so despite my principal's protests I left my teaching job. I set myself up in business as a potter and joined various groups. I became the activities officer for the Victorian Ceramic Group and organised workshops throughout the state.

I then spent two special years travelling in Europe, connecting with family, working in pottery in Wales, Scotland and South Africa. When I returned to Australia, I set up my own successful pottery business in Upper Beaconsfield, selling my work throughout Victoria and interstate while getting involved in the craft and ceramic groups in my area.

By this time, I had discovered more about myself and regained some of the self-worth that I had lost in my formative years. I was strong and independent. Running my own business made me feel confident; I was respected as the person I had become. Some days, I had no food in the pantry or petrol in my car, but I was happy. Every day, I kept faith that an order would be paid just in time, and it always was. I survived. It was around this time that I met my soon-to-be husband and started our family. Motherhood was an amazing experience. However, when you become a mother all of your focus is on your children. Everyone wants to give their children the best they possibly can, so I put pressure on myself to do everything 'right'. I did not make time for myself.

I began to revert back to my old 'people-pleaser' ways and lacked the confidence to see myself as anything other than a mother and wife. I was always questioning myself and little things started to affect me and I continually self-sabotaged. I became a stay-at-home mum, got involved in the community organising the boys' playgroup, kindergarten, primary and eventually high school commitments. While it was good to know I was doing all I could in my role as a mother, I was exhausted and miserable.

When the boys were teenagers, I had to go back to work. Once again, I was yearning for more in my life so I started teaching at a primary school; however, it was a very negative environment. I stayed there for seven years and slowly became more and more depressed. I gained a lot of weight and found it exceptionally challenging to enjoy my life and the depression set in. My life was totally out of balance. What had happened to me? Where did the happy independent me go?

I decided enough was enough. I weaned myself off antidepressants and began my journey through personal development and education so that I could be the best version of myself. The actions I took to turn my life around changed me forever. Fast forward to today, and I am not the person I used to be. I love who I am and what I'm doing. I am passionate about mental health awareness and education. And it all started with one tiny decision to take my life in my hands; to gain control of myself first.

I am now a Master Practitioner of N.L.P., Time Line Therapy and Hypnosis, a teacher, a counsellor, an artist, a published author, a teacher of meditation, a mum and a wife. I do the best that I can at any one point in time and I am passionate about teaching and supporting others to be empowered to live their best life.

Through awareness, education and action, I changed my life. I am excited to share my journey in the hope it will inspire others to empower themselves, and drive their own bus.

Understanding your journey from here

We all have a past and a childhood that shaped us to who we are today and the reason you picked up this book prompts me to ask you some questions.

- Do you want to get more out of life?
- Do you feel things are okay but could be better?
- Are you unhappy?

PART ONE

- Are you feeling stressed?
- Are you suffering physically or emotionally, overwhelmed, angry, frustrated or out of control?
- Do you know why you feel this way?

Action or regret
If you don't change something now, will you regret it later?
Many people make the mistake of letting their past define their future. They stay in their comfort zones where they have always been content rather than branching out and experiencing something new. Often, this inaction leads to regret further down the track.

Using the unique perspective she was privy to, Australian palliative care nurse Bronnie Ware identified the most common regrets we have in our lives after a series of interviews with her elderly patients. Ware published her findings on her blog, which she then turned into a book entitled *The Top Five Regrets of the Dying: A Life Transformed by the Dearly Departing*[2]. She highlights that many of her dying patients wished they had lived their lives on their own terms rather than the ones expected of them. Many wished they had allowed themselves to be happier. If you are feeling that something is not quite right, then it doesn't matter what you didn't do yesterday. You have the power to change your life right now and take yourself in a whole new direction. The choice is yours, and whatever you choose is okay. Just know that you and only you are responsible for the choices you make. Just know that staying where you are may not make you truly happy. Believe it or not, you are in the driver's seat.

One of the most important things to understand and remember throughout the process is that you are in control of your own life, your thoughts and your actions. It is possible to change whatever you need to. Whether you want to start a new business, land a great new job, get promoted, travel, master a new language, be the best parent you can be, further your education, take your talent to the next level, make a living from your passion, live a balanced life or simply be happy, it's up to you to take control of your personal growth and your experiences in life. You don't need to wait for anyone or anything else to change and be different. You don't need permission and you don't need approval. One day, you might regret it if you don't change what needs to be changed right now.

Becoming aware is the key

I want to introduce an important concept that I talk about throughout this book: awareness. Awareness is about increasing your knowledge or understanding of a subject, issue or situation. It involves taking a step back from the speed of life and looking at things from a wide, objective standpoint. To be truly honest with yourself is one of the hardest things to do. You may ask: "Become aware of what?"

- Who are you?
- What do you want?
- Why haven't you got it now?
- What is your truth?

For example, if someone says, "I can't do it," I ask them, "You can't do it, or you don't want to do it?" Your answers depict why you do the things you do, how you react to life's challenges, at least for those problems that have a solution. Sometimes there is nothing that you can do. Evaluating how you live your life, the choices you've made, who is in your life and how you spend your time each day, will help you to understand who you are, what you want, and why you haven't got it now. **Awareness through self-reflection can offer the most valuable insights and direction for your future.**

> *"Find your why and you'll find your way."*
> **John C Maxwell**

You must control the authorship of your destiny. The pen that writes your story must be held in your own hand. Your words and your thoughts depict who you are and how you live. Your mind and attitude determine the next chapters you write.

PART ONE

And you do have a choice

We make choices every day and if they are aligned with who we are then life is good. Sometimes though we can make choices for the wrong reasons, our why may not be clear. The key is to accept responsibility for the choices we have made in the past and through awareness and self-reflection we can gain the most valuable insights, receive our learnings and move in a more positive direction for our future.

> *"Everything that is happening at this moment is a result of the choices you've made in the past."*
> **Deepak Chopra**

Understanding when enough is enough

In a world of unlimited possibilities, how do you know when to stop and walk away from something? Is there anything in your life that makes you think: enough is enough; I can't go on the same way anymore because it does not bring me happiness? If there is, what is the first thing that comes to mind?

It could be enough of work, parenting, unhelpful habits, sex, social media, trying to look a certain way, trying to lose weight, depression, anxiety, illness or any aspect of your life that feels unfulfilled or out of alignment. Sometimes, it's like we've jumped on the fast track and can't get off. Life in the fast lane often leads to burnout. We often fall into the trap of thinking that our lives aren't about us – they're about everyone else. We constantly push our needs aside and fail to prioritise the things that enrich our existence.

This leads to feelings of stress, frustration, anxiety and unhappiness. Even when we become aware of these negative feelings, we keep going and push our doubts aside. Trust me, eventually you will need to let it all out – and you might find yourself erupting when you do. It's tough work admitting feelings you may have buried for a long time.

> *"When it's time for me to walk away from something, I walk away from it. My mind, my body, my conscience tell me enough is enough."*
> **Jerry West**

WELCOME TO THE JOURNEY OF YOUR LIFE!

> WHEN YOU ENJOY THE PROCESS
> AND TAKE ACTION – THE POSSIBILITIES
> ARE UNLIMITED.

Where are you sitting on the bus right now?

"I take responsibility for who I am and change the things I must to be happy. It's a hell of a start being able to recognise what makes you happy."

Lucille Ball

Clarification on this point is imperative. Figuring out what you want and where you want to be can only be done by evaluating where you are right now. It's time to get real. The entire journey is all about you and where you are going. Which destination are you heading towards? Are you in control or do others keep taking the wheel and sending you on detours?

You can choose to be the passenger in your life, and that's okay as long as you understand that if something does not feel right and you are unhappy, you can make the choice to do something about it, the challenge is, "Where do you start?"

This first exercise may make you feel a bit uncomfortable, and that is actually a good thing, meaning you're on the right track to changing how you feel. You have to know where you are before you can depart. If I asked you right now, do you know what you want from life? Do you know what you want to achieve in life? Do you know how you want to live your life? How would you like others to remember you when you are gone? How would you answer these questions? What would you say?

The first time I was asked those questions I just said I wanted to be happy. Well! Did that open up a can of worms! Why do you want to be happy? Why are you not happy now? And so started my journey. I had never asked these questions of myself before and it changed my life. In order to know what you want from your life, you need to continue to ask the right questions and truly

 PART ONE

get to know who you are, why you do the things you do and the way you do them. Get to know yourself inside out and let your light shine. Life is what you make it; the journey is an adventure.

These four important questions and the feelings associated with them is a good place to start, answer them if you can:

1. **What do you really want?** (You may say you don't know, and that's okay.)

Now ask:

2. **If you were to know, what is it you really want?**
   Is it spending time with the special people in your life? Spending time in your favourite environments? Creativity? Connecting? Laughter? Trying new things? Travel? Personal or professional accomplishments? What moments in life bring you joy, peace and purpose?

Now ask:

3. **Why do you want it?**
   Your why is the motivation for you to get what you want.

Now ask:

4. **Have you got it now? If not, why not?**
   Work through your answers, and keep them in mind as you begin the practical side of your journey by evaluating where you are in life right now.

Your Life Circle

The practical side of your journey begins with a concept called **Your Life Circle**. Do this exercise now and then repeat it in 6 months' time after you have worked through this book on your new adventure.

Life for most people can be categorised into seven main areas:

1. Relationships
2. Emotions
3. Finances
4. Spirituality
5. Health/wellbeing
6. Fun/social life
7. Career/business

In order to go somewhere new and make a change, you need to be very clear on where you are right now in each area. Remember, taking time to savour your past and clarify your present will revitalise you for the next phase of your life. Just be honest with your reality of NOW.

I will explain a little about each area and then I want you to use the questions at the end of each section to reflect deeply on whether you are feeling balanced and fulfilled in each area.

1. Relationships

While relationships, both personal and workplace ones, can be the source of acute and extreme life stress, it is often how we choose to deal with our difficulties that determines if and how our problems can be resolved. When problems persist within our relationships, self-esteem, respect, trust and unconditional love are tested and can have an effect on other areas of our lives.

There are three types of relationships relevant to our Life Circle: personal/partner, family, and friends. Having strong, productive relationships and the ability to get along well with others is of crucial importance in order to experience a strong level of self-esteem and a sense of belonging that can insulate us from the challenges we may face on our journey through life.

- Do you have rewarding, close and loving relationships?
- Do you make friends easily?

PART ONE

2. Emotions

Feeling emotion is life's barometer for measuring a life well-lived full of natural highs and lows that are unique to you. It is not the events around you that determine who you are but rather your reactions to them. You choose how you handle your emotions. People with good emotional health are in control of their thoughts, feelings and behaviours. They feel good about themselves and have good relationships. They are able to handle life's challenges, build strong relationships and recover from setbacks.

However, just as effort is required to build and maintain physical health, the same is true with mental health. Improving your emotional health can add to your overall enjoyment of life. Taking time away from work to refresh our mind, body and soul is a critical practice to support us in being the most effective and productive at all we do.

- Are you in control of your thoughts, feelings and behaviours?
- Do you take the time to do the things that you love to do?
- Do you have hobbies or passions that you enjoy doing?
- Do you take time out to balance work and play, or do you just work excessively?
- Do you get emotional on a regular basis?

3. Finances

Finances relate to your personal beliefs and situations surrounding money.

Are you earning enough to do the things you want to do and need to do? Are you in control of your finances? Having a solid, stable financial situation provides a reserve that is essential to feeling good about who you are, with positive expectations for your future state of abundance.

- Are you happy with the financial benefits of your job, career or business?
- Do you have enough money to pay the bills?
- Have you created a stable financial situation for yourself where your personal assets grow on a monthly basis?

4. Spirituality

Spirituality is LIFE:

L<small>IVING</small> I<small>N</small> F<small>ULFILLED</small> E<small>XISTENCE</small>

One needs to live with purpose and with meaning. The undisputed reality is everyone has a spiritual need. Some people are fulfilled by organised religion, and others choose to explore options on their own terms. One can be open to everything and attached to nothing at the same time. Spirituality is about tuning in, recognising your unique needs through meditation or just asking the right questions. Spirituality can be defined as thoughts, beliefs and actions that give our life its deepest meaning. You need to nurture and explore your inner self alongside your external reality in order to find balance, realise how perfect your life is and grow your relationship with yourself.

- Are you living a fulfilled existence?
- Do you nurture your unique spiritual needs on a regular basis?
- Do you take time to read uplifting books or work on your own personal development?

5. Health and wellbeing

Health and wellbeing refer to fitness, vitality, energy, and how we balance these to look after ourselves. There are ways to keep the blues at bay and to keep your body, mind and spirit healthy. Eat well, keep fit, do something you love, make new friends, learn how to handle stress, stay positive, have an attitude of gratitude, love yourself, have fun, be silly, and laugh often. A positive, vibrant and confident feeling comes from taking the best possible care of your health.

- Do you love yourself enough to do the things you need to do to take great care of your physical health?
- Do you exercise regularly?

PART ONE

- Is your diet conducive to optimum health, or do you regularly eat junk food?
- Do you live a balanced lifestyle?

6. Fun and recreation

These experiences create positive reactions in our minds and bodies as well as beautiful relationships and memories.

- Do you create time to have a social life, time to just be and do the things you really enjoy in life? Those things that make you feel alive?
- Do you prioritise fun? To live, laugh and love whether it be having coffee with friends, playing sports or enjoying your hobbies?

7. Business/career

The perfect job or career is one that keeps you fulfilled and creates balance in your life. Do you want to live to work or work to live? The context in which you use your skills and talents is a choice. Do you want to work in order to receive, a) - something of value, monetary or in kind, or b) - for your own satisfaction or as a duty of care?

Balance is about what you want to do, what you have to do and what you need to do. If you are not happy at work, then ask yourself why. The key is to become aware of the issues and know that you have the ability to make a choice and find balance in your life.

- Are you happy in your business/career?
- Do you know why you do what you do?

Your Life Circle map

Now with knowledge of what your Life Circle is made of, you are ready to evaluate where you are at in your life right now! On the your Life Circle map there are nine lines radiating from the centre, each line representing an area of your life.

WELCOME TO THE JOURNEY OF YOUR LIFE!

1. On each line, mark a dot and number it from 1 – 10. Zero being the centre and 10 landing on the inner circle. 1 represents the least amount of time/energy and 10 represents the best it can possibly be.

2. Join the dots and this will create the map of where you are now and it represents where your starting point is.

3. When completed, pick three sections based on the explanations below, fill in the appropriate score and ask yourself the questions that follow.

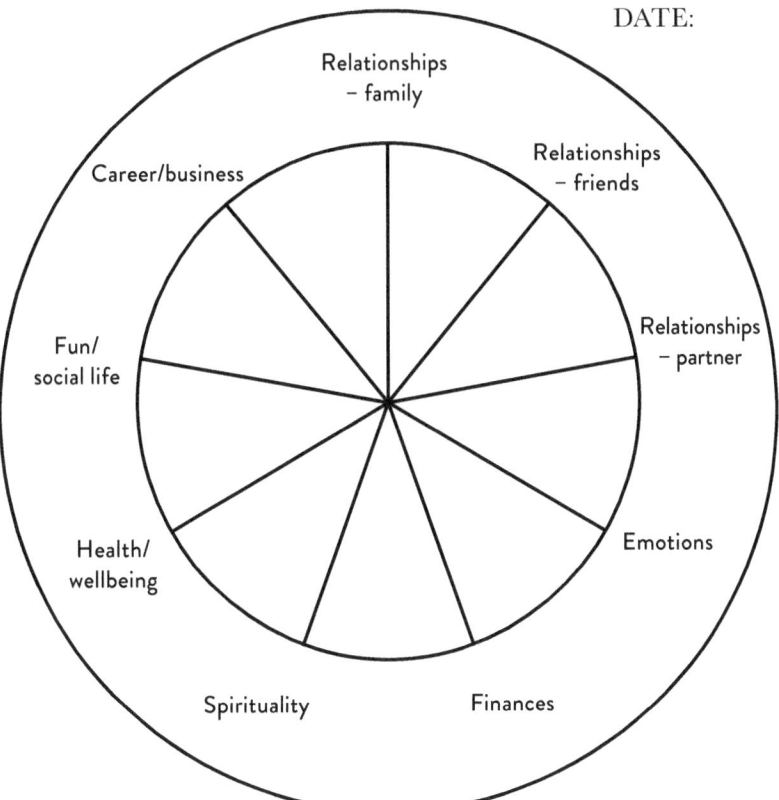

Please refer to the Bonus Content for an example of a completed Life Circle and one for yourself to print out.

PART ONE

Your first five steps to your Life Circle solutions

Step 1: First, choose your lowest-scoring section and ask yourself the questions that follow.

The lowest-scoring area in my Life Circle is:

Area 1: ....

Currently rated: /10

Step 2: Now, choose the most important area of your life that you would like to improve right now (note: it doesn't need to be the lowest ranked).

The most important area to me in my Life Circle is:

Area 2: ....

Currently rated: /10

Step 3: Now, choose the area of your life that you are feeling most challenged in right now.

The most challenging area in my Life Circle is:

Area 3: ....

Currently rated: /10

Step 4: For each area of your life you have chosen: [the lowest, the most important and the most challenging] answer the following questions:

1. How specifically, is it a challenge?

2. How long has it been a challenge?

3. What is the purpose of the challenge?

4. Is there anyone else involved in this challenge?

5. What is the first event that you can remember where this challenge was present?

6. How is this not a challenge?

7. How do you handle the current challenge?

8. How do you feel about the challenge?

9. What have you been thinking lately, saying lately or doing lately that is affecting your behaviour and your feelings about this challenge?

10. What do you need to change to overcome the challenge to get what you want?

Step 5: Reflective Exercise

Once you have finished answering the questions in all three areas, write down what you have learnt about yourself in regards to what is working and what is not working in your life right now. The following questions should provoke some illuminating answers for you:

- What have you learnt about yourself?

- What is most important to you right now?

- What do you specifically want?

- When do you want it?

 PART ONE

Make a commitment

Nothing in your life changes until you do. Before you go on to the next chapter and grab the steering wheel of your life, you must be prepared to make a commitment to yourself. Why? Because when the road gets bumpy you may try and jump off before you reach your destination. And we both know that won't result in what you want. Therefore I have taken the liberty of preparing a little agreement for you, one that you can use and read along the journey. You can look at it as often as you need, but I strongly suggest you make the agreement within your own heart first and just use this one on paper as a reminder.

> *"The only impossible journey is the one you never begin."*
> **Tony Robbins**

WELCOME TO THE JOURNEY OF YOUR LIFE!

MY AGREEMENT WITH SELF

I, ..., am committed to discovering my flow and recharging my life so that I can be empowered to live my best life.

I agree to commit 100%, be honest with myself and follow through on the tasks required to achieve my desired outcome.

I understand that I am responsible for the changes I need to make, and if I don't take action nothing will change.

I understand that change does not happen overnight and that I need to be committed to my outcomes.

I understand that I need to be consistent with my actions, and I know that if I need help, I need to ask for it.

One step at a time, I know I will reach my dreams.

Signed..........

Dated..........

> We all ... have an obligation to daydream. We have an obligation to imagine. It is easy to pretend that nobody can change anything, that society is huge and the individual is less than nothing. ...But the truth is, ... individuals make the future, and they do it by imagining that things can be different.
>
> ## Neil Gaiman

Imagine you are approaching a wall and see a huge doorway going through to the other side. You know, one of those mysterious, impressive entrances – exquisitely carved, ornate and inviting.

You stop and observe and take it all in.

What are you feeling? Scared, curious, brave, courageous, or even wonder?

I know how that feels; I have been there. It's that first step outside your comfort zone. You grab hold of the door handles, and they seem to have a power of their own. They swing open, and you quickly move to get out of the way.

Are they inviting you in? Of course, they are.

You take a few steps cautiously through the door. With each step you take, you seem to get more excited and begin to trust yourself, you notice how good, strong and confident you feel.

You reassure yourself knowing that you have made the right decision, you do have everything you need for the journey, and you feel good. Whatever it takes, you know you are ready.

As you stand there, just through the doors, the emotions settle, and there it is – you can see it clearly: a big, yellow bus with your name on it.

*Before you get on board, a voice from nowhere announces, "The bus is not taking passengers just yet. Please take a seat." You look around, and there is a seat in the sun at the bus stop. As you sit down, a young man in a uniform comes up and hands you a clipboard with some paperwork on it. At the top of the first sheet is the heading Itinerary. Then he hands you your **Journey Handbook**.*

PART TWO

THE JOURNEY HANDBOOK

What you need to understand for your journey from where you are now to living your best life

"

Life is a journey and it's about growing and changing and coming to terms with who and what you are and loving who and what you are.
Kelly McGillis

"

Contents

Introduction 29

Your journey preparation 29

Let's look inside your toolkit 30

Your journey to success 30

1. WHAT YOU NEED TO UNDERSTAND
Building a strong foundation 31

Our internal wiring 33

The brain 33

The filters and how they work 33

The conscious and unconscious minds 35

2. HEALTH CHECK 37

The chakra system 37

Understanding the importance of cultivating a growth mindset 41

Understanding positive versus negative thinking 42

To understand your Life Balance 44

To understand values 47

To understand self-awareness and your roadblocks 49

To understand triggers 50

3. WHAT YOU NEED TO KNOW 51

Choice and responsibility 52

Living at cause or effect 54

Permission 55

Acceptance is the key 56

Resistance to resilience 58

Intention 59

Clarity of communication 60

4. THE CONNECTION TO THE SOLUTION 62

Being you: the primary purpose of life 62

Awareness: to go within 63

Self-belief and self-worth 65

Intuition and wisdom 66

Flow and creativity 67

5. THE RULES TO GUIDE YOU 69

6. THE ROAD TO SUCCESS 81

Know your outcome 81

Make a commitment to yourself 81

Take action 82

Dare to dream! 83

Adventure calls 83

Your Success Circle Map 84

Eight invaluable mindset qualities for success 84

Creating your Success Circle Map 86

Time to reflect 88

Introduction

Your journey preparation

Are you prepared for the driver's seat? The big question now is working out which bus you need to catch and to prepare you for the journey that lies ahead. When you are overwhelmed by the results from the past, negative or unhealthy emotions, behaviours and feelings, it's very hard to think clearly about anything.

When I made the decision that something needed to change, I was in such a negative state, I didn't recognise that I had most, if not all, of the tools that I would need for my journey back to myself. Like me, you have a lot of skills and understanding already for your journey but maybe you just don't know what they are yet – and that's okay. You know how to drive, but you've been the passenger on the bus for so long that the move to the driver's seat can seem scary. It's just about realising how amazing and unique you are right now.

As you read on, you will realise there are a few aspects of personal development you may like to brush up on and become aware of that will give you the freedom to move forward in your journey. You see, all along I had the skills – lots of them. Deep down, I knew I had something special and could not understand why I was still having trouble being where I truly wanted to be. I had lost the ability to live in awe of what surrounded me, to get excited or just be me. I knew how to drive my bus but something was stopping me. With education and training I discovered my roadblocks.

I am a teacher. I am a creative thinker. I can work well with my hands. I have the ability to see other people's needs. I am a positive thinker even though I had low self-esteem. I can make pots, run a business, draw and paint, and I have a curious mind. Somewhere, hidden away, I have a sense of humour and am able to have fun. I am a hard worker. I take action. I am calm most of the time.

Along with the tools and skills I already had, I learnt more about myself; I put these tools and skills into context and took action. I needed to accept who I was in order to keep moving forward. I discovered I

PART TWO

loved to learn, be around people, have fun, relax and, especially help others be social and enjoy life. These things needed to be in my life, for me to be me.

Now it's time for you to think about and acknowledge the skills, achievements and understandings you already have in your toolbox for this journey.

Let's look inside your toolkit

So, here is the big ask: write down at least 50 skills and achievements you already possess, from paying bills on time to organisational skills, becoming a parent to being the CEO in your career. Think outside the box, you may be surprised by the tools you already have – and you should celebrate them! Have fun and see if you can think of more than 50.

It might help to close your eyes and breathe deep into your belly. Breathe in for six, hold for three and breathe out for nine. Repeat this several times; you will feel yourself starting to relax. It will clear your mind and allow you to go within to ask the question: what skills and achievements do I already have to take me on my journey?

Enjoy the process. While it would be great if you came up with 50, don't worry if you don't. Leave space to add more skills as more things will come to you as you continue to read. Remember this is a journey. What you see, hear and feel along the way is an adventure. It can only be as difficult as you make it – it's up to you.

Your journey to success

After you have created your skills list, you might feel uncertain about whether you have what it takes to achieve your dreams.

Along the journey to success there inevitably will be bumpy roads and roadblocks. But you can travel more smoothly if you prepare in advance and know that the journey won't always be easy. Like any skill in life, mental preparation is also a skill. I believe anyone can be good at something if they so desire. Skills come from practice and patience, along with the desire to live a fulfilled life without regret.

You can set in motion a new start or lifestyle by changing your thinking and your behaviour. Success is reaching your destination, facing your challenges and fears, embracing them and using them to grow, evolve and keep moving forward. Acknowledge that you are capable and can become the best version of yourself, and accept the responsibility for being in control of your life. It's an adventure. It's exciting!

We all need an adventure in our lives, right? Embrace and accept who you are right now, and open yourself up to the future and what you can achieve even if you may not believe it yet. You can if you desire it and are willing to put in the effort, upgrade your knowledge and develop the skills you need to go on your journey, and believe that anything is possible.

The challenge here is to understand what you need for your journey. You must understand and have good judgement in order to recognise and connect with possibilities that present themselves along your journey.

The Journey Handbook is divided up into 6 sections that will clarify and support you to understand what you need for your journey and build a strong foundation. You know there will be some bumps and potholes along the way; and the Journey Handbook will help you be prepared! At the beginning of each section is a quote to motivate you and at the end of each pillar is an affirmation to support what you have learnt.

1. What you need to understand

Building a strong foundation

If a house does not have an adequate structural foundation, it will crumble under stress; a plant without an ample root system will fall in a heavy wind. A strong personal foundation is a structural base that

PART TWO

supports one who is secure in their identity and through that security, chooses to affect rather than be affected by their challenges in life.

Your personal foundation assists you in getting through your day with ease and success. It becomes the platform from which everything else in your life develops and grows – resilience, happiness, fulfilment and the right to be who you really are.

Your personal foundation consists of the following:

- WHO you are on the inside (your authentic self).
- WHY you do what you do (how you align with your values and beliefs).
- HOW you do it (your thoughts and behaviours) and present yourself to the outside world.

A strong foundation empowers you to overcome challenges, to defy the odds and to move forward easily and effortlessly.

"Rock bottom became the solid foundation on which I rebuilt my life."
J. K. Rowling

Our foundation is developed through our life experience from birth and beyond.

Everyone is different and unique in their own way. How you show up in the world is determined by your programming since birth. It is an ongoing process and results in thoughts that create internal representations that are determined by the sum of your experiences throughout your growth and development, your life experiences and how you have processed them in the past. Determining how strong your personal foundation is relies on how well you understand how your processing system works.

We as human beings are blessed by the fact that we have this amazing computer/brain that runs our lives either consciously or unconsciously. It stores our memories, gives us the power of thought, harbours our emotions and allows us to express our feelings. It also runs our central nervous system and every process that regulates our body and more.

Our internal wiring
THE BRAIN

Firstly, you need to understand that your life is driven by you, and how your mind works; whether you are feeling happy, sad, angry, creative, stressed, depressed or scared. The wiring and chemistry of our brains are what define our experiences and our behaviour. Once we have an understanding of how the neurological thought process works, we begin to understand why and how we do the things we do.

The brain functions as the primary receiver, organiser and distributor of information for the body. The brain attains knowledge from our experiences and stores it in our unconscious mind, where the information prompts our thought processes and our behaviours.

THE FILTERS AND HOW THEY WORK

As far as personal development goes, the neuro-linguistic programming (NLP) model of communication does a good job of explaining the process of our development. As humans, we take in information with our five senses. The vast majority of information is taken in unconsciously. We absorb information at an average rate of up to 4 million bits per second, but we can only process 134 bits in around seven chunks at a time. Consciously taking in all this information could be fun, but it is probably a little impractical and for many overwhelming.

That's why we have filters that help us to distort, delete and generalise the abundance of information. In general terms, the brain tends to sort and filter in one of the following ways:

- **Deletion:** helps us to focus on what is most important at any point in time, and delete the rest. For example, you may have noticed this when people have 'selective hearing'.

- **Distortion:** we reframe or misrepresent reality through distorting our experience of sensory information, ie, fears, phobias.

- **Generalisation:** the process of learning and drawing conclusions can be used and applied to another task. For example, when a child first learns to open a door, they then know that all doors can be opened. The negative experience of being bitten by a dog could mean that all dogs will bite and, thus, create a phobia.

Our individual filters are determined by time, space, matter, energy, language, our understanding of words and gestures, memories, our programming and the unique way we go about making decisions.

Our internal representations trigger corresponding states, which in turn motivate all of our behaviours. Knowing about the various factors that can affect human communication enables us to communicate with greater flexibility. We are able to run our own minds and create a more fulfilled life for ourselves, where we are less affected by external circumstances because we have gained awareness, and even control of our internal processes.

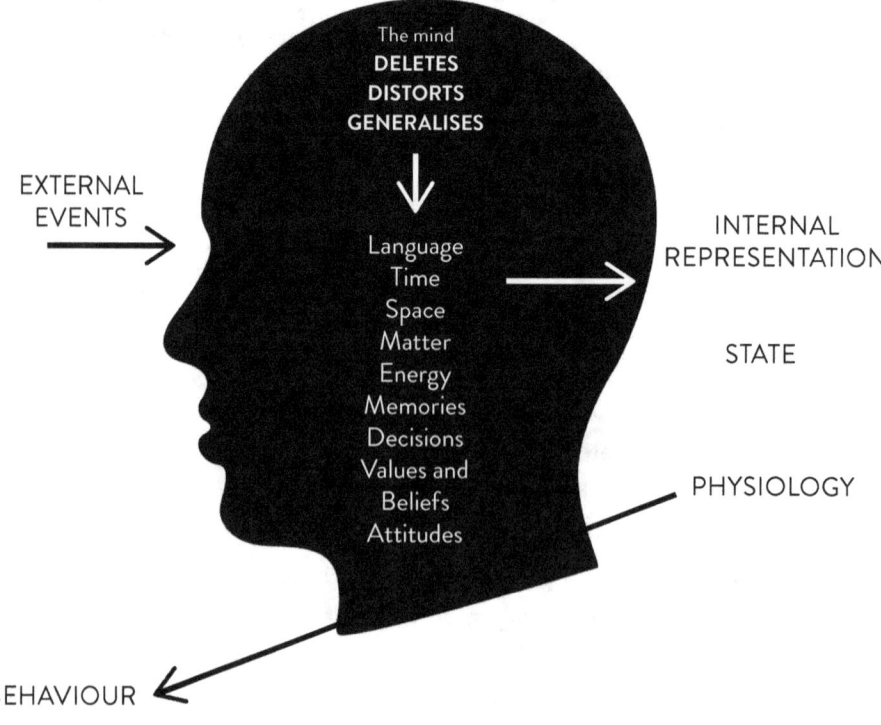

EVERYONE HAS DIFFERENT FILTERS

We can never assume what someone else perceives, as their experience is different from ours. We have not walked in their shoes. Have you ever watched a movie with someone who took a completely different spin on the context of the movie? Or did you exclaim how amazing a particular part was while the other person had not even noticed it? Our thoughts and our behaviours are uniquely ours and have been developed through our life experiences. So, yes, we are responsible for them, and yes, we do have the ability to change them if we so desire, becoming aware is the key.

For example, I often use this exercise in my programs. Now, just for fun, close your eyes and think of a blue car.

- What is the first mental picture that comes to your mind?
- What shade of blue is it?
- What model?
- How old is it?
- Is there a memory attached to it?

In one instance, one lady thought of her first car, a pale blue Mazda, whereas another lady had just seen a blue police car on her way to the program. Interesting, yes? Ask a friend the same question just for fun.

> I AM DEDICATED TO DISCOVERING
> WHO I AM AND HOW GREAT I CAN BECOME.

The conscious and unconscious minds

Let me explain a little about the unconscious versus the conscious mind.

Our conscious mind is our critical consciousness, which gives us the power of logic and reasoning. It is the part of the mind that you

PART TWO

are aware of and use to problem-solve your daily tasks and forms a conscious process of understanding and gathering relevant information so that we can form a judgement, being able to discern what's right or wrong (according to the values and behaviours stored in our unconscious mind). It helps us evaluate and learn.

Our unconscious mind consists of the processes of the mind that occur automatically and exist well under the surface and are not readily available for introspection.

THE PRIME DIRECTIVES OF THE UNCONSCIOUS MIND:
- Stores and organises memories.
- Releases memories with unresolved negative emotions.
- Presents memories to our conscious mind to release negative emotions.
- Preserves the body and keeps our body functioning.
- Represses emotions for protection.
- Takes everything personally (perception is projection).
- Works on the principle of the least effort.
- Does not process negatives (for example, 'don't').

It stores all of our information, beliefs and programming, and has the ability to sabotage us if we are not aware. It can set off a trigger; a trigger being a pattern of behaviour (a habit) or thought (that little voice in our head sometimes called the little itty-bitty-shitty committee by a colleague of mine) that trigger comes from our unconscious mind and can determine our behaviour and thoughts around certain events or desires we might have.

These triggers are unconscious. Have you ever experienced a time when someone said something and triggered a response that you had no conscious control over? It can be positive or negative. The emotions rise up into our consciousness and create a reaction, an emotion or a behaviour. A hurt feeling bubbles up, if it is negative, you can feel angry; if the response is positive, you can go to your happy place.

Often, we don't notice that we have been triggered or question why we have behaved in a certain way.

Once we become aware of what our triggers are and where they come from, we can take control of our behaviour. How exciting is that!

- Have you noticed if you have been triggered lately?

2. Health check

You need to understand that your life needs to be a do-it-yourself life. No one else can do it for you. No one else can eat or breathe for you. If you are not doing it for yourself then your body will become sick or you will experience pain of some kind. When we are not doing or thinking as we should, we are not aligned with our true selves. When we follow our true feelings, we are doing what is best for ourselves, and we are in control of our own life journey. When we experience emotions, whether they be positive or negative, we are experiencing an internal reaction to whatever is happening in our lives in our external world.

We all need to check in on our mental, emotional and physical health regularly and understand that whatever we do or say is aligned with our beliefs and values. If we don't, then roadblocks will start to appear whether we are aware of them or not. Through my personal journey, I have opened up to the chakra energy system, and it works for me every time. It is a way for us to look inside for what feels right and to understand that we have all the answers if we ask ourselves the right questions and listen to what our body is telling us.

The chakra system

The chakra system is a crucial checkpoint in the process of discovering what our body is telling us when we are out of balance. When we are experiencing some form of dis-ease in our lives (stress, anxiety, unhealthy diet, bad habits etc long term) our bodily functions become blocked and so starts the journey to ill-health. Once we become aware

PART TWO

of what we are experiencing at any one point in time, then we can take action to counteract the effects of our negative experiences, open up our chakras and allow our energy to flow.

"There is deep wisdom within our very flesh, if we can only come to our senses and feel it."
Elizabeth A Behnke

The chakras are circular vortexes of energy that occur in seven different points on the spinal column. All seven chakras are connected to various organs and glands within the body. These chakras are responsible for distributing life energy, which is also known as Qi or prana. When a chakra is disrupted or blocked, the life energy also gets blocked, leading to the onset of mental, physical and emotional ailments. Each of the seven major chakras carries a specific meaning and colour. I have only scratched the surface of learning about the chakras. On my journey, as I became more curious it all seemed to make sense to me and helped me to a greater understanding of myself. It continues to guide me as I learn more and more. It helps to give me clarity, which is vital to understanding what I need to do next.

I have included here a very basic explanation of what each chakra represents, which might help you understand what's going on when you ask yourself the right questions. Generally, when we look at our chakras – when we are unwell or when our energy is low – we can relate our physical ailment to a chakra. It can tell us which area of our life we need to be working on. The following health check will give you an idea of how it works, what happens when a particular chakra is

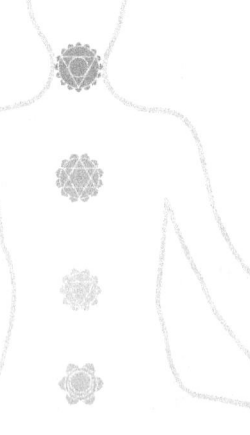

out of balance and the area you need to work on. This health check is not about judging yourself in any way – it's about awareness. The more conscious we become of where our energy is, the more we can make the changes necessary for a more balanced and healthy life.

PURPLE REPRESENTS THE CROWN CHAKRA (SASARARA)
Purpose: connection to the divine; this chakra represents the ability to be fully spiritually connected.
Location: the very top of the head.
Emotional issues: inner and outer beauty, pure bliss, self-acceptance.
Physical associations: pineal gland, brain, nervous system.

INDIGO REPRESENTS THE THIRD-EYE CHAKRA (AJNA)
Purpose: intuition; sense of purpose and direction in life; the ability to focus on and see the big picture.
Location: forehead, between the eyes.
Emotional issues: intuition, imagination, wisdom, the ability to think and make decisions.
Physical associations: pituitary glands, eyes, sinuses.

LIGHT BLUE REPRESENTS THE THROAT CHAKRA (VISHUDDHA)
Purpose: self-expression; our ability to communicate, relating to others.
Location: throat.
Emotional issues: communication, self-expression, feeling the truth.
Physical associations: thyroid, respiratory system, teeth, vocal cords.

GREEN REPRESENTS THE HEART CHAKRA (ANAHATA)
Purpose: love; relationships and self-acceptance; our ability to love; devotion to self.
Location: centre of chest, just above the heart.
Emotional issues: love, joy, inner peace.
Physical associations: heart, thymus, lower lungs, circulatory system, immune system.

PART TWO

YELLOW REPRESENTS THE SOLAR PLEXUS CHAKRA (MANIPURA)
Purpose: personal power, identity and ability to channel; ability to be confident and in control of our lives.
Location: upper abdomen in the stomach area.
Emotional issues: self-worth, self-confidence, self-esteem.
Physical associations: central nervous system, pancreas, liver, digestive tract, skin.

ORANGE REPRESENTS THE SACRAL CHAKRA (SWADHISTHANA)
Purpose: sexuality and pleasure; needs; our connection with and ability to accept others and new experiences.
Location: lower abdomen, about two inches below the navel and two inches in.
Emotional issues: sense of abundance, wellbeing, pleasure, sexuality.
Physical associations: reproductive organs, kidneys, bowels, immune system.

RED REPRESENTS THE BASE CHAKRA OR ROOT AREA (MULADHARA)
Purpose: career, money, mindset, wants and a sense of belonging; represents our foundation and the feeling of being grounded.
Location: base of spine in the tailbone area.
Emotional issues: survival issues, such as financial independence, money and food.
Physical associations: spine, rectum, legs, arms, circulatory system.

What does each area say to you? Is one area 'blocked' more than another? Do you listen to what your body is telling you on a regular basis? If not, why not?

Use the affirmation below for taking care of your wellbeing.

> I MAKE MYSELF A PRIORITY IN MY OWN LIFE. I LISTEN TO MY BODY, AND I AM GRATEFUL FOR ITS MESSAGES.

THE JOURNEY HANDBOOK

> *"In a growth mindset, people believe that their most basic abilities can be developed through dedication and hard work; brains and talent are just a starting point. This view creates a love of learning and resilience that is essential for a great accomplishment."*
> **Carol Dweck**

Understanding the importance of cultivating a growth mindset

From becoming aware of your body and improving your mind-body connection, we move onto exploring your outlook and attitude. Having a growth mindset (the belief that you are in control of your own ability and can learn and improve) is the key to success. Yes, hard work, effort and persistence are all important but not as important as having that underlying belief that you are in control of your own future.

Developing a growth mindset will teach you to embrace failure and find new ways to succeed. Think of it as your brain's new superpower. Carol Dweck is a famous researcher and psychologist who pioneered the terms 'growth mindset' and 'fixed mindset'. Dweck's research began some 30 years ago from working with students. She noticed that some students quickly bounced back from perceived 'failures' while other students seemed very upset by small setbacks. Why did some students bounce back and others didn't? The research led her to discover something that is now commonly called a growth mindset.

People with a fixed mindset often believe that they cannot change because their traits and

FIXED MINDSET
"MY INTELLIGENCE IS FIXED AND WON'T CHANGE."
"I AM EITHER GOOD OR NATURAL AT SOMETHING OR I'M NOT."
"I TAKE CRITICISM PERSONALLY."
"IT'S DIFFICULT TO IMPROVE."
"THERE'S NO POINT IN EVEN TRYING."
"I'M REALLY NOT GOOD AT THIS."

GROWTH MINDSET
"I CAN IMPROVE IF I KEEP TRYING."
"OTHER PEOPLE'S SUCCESSES INSPIRE ME."
"MISTAKES HELP ME LEARN AND GROW."
"I LEARN A LOT FROM CHALLENGES."
"FEEDBACK IS VALUABLE AND MAKES ME BETTER."
"I CAN LEARN ANYTHING IF I PUT MY MIND TO IT."

Adapted from the work of Carol Dweck

PART TWO

qualities are 'fixed'. They don't develop or improve their skills because they believe that's just the way they are. Those with a growth mindset are quite the opposite; they believe that they can improve with effort, education and training. Dweck realised that individuals can be placed on a continuum according to their inner views of where ability comes from.

> I AM A PROBLEM SOLVER, AND I EMBRACE EVERY CHALLENGE THAT COMES MY WAY.

Understanding positive versus negative thinking

POSITIVE THINKING

Positive thinking is a mental attitude in which you expect good and favourable results. In other words, positive thinking is the process of creating thoughts that create and transform energy into reality. A positive mind chooses happiness, health and a happy ending for any situation. Positive thinking is therefore beneficial for our mental health, primarily because it eliminates any form of paranoia and negativity that could cause depression and stress. The process is actually a domino effect in terms of overall health. Those who think positively feel happier and are more content with their lives.

"Life's battles don't always go to the stronger, faster man. But sooner or later, the man who wins is the man who thinks he can."
Vince Lombardi

NEGATIVE THINKING

Negative thinking is a thought process wherein people tend to find the worst in everything or reduce their expectations by considering the worst possible scenarios. While everyone experiences negative thoughts from time to time, negative thinking seriously affects the way you think about yourself and the world and even interferes with work/study, relationships and everyday functioning. Negative thinking could be a symptom of mental illness, such as depression, anxiety disorders or personality disorders. Focusing on the negative leaves no room for fun whatsoever in everyday life.

A positive growth mindset means focusing on the bright side of life, taking responsibility for your thoughts and flicking that switch from negative to positive, while accepting that the negative is showing you the way, and understanding that without the negative you will not be able to recognise the positive.

One needs to be able to focus on the positive and develop an attitude of gratitude. More importantly connect to the feelings you experience in recognition of that which you are grateful for. Accept the things you can't change and recognise the things you can change. As the well-known 'Serenity Prayer' from Reinhold Niebuhr explains: "God, grant me the serenity to accept the things I cannot change, the courage to change the things I can, and the wisdom to know the difference."

Surround yourself with positive people and look for the positives in life, remain optimistic and refrain from being judgemental, as you have not walked in their shoes. Recognise what does not support you and move away. For example, one of the most challenging experiences we can face is a breakup in a relationship. Rising above the hurt, disappointment and guilt you may feel to find the positive in this experience is difficult.

See the experience as a challenge, as you move through the challenge, you may begin to realise that the relationship you had has created some positive lessons worth learning. These lessons could include how strong you are to have made the decision to end the relationship; the awareness of the fact that the person did not meet your needs or that you did not meet theirs; that you discovered what truly makes you happy (and it was not them); that you did all you possibly could to make it work but that it takes two to communicate well; and the understanding that each person in a relationship has the right to be themselves.

PART TWO

If it had not been for that person, you would not be the person you are today. How exciting is that! I remember going through the relationship conundrum. Once I found the right one, I realised that each relationship I'd had had prepared me for my current one. I learnt so much about myself and am so grateful for those relationships, as I would not be in the relationship I have now if it had not been for each one of them.

For every negative there is always a positive.

> I FOCUS ON THE POSITIVE IN MY LIFE, PERSONALLY AND IN OTHERS. I APPROACH LIFE'S CHALLENGES WITH A POSITIVE OUTLOOK.

To understand your Life Balance

A healthy lifestyle aligned with who you are and what you want out of life, is imperative to achieving your life balance. Primarily, eat well, include physical activity into your daily routine and get enough sleep.

Life Balance is about your own happiness and fulfilment. To achieve this, you need to feel good about yourself, be in control of your life and career path, it's about being happy and acknowledged for who you are and having real meaning in your life. First, we need to look at and question if our primal human needs are being met. A primal human need is what nature and human evolution says you need to have to ensure a productive and happy life.

As humans, we have basic survival needs: water, food and shelter. However, in addition to the obvious basic needs, we have other important needs that are not as obvious, but just as essential to our health and wellbeing.

Abraham Harold Maslow was an American psychologist who is best known for creating Maslow's hierarchy of needs, a theory of psychological health, based on fulfilling innate human needs by priority, in order to achieve self-actualisation. It is a motivational theory in psychology that illustrates a five-tier model of human needs, often depicted as hierarchical levels within a pyramid.

In 1943, Maslow initially stated that individuals must satisfy lower-level deficit needs before progressing on to meet higher-level growth needs. He later clarified that satisfaction of needs is not an all-or-none situation. The definition of growth is a variable state that one can move through; depending on what one is experiencing at the time. Maslow presented the hierarchy of needs in his 1954 book *Motivation and Personality*[3].

Needs lower down in the hierarchy must be satisfied before individuals can attend to needs higher up. From the bottom of the hierarchy upward, the needs are: physiological, safety, love and belonging, esteem, and self-actualisation.

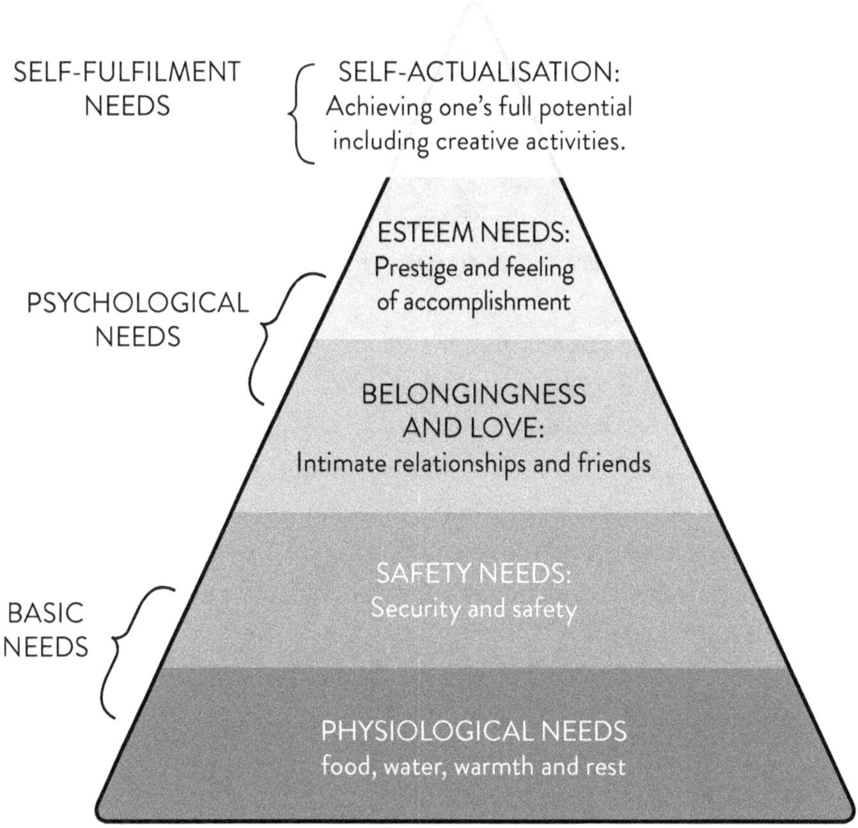

SELF-FULFILMENT NEEDS
- SELF-ACTUALISATION: Achieving one's full potential including creative activities.

PSYCHOLOGICAL NEEDS
- ESTEEM NEEDS: Prestige and feeling of accomplishment
- BELONGINGNESS AND LOVE: Intimate relationships and friends

BASIC NEEDS
- SAFETY NEEDS: Security and safety
- PHYSIOLOGICAL NEEDS: food, water, warmth and rest

I use Maslow's hierarchy when I know something's getting me down and I'm not sure what it is. It's a simple way to identify what I need at any one point in time. Running through the different needs can help me pin down what it is that I'm missing, whether I'm feeling the cognitive need to stretch brain cells or the need to catch up with some friends and feel a sense of social belonging. Maslow's hierarchy puts things into perspective for me; you might also find it useful.

Would you wonder why a plant was wilting if it didn't have water or sunlight? Would you take your car to the mechanic before checking it had fuel in its tank and air in its tyres? Of course not. We are all unique, and our needs vary. The purpose of understanding our needs is to understand what is missing when our life is out of balance and things just don't feel right. The next time you are faced with the knowledge that things are not quite right, just stop, breathe, go inward and ask yourself, *Is my life in balance? If not, why not?* Allow your inner self to have a say, reveal your truth, and trust yourself.

The first step to living a **BALANCED LIFESTYLE** is to focus on the mind-body connection, sleep, proper nutrition, rest and exercise. Once you have the first step under control you also need to take into account other inherent aspects of what we need to live a fulfilled Life. The second step is understanding that for each area of your Life Circle you need to:

- Have your basic needs met, the things you need to survive in the specific area in question.
- Feel safe and secure.
- Check you have a supportive environment that will support and acknowledge you for who you are, giving you a sense of belonging and that it is aligned with your values and purpose in life.
- Be a part of a community and be able to contribute to that which is bigger than us.
- Be challenged and achieve goals; we all have innate skills, and we need to use them, because without a sense of progress and achievement, we can feel worthless.
- Have at least one person with whom we can be intimate, share

ideas, hopes and dreams and experience unconditional love and growth with.
- Recognise what we love and enjoy doing and do it; these activities lead to fulfilment.
- Have and enjoy good communication to fulfil your social, personal and work needs.

So, why is it that sometimes we forget what we need to survive and be happy? What we 'need, want and have' to do in each area of our life can be different. Clarity and focus around these points will create a strong foundation.

> I AM WORTHY OF HAPPINESS AND LOVE.
> MY FUTURE IS UNDER CONTROL.

To understand values

Most of the time, we move through life without even thinking to examine our values, however values are important because they act as a set of rules and guidelines for our life experiences. Your values are the principles/standards of behaviour that give insight into what's important; the convictions and beliefs that we adopt as our guidelines in daily life. They are a set of consistent measures and behaviours that individuals choose to practise in the pursuit of doing what is right or what is expected of them by society.

Often, values are passed from parents onto their offspring soon after childbirth and instilled throughout childhood. As they grow, children learn more values from their peers, teachers, friends and society. These attributes include honesty, trustworthiness, diligence, discipline, fairness, love, peace, justice, care for one another and being mindful of the environment (including plants and animals). Additionally, selflessness and being considerate of others are desirable human values.

When you take the time to clarify your values, you can better understand what motivates you and why you do what you do.

You may even find that your values change on your journey as you experience different things. If you feel disharmony and unease, your values may not be in alignment with your actions. A good strategy for success is knowing what your values are and living by them. We also need to understand that people value different things because of their past programming, life experiences etc, they think in different ways and their experiences are different to yours, their brains process information differently (remember the NLP communication model: distort, delete and generalise).

Accordingly, it is important to manage and communicate with people in different ways so that you are speaking 'their' language. Understanding and communicating within other people's models of the world allows for the best result. I refer to my core values in times of both happiness and hardship. These values form my moral compass. They allow me to make difficult decisions with conviction and confidence. When our actions or circumstances are not aligned with our values, life can trigger negative reactions, stress, illness and that uncomfortable feeling that things are not quite right. You need values to declutter your life, to know how to respond in tough situations. You need values to forge lasting relationships with those around you. Your values determine what is important and acceptable in your everyday life.

On the flip side, once you clear the clutter and have clarity on what you want to achieve at any one point in time, it is possible to realign your values to support you to reach a desired outcome. For example, if you are running a business and you are finding it hard to price your worth and not making enough money to exist, you may find that your value around money is not in your top five values in the business section of your Life Circle. Interesting, yes!

MAKE A LIST OF AT LEAST 10 OF THE MOST IMPORTANT THINGS YOU VALUE IN YOUR LIFE

When you go through the process of recognising the values that are most important to you, you generally find clarity on why you do the things you do, and what you might need to change if things are not working out the way you expect them to or want them to.

To discover your core values, complete this Values Exercise.
- Think about the values that are important to you in everyday life.
- Make a list of at least 10 then choose the top 5.
- Put them in order from most important to least important.
- My top 5 core values are........
- What did you learn?

If you are having trouble, refer to the Values List in the Toolbox at the back of the book. Read through it once, then do it again and write down a list of the values that align with you. Choose the five most important ones, reorder them from most important to least important. Repeat this exercise for each area of your Life Circle. What did you learn?

Please note I have a process that will help you to realign your values to support you to achieve your desired outcome, check out the Bonus Content for more details.

> ALL AREAS OF MY LIFE ARE IN BALANCE
> WITH MY CORE VALUES. I FAITHFULLY
> FOLLOW THE GUIDANCE OF MY TRUE
> VALUES IN ALL THAT I DO.

To understand self-awareness and your roadblocks

A roadblock is that which is stopping you from achieving your goals and living your best life. Become aware of what is stopping you. Review your situation, accept the challenge and get excited because you know how good it will feel when you move through it and get closer to a life you can love.

PART TWO

THERE ARE TWO TYPES OF ROADBLOCKS:

1. Those that come from within.
It could be that little itty-bitty-shitty committee, a negative belief, a negative environment or an attitude that does not serve you. You need to be aware that they can show up in the form of: ill health, stress, anxiety, depression, procrastination, overwhelm, excuses, not enough time, etc etc. Roadblocks are a warning that something is not quite right. They inform you that you need to delve in a little deeper, go within and find the root cause, become aware and change what you need to and clear the road to your destination.

2. Those that are external.
Those things you have no control over ie: your house burning down, floods, and natural disasters. With the external, it is how you deal with them that is the key. Once you become aware of what your roadblock is you can begin to trigger a new start, a new lifestyle by changing your thinking and your behaviour.

Success is reaching your destination, facing your challenges, recognising your fears, embracing them and using them to grow, evolve and keep moving forward.

> TODAY IS GOING TO BE A GOOD DAY.
> I CAN DO THIS.

To understand triggers

Have you ever experienced a time when someone has said something and triggered a response that you have no control over consciously? A trigger is an unconscious pattern of behaviour (a habit) or thought (that little voice in our head) that comes from nowhere and can determine our behaviour and thoughts around certain events or desires.

Our response can be positive or negative and the emotions rise up into our consciousness and create a reaction, an emotion or a behaviour. A hurt feeling can produce a negative response and you can feel angry or your happy place appears out of nowhere if the response is positive. We often don't notice that we have been triggered and continue on with whatever we are doing.

The scary thing is our body holds onto that trigger and it continues to trigger us unless we become aware and start to understand what is happening and take control. As we are all unique in our own right, our response can be different to someone else's. On the downside, one way to control our neuro-chemical response is with alcohol, recreational drugs, antidepressants etc. The danger here is that our brain adapts to these chemicals and the ability for the brain to produce the happy natural chemicals naturally can be limited (serotonin oxytocin and dopamine), this can create a habit of dependence that can be detrimental and turn into a major roadblock.

Become aware of your triggers, listen to what your body is telling you, find the root cause and let go of that which does not serve you.

> I AM DEDICATED TO DISCOVERING WHO I AM AND HOW GREAT I CAN BECOME.

3. What you need to know

One of the hardest things to do in life is to be truly honest with yourself. When we have a dream for our future, we need to be aware of what is needed to overcome any difficulties that might get in our way. The following areas are

"Your aim is to thrive emotionally, physically and mentally. It will take time, so don't be hard on yourself. Take one step at a time."

Unknown

PART TWO

aspects of our everyday life that we need to understand to reach a successful outcome.

Choice and responsibility
YOU NEED TO TAKE RESPONSIBILITY FOR THE CHOICES YOU MAKE

On my journey through self-development, the realisation that I was responsible for all the choices that I made was a challenge. Think about this:

> Everything that is happening at this moment is a result of the choices you've made in the past.

There are two primary choices in life: to accept conditions as they exist or to accept and take responsibility for changing them. Good choices are decisions that keep you heading in the right direction, the direction in which you want to go. (Please note! A good choice for you may not be a good choice for someone else.)

Every day we make endless choices. For example, we choose what we have for lunch and what time we get out of bed. Where we go and what we are going to do next. On a deeper level though, the big decisions we make, can make or break what happens next. And that's okay. Some people just make better choices by understanding the circumstances and taking responsibility for the outcome, good or bad.

For example, a friend was telling me the other day that she had put on 5kgs in the last couple of months because her mum was serving up large meals and dessert every night. Did she have a choice about actually eating all of it? Yes. Did she take responsibility for her actions? No. What are the other choices could she have made?

When she realised she was putting on weight perhaps she could ask the following questions:
- Why am I eating all this food?
- Do I really want to keep eating all this food and gain more weight?
- What do I need to do to change this outcome?

Responsibility takes courage

We need to take responsibility for the choices we make. Yes, we have programming from the past, and yes, we have had challenges and maybe trauma in the past. Every life experience we have had to date has made an imprint on the person we are today. We can't change that fact. However, it is how you deal with your trauma and the way you address each challenge that comes your way that determines the outcome and the experience that is imprinted in your mind. Don't be too hard on yourself as your experiences are in the past and you did the best you could with what you had at that point in time. Take your learnings and move on.

Asking the right questions is a way to delve deeper and discover the truth that only you can be aware of, which allows you to resolve the issue. It's like going to the doctor to diagnose an ailment, after you get the diagnosis, you know what you are dealing with and it's easier to find the solution.

Notice how you react to what other people say and when it triggers an uncomfortable feeling inside you. Do you hang on to the feeling? Do you push the feeling away rather than dealing with it? Or do you ask yourself, *Why am I allowing that to bother me?* Good questions create clarity. I use this exact question in my life and it reminds me to take responsibility for my thoughts and look at whatever is in the way – whether that be emotions, self-doubt, or negativity.

The greatest courage in life is the courage to take responsibility for your own life. Like it or not, you are responsible for the person you are today – your thoughts, your behaviour, and how you feel at any one point in time. When we become aware of how we think or react, we can change our dysfunctional thoughts and begin to think in a different way, creating a more positive reaction or outcome.

> *"You may believe that you are responsible for what you do, but not for what you think. The truth is that you are responsible for what you think because it is only at this level that you can exercise choice. What you do, comes from what you think."*
> **Marianne Williamson**

PART TWO

> *"Most people do not really want freedom, because freedom involves responsibility, and most people are frightened of responsibility."*
> **Sigmund Freud**

Remember you do have a choice,
take responsibility for who you are
and be empowered to live your best life.

> I TAKE FULL RESPONSIBILITY FOR MY
> THOUGHTS, MY ACTIONS AND THE CHOICES
> I MAKE. I CHOOSE TO BE HAPPY.

Living at cause or effect
YOU NEED TO LIVE YOUR LIFE AT CAUSE

There are two sides from which you can live your life: the cause side and the effect side. If you're on the CAUSE side of the equation, you accept responsibility for your thoughts, your actions and the results you achieve throughout your life. You are in control, and driving your own bus.

> *"Ninety-nine percent of all failures come from people who have a habit of making excuses."*
> **George Washington Carver**

If you're on the EFFECT side you lay blame, make excuses and say that someone else is responsible for YOUR outcomes. The 'reasons/excuses' side in life is not the best side to be on – it keeps a person stuck. It won't be the most satisfying side to be on in the long term. People are very quick to lay the blame on something outside of themselves.

When you are living at cause, you are in control of the results you achieve.

If you are living on the Effect side, you are continually making excuses and encouraging a victim mindset.

> I AM THE CREATOR OF MY LIFE EXPERIENCE.

Permission
YOU NEED TO GIVE YOURSELF PERMISSION

Permission is the action of allowing someone to do a particular thing, to give consent or authorisation. The reality is that you need to give yourself permission to start your journey of self-growth and development. By looking outside of yourself for someone else to give you permission, you are putting the brakes on because their permission or approval may never be given. There are four main areas in which you need to give yourself permission.

1. Permission to fail: in reality, there is no failure, only feedback. You see, it depends on how you look at it. If you never have a go, you will never know, right?

2. Permission to succeed: decide what success means to you. It can be as small as paying your bills on time or as mammoth as having your first six figure month in your business. See each achievement as a success, no matter how big or small. Get excited, celebrate each step, and have fun.

3. Permission to take care of yourself: when a person is thoughtful and generous and prioritises other people's needs over their own, they can find it difficult to give themselves permission to look after their own needs. There is a belief that it can be selfish to consider your own needs first. It can be seen as being above everyone else and thinking you matter more than them. When you put your needs into the equation, you are saying 'me as well', not 'me first'. Find the balance because when you care for your own needs and do what you need to feel nurtured and

supported, you are better able to be the best version of yourself and to take better care of those around you.

4. Permission to feel however you are feeling: it's okay. We are all human, and we can feel and experience all types of emotions (joy, hope, excitement, love, gratitude, sadness, grief, jealousy, loneliness, stress, and anxiety). As long as we don't get stuck in one of the heavier emotions for too long, it's okay. And if you need to, ask for help.

The only person who can truly give permission is you. Give yourself permission to be curious and explore. Listen to yourself. Everything you feel and experience, it's your choice and you do have a choice to live your life to your fullest potential. Ultimately, when you give yourself permission to be yourself, to be who you want to be in this world, you free yourself to love in a way that's true to you, to fulfil your potential and to experience all the joy and happiness that's available to you at this moment in time and in the future. Once you give yourself permission, a whole new world opens up. You see more, feel more and hear more. How exciting is that!

> I GIVE MYSELF PERMISSION AND THE POWER TO CREATE THE FREEDOM AND LIVE TO MY FULL POTENTIAL IN A LIFE I CAN LOVE.

Acceptance is the key
YOU NEED TO BE ABLE TO ACCEPT WHAT YOU CAN'T CHANGE

Acceptance is the willingness to tolerate a difficult situation that you cannot change. Acceptance unlocks the denial, the fear and the negativity of the challenges we face; too often, we can get stuck feeling stressed and powerless about our outcomes.

Acceptance is the power we give ourselves to move through

challenges peacefully in a positive way. Then we can see other possibilities clearly.

Acceptance is also a choice.

If you choose to accept what's happening, at the same time understanding, that no matter what you say or do, nothing will change and that you can only do your best at any one point in time. It becomes easier to accept the outcome, get your learnings and keep moving forward in a positive way.

> *"God, grant me the serenity to accept the things I cannot change, the courage to change the things I can, and the wisdom to know the difference."*
> **The Serenity Prayer**

If you choose to fight it, dwell on it when you can't do anything about it, you choose to be miserable, emotional and struggle daily to overcome the negative.

When you take action and communicate in an honest authentic way with yourself and others, you can look at the situation honestly and understand that you have a choice.

For example: When challenged on your journey an important question you need to ask is

"Can I do anything to change the situation?"

If you answered **YES!** Ask "What action can I do to improve the situation?"

If you answered **NO!** and nothing you can do will change the situation – **ACCEPT** the situation get your learnings and let it go.

Remember: it's how we think about what we do that creates what we focus on each day. What we think, we become. What you focus on, you get, negative thinking is typical human behaviour and negative emotions generally take up a lot more brainpower and are processed more thoroughly than positive emotions.

PART TWO

> I LOVE, APPRECIATE AND ACCEPT MYSELF FOR WHO I AM.
> I WILLINGLY ACCEPT AND RELEASE MY
> PAST, AND EVERYTHING IN MY LIFE THAT IS
> BEYOND MY POWER TO CHANGE.

Resistance to resilience
YOU NEED TO MOVE FROM RESISTANCE TO RESILIENCE

Resistance

Resistance is the refusal to accept or comply with something. Resistance is your body and mind's attempt to preserve your current state, even if that state is negative. Your mind generates resistance by creating excuses for why you can't or shouldn't do something, either consciously or unconsciously. Interestingly, I remember doing an exercise at one of my trainings and I just couldn't get into the process and let go. The trainer had relaxing music going. There was too much noise; everybody was talking at once. I asked if the music could be turned down so that I could focus on what we were meant to be doing, and he said, "Gillian, stop resisting the process."

Interesting, yes? You see, your mind can resist, even when you are not aware of what is happening, and create a mental block in the form of an excuse, especially when you are doing self-development work. Resistance can appear in many forms; you just need to be aware and ask questions, especially if you are not achieving your outcome, whatever that may be.

The tricky thing about resistance is differentiating the valid excuses from the invalid ones. But calling everything an excuse is too simple. Once you become aware and realise the difference, you can take the appropriate action. The worst thing that can happen is that you get so distracted and out of control that you lose sight of whatever it is you want to achieve and get stuck.

Resilience

Resilience is the capacity to recover quickly from difficulties. When we are resilient, we adapt well in the face of adversity, trauma, tragedy, threats or significant sources of stress. Resilient

> *"Life doesn't get easier or more forgiving, we get stronger and more resilient."*
> **Steve Maraboli**

people don't get stuck, wallow or dwell on their failures. They acknowledge the situation, learn from their mistakes and then move forward. Living with a strong foundation and understanding the need to live a balanced lifestyle (mentally, physically, socially and spiritually) will strengthen your life. Allow your light to shine so that you can live your best life.

> I AM UNIQUE. I HAVE WISDOM AND STRENGTH, AND I CAN ADAPT TO CHANGE EASILY AND EFFORTLESSLY.

Intention
YOU NEED TO LIVE WITH THE POWER OF INTENTION

An intention is to have an aim or plan, something that is intended and aligned with a purpose, your reality; it can be driven by a feeling, an action or actions that will take place. An intention is powerful because when you change the way you look at things, the things you look at change.

When you have an aim or a plan/goal for your day, week or year, the plan develops a positive energy of its own. It creates baby steps of focus and the belief that you can achieve your outcome whenever that might be. For example; a daily intention to raise your energy might be to smile at everyone you meet (notice how you feel at the end of the day). A weekly intention might be that each day you will do one positive action towards your weekly goal.

If we live with an expectation of a particular result/outcome and it does not turn out the way we expect it to, then our energy levels dive, and this can propel us into a downward spiral of negativity. But to plan and hold intent with no expectations leads us to success at whatever level we want to reach during the day, and we can accept the fact that it is okay no matter what happens.

We need to ask ourselves these two questions:
What is my intention, value or desire today?
How many ways can I continue to achieve my intent today?

> I WOKE UP TODAY WITH STRENGTH IN MY HEART AND CLARITY IN MY MIND. I AM GOING TO HAVE A GREAT DAY.

Clarity of communication
YOU NEED TO BE A GOOD COMMUNICATOR

"The way we communicate with others and with ourselves ultimately determines the quality of our lives."
Tony Robbins

Communication is the process of passing information and signals between people. We use communication to share information, comment, ask questions, express wants and needs, and develop social relationships. It is a process of transmitting and sharing ideas, opinions, facts or values from one person to another or one organisation to another. Every communication involves (at least) one sender, a message and a recipient.

Personal relationships rely on effective communication to deal with the various concerns and problems of daily life. Good communication in relationships reduces conflict, builds trust and strengthens bonds. The functions of communication in an organisation are to inform, persuade and motivate. It is this type of communication that helps us build healthy relationships and credibility, both in our personal lives and work lives.

To be a good communicator, you need to:

Be a good listener: active listening involves paying close attention to what the other person is saying, asking clarifying questions and rephrasing what the person says to ensure understanding.

Understand nonverbal communication: your body language, eye contact, hand gestures and tone of voice all colour the message you are trying to convey.

Have clarity and be concise: don't talk too much or too little. Say what you want, clearly and directly.

Be friendly: speak or use a friendly tone, ask a personal question, or simply smile. Ask questions, gain rapport, and show an interest in the other person.

Be confident: confidence shows that you believe in what you're saying.

Show empathy: using phrases as simple as, "I understand where you are coming from", demonstrate that you have been listening to the other person, respect their opinions and have empathy for their situation or emotions.

Have an open mind: listen to and understand the other person's point of view.

Be respectful: simple actions like using a person's name, making eye contact and actively listening when a person speaks will make the person feel appreciated.

Give and receive feedback: being able to give and receive feedback appropriately, give praise and thank the other person is important.

PART TWO

Pick the right medium to communicate with: know what form of communication to use for the right purpose, be it your boss or the girl next door (text, email, letter, face-to-face and more). Would you quit your job or propose marriage with a text?
Do you have trouble communicating with others?
In which area of your life is communication the most difficult?

> I AM AN EXCELLENT COMMUNICATOR.
> OTHERS LISTEN TO ME, AS I LISTEN TO THEM.
> I AM ASSERTIVE AND SAY WHAT I NEED TO
> SAY EASILY AND EFFORTLESSLY.

4. The connection to the solution
The answers come from within

It's easier than ever to get lost in everyday life activities and the stress of the external world. Our focus is almost always on anything and anyone other than ourselves. Reconnecting with yourself is something you must do. It gives you a chance to celebrate your gifts and understand what really drives you. When you know this, the more you can show up for others and let your light shine.

"Understanding your traits, feelings and behaviours, both good and bad, is vital if you want to build better relationships, achieve your goals and lead a contented life. It takes bravery but the payoffs are worth it."
Nikki Williamson

BEING YOU: THE PRIMARY PURPOSE OF LIFE

Being authentic is when your actions and words are congruent with your beliefs and values. It is about being yourself, liking who you are, and living your truth by understanding who you are and why you do what you do. It does not mean you are selfish, and it does not mean you don't care about others. It means that you can do everything you want with

THE JOURNEY HANDBOOK

confidence and clarity, and be happy within yourself, so being yourself is a good thing, right! No one else can do it better than you. To be authentic is to understand and just be who you are; it makes life easier.

> "Be yourself; everyone else is already taken."
> **Oscar Wilde**

To be authentic:
- Get to know your needs and wants and how to fill your cup.
- Check that your values, beliefs, emotions and behaviour patterns are aligned with who you want to be and where you want to go. You are in control.
- Get to know your story. Then understand that the past is gone, the future has not happened yet and the power of now is where you are at any one point in time.

> I HAVE THE COURAGE TO BE MYSELF
> IN EVERY AREA OF MY LIFE.
> I AM POWERFUL, CAPABLE AND STRONG,
> AND I BELIEVE IN MYSELF.

Awareness: to go within
BECOMING SELF-AWARE IS THE KEY TO HAPPINESS

Self-awareness and getting in touch with your intuition is about being honest with yourself. It involves keen introspection, curiosity and adventure into the unknown. It's not about overthinking everything you do or say – it's about listening, feeling, recognising and acknowledging what your body and your mind are telling you and taking appropriate action when needed.

Self-awareness is conscious knowledge of one's own character and feelings. It refers to your ability to recognise your emotions, beliefs, motivations,

> "Connecting with yourself is something that requires daily love, care and attention. To be kind and compassionate with yourself while letting go of judgement and comparison."
> **Gillian Gorrie**

PART TWO

strengths and weaknesses. When we connect to ourselves, we're also able to create lives that are more meaningful and fulfilling.

When you are feeling out of sorts, and things are not quite right, to go within and connect with our authentic self is the only solution. It allows you to motivate yourself, manage your stress better and helps with intuitive decision-making.

There are eight steps we can take to strengthen our connection to ourselves:

1. Breathe away your negative emotions when you need to think clearly. Breathe in for six, hold for three, breathe out for nine. Repeat until a feeling of calm comes over you.

2. Notice what you are feeling at any given time. Ask the right questions. Do you have tension in your body? Where is it? What caused it?

3. Acknowledge your feelings/emotions. Give them a name (anger, frustration, sadness, anxiety).

4. Accept your thoughts and emotions without judging your reasons, feelings or experiences. Understand that they have a purpose.

5. Recognise your triggers and continue to ask the right questions. Why am I allowing myself to feel this way?

6. Give yourself time out. Engage in enjoyable solo activities that you find energizing or calming, such as creative activities or walking, time with pets.

7. Meditate, practise mindfulness, and enjoy every moment of your life.

8. Practise self-compassion and being warm and understanding towards yourself. You can only do your best at any one point in time. Don't beat yourself up. Learn to love who you are and celebrate. Contrary to popular belief, self-compassion isn't self-indulgent.

> I AM EXPERIENCING MY LIFE AND HOW IT
> IS CREATED THROUGH MY THOUGHTS AND
> MY FEELINGS EVERY DAY.
> I LOVE, APPRECIATE AND ACCEPT MYSELF
> FOR WHO I AM, I AM FREE TO BE ME.

Self-belief and self-worth

"If I have the belief that I can do it, I shall surely acquire the capacity to do it even if I may not have it at the beginning."
Mahatma Gandhi

Self-belief can be defined as confidence in your own skin, abilities and judgement. When you believe in yourself, you can accomplish so much more in life. Sometimes, we feel uncomfortable when we are not aligned with our beliefs and values around a said situation/challenge, if we don't have a belief in self or feel worthy, it can be easier to just pull the plug. You may feel like you don't deserve to be successful. This is the point in time where you need to reset and ask yourself: What will I gain if I make the effort and do what I need to do to be truly happy? What will happen if I don't do anything?

The reality is that it's a choice. When our actions line up with our desires and our goals, we become more powerful and confident, knowing that we have the tools and resources to overcome any challenge we encounter. Sharpening those tools and gaining the confidence to choose a different path (if that is what is needed) involves seeing yourself as a success, seeing a problem as a challenge that can be overcome, and realising that every mistake or failure is actually an opportunity to do it better next time with the wisdom you have gained in the process.

PART TWO

Make time, slow down and get into a space where you can allow your intuitive mind to flow, trust it and believe you CAN, take your learnings and keep moving closer to a life you can love.

Be empowered to live your best life – you just need to want it enough.

> WHEN I WORK ON MYSELF,
> I AM HONOURING WHO I AM.

Intuition and wisdom

Intuition is the ability to understand something instinctively without the need for conscious reasoning. Your intuition can be that knowing feeling of danger or accomplish-

"There is a voice that doesn't use words. Listen."
Rumi

ment aligned with your core values and your true sense of purpose. You just need to listen to it, feel it. Pay attention. Stop and listen; breathe and be mindful of what your body and mind are telling you.

Have you ever felt that peace or fulfilment when your cup is full? It can just be that 'ah-ha' moment. It can be a strong physical feeling as well as a feeling of wholeness – doing the right thing at the right time in the right place. I've felt it – for me, it's a feeling of completeness along with an empowering sense of calm. It's enlightening and real, and then you know you have a connection to your inner wisdom. The more you love and trust yourself, the more in touch you will be with your intuition.

An intuitive message can come to you in many ways:
- It can pop up in the form of an 'ah ha' moment: thoughts can just pop up at any time, especially when you are not emotionally charged.
- It may come in the form of a number of coincidences or patterns throughout the day.

- It can be a feeling of peace and flow.
- Confidence: a knowing that you're doing the right thing at the right time.
- Lucid dreams: the answer to a question you ask can come in the form of a dream.
- A thought that comes out of the blue: acknowledge it, journal it. I often get mine in the shower or while I am driving.
- Your thoughts may be pulling you in a certain direction: they want to guide you. Work on the negative, celebrate the positive.

Listen to your intuition; it comes from your inner truth.

Develop your intuitive muscle:
- You can choose to do this through meditation.
- Become aware of what your body is telling you.
- Notice those niggling feelings, and when they occur. Simply ask the right questions and journal it out
- Practise responding instead of reacting.
- Question your feelings without judgement.

If you choose to ignore your intuition, a feeling of uneasiness can come over you, it can be a sneaking feeling that something is not quite right. You may choose to listen to this voice, your ego, the little itty-bitty-shitty committee, because it feels safe and it's easy. Understand your intuition is a voice of wisdom from within, the connection can be really awesome.

> I TRUST MY INTUITION AND AM ALWAYS
> GUIDED TO MAKE WISE DECISIONS.
> I FIND ALL THE ANSWERS THAT I NEED FOR
> MY LIFE FROM WITHIN.

Flow and creativity

Flow is the mental state in which a person doing an activity is fully

PART TWO

immersed, feeling energised and focused. But flow can also apply to your entire life, and when this happens, you have found your way. Have you ever experienced that feeling of flow when you are completely immersed in an activity, when you are in 'the Zone'? Allowing yourself to be in the right place, doing the right thing, at the right time.
When you are in flow, creativity flows.

> *"Life is a series of natural and spontaneous changes. Don't resist them – that only creates sorrow. Let reality BE reality. Let things flow naturally forward in whatever way they like."*
> **Lao Tzu**

To be able to experience flow in everyday life is important. Developing the ability to enter a state of flow is life-changing. When you are fully immersed in the present moment and lose track of the world around you, time flies, productivity and creativity skyrockets and you experience a deep sense of fulfilment.

One thing I love about flow is that it encompasses being completely in the moment and experiencing a sense of calm and happiness in your work and daily activities. Once you've learnt to focus on the important things, instead of being constantly interrupted, you can easily focus on and immerse yourself in the task at hand. By believing in yourself, you can enjoy yourself even more, reduce stress while increasing quality output, get important stuff done and actually achieve your goals (rather than working for the sake of it).

A few steps to keep in mind on the journey to flow are as follows:

1. Have clarity around what you want to achieve in life.

2. Choose work you love. If your job is made up of stuff you hate, you might want to consider finding another job. Make sure it's challenging, but not too hard, so that you can learn and grow.

3. Find your quiet time. Which part of the day is your most

- It can be a feeling of peace and flow.
- Confidence: a knowing that you're doing the right thing at the right time.
- Lucid dreams: the answer to a question you ask can come in the form of a dream.
- A thought that comes out of the blue: acknowledge it, journal it. I often get mine in the shower or while I am driving.
- Your thoughts may be pulling you in a certain direction: they want to guide you. Work on the negative, celebrate the positive.

Listen to your intuition; it comes from your inner truth.

Develop your intuitive muscle:
- You can choose to do this through meditation.
- Become aware of what your body is telling you.
- Notice those niggling feelings, and when they occur. Simply ask the right questions and journal it out
- Practise responding instead of reacting.
- Question your feelings without judgement.

If you choose to ignore your intuition, a feeling of uneasiness can come over you, it can be a sneaking feeling that something is not quite right. You may choose to listen to this voice, your ego, the little itty-bitty-shitty committee, because it feels safe and it's easy. Understand your intuition is a voice of wisdom from within, the connection can be really awesome.

> I TRUST MY INTUITION AND AM ALWAYS
> GUIDED TO MAKE WISE DECISIONS.
> I FIND ALL THE ANSWERS THAT I NEED FOR
> MY LIFE FROM WITHIN.

Flow and creativity

Flow is the mental state in which a person doing an activity is fully

PART TWO

immersed, feeling energised and focused. But flow can also apply to your entire life, and when this happens, you have found your way. Have you ever experienced that feeling of flow when you are completely immersed in an activity, when you are in 'the Zone'? Allowing yourself to be in the right place, doing the right thing, at the right time.
When you are in flow, creativity flows.

> *"Life is a series of natural and spontaneous changes. Don't resist them – that only creates sorrow. Let reality BE reality. Let things flow naturally forward in whatever way they like."*
> **Lao Tzu**

To be able to experience flow in everyday life is important. Developing the ability to enter a state of flow is life-changing. When you are fully immersed in the present moment and lose track of the world around you, time flies, productivity and creativity skyrockets and you experience a deep sense of fulfilment.

One thing I love about flow is that it encompasses being completely in the moment and experiencing a sense of calm and happiness in your work and daily activities. Once you've learnt to focus on the important things, instead of being constantly interrupted, you can easily focus on and immerse yourself in the task at hand. By believing in yourself, you can enjoy yourself even more, reduce stress while increasing quality output, get important stuff done and actually achieve your goals (rather than working for the sake of it).

A few steps to keep in mind on the journey to flow are as follows:

1. Have clarity around what you want to achieve in life.

2. Choose work you love. If your job is made up of stuff you hate, you might want to consider finding another job. Make sure it's challenging, but not too hard, so that you can learn and grow.

3. Find your quiet time. Which part of the day is your most

productive, morning or evening? Choose to do the right jobs at the right times.

4. Clear away distractions. Turn off loud and distracting music and put away your phone.

5. Live and learn to focus on the right tasks for as long as possible. Learn your concentration limits and work within them.

6. Take a break when you need it.

7. Enjoy losing yourself in the flow. Be in the Zone and appreciate the feeling.

8. Keep practising each step with awareness of who you are, what you can achieve, what you need to achieve, what you want, what you are good at and what you love to do.

Energy flows where intention goes. Understanding who you are, what you want, and how you are going to get it, is the first step and will get you closer to experiencing flow in your life. The next step is to allow yourself to go with the flow, and give yourself permission to be the best that you can be. How exciting is that!

> I AM RELAXED, INSIGHTFUL, PRODUCTIVE
> AND FOCUSED ON THE FLOW OF MY LIFE.
> EVERYTHING IS COMING EASILY AND
> NATURALLY FOR ME.

5. The rules to guide you

Finding the best way to get the task done can be challenging and the simpler we make it the easier it is to achieve our wants and desires.

PART TWO

Rules keep us accountable, eliminate the time and effort you spend on distracting activities and other unproductive behaviour that can waste your time.

Focus
THE RULE: FOCUS ON WHAT YOU WANT TO DO/ ACHIEVE. FOCUS ON EACH STEP ALONG THE WAY.

"No matter how much it hurts, you gotta stay focused on what you're there for and your goals, just don't give up."
Stephen Thompson

To focus is a state or a point of concentration, directed attention, or a centre of activity. It is important to be focused, as this is the gateway to all thinking, perception, learning, reasoning, memorising, problem-solving and decision-making. What you focus on is what you get! Different meanings can be given to every event you experience in your life. You choose which meaning you put to it by deciding what aspects and emotions to focus on, and realise the consequences of that thought. Without good focus, all aspects of your ability to think will suffer, and the likelihood of what you want to achieve will decrease.
What you focus on is what you get!

> I AM CALM AND FOCUSED IN ALL THAT I DO.
> I CONCENTRATE AND FOCUS ALL MY
> EFFORTS ON THE THINGS I WANT TO
> ACCOMPLISH IN LIFE.

Motivation
THE RULE: STAY MOTIVATED AND UNDERSTAND WHAT MOTIVATES YOUR ACTIONS AT ANY ONE POINT IN TIME.

The word 'motivation' is derived from the word motive, which means needs, desires, wants or drives within an individual. Motivation is a process to stimulate one into action to accomplish a desired outcome or goal. Your motivation is always based on your why; why you desire this specific thing or goal. When your why is strong enough, then your motivation is stronger to do the things you need to do, to achieve whatever you want, to be happy, to live your best life and to achieve your goals.

Most conscious actions require motivation, and there are four types of motivation; two of which are basic: intrinsic and extrinsic.

> *"When you find the reason to do it, you will feel that fire within you. That kind of motivation that makes you keep going while others give up."*
>
> **Gymaholic**

1. **Intrinsic motivation** is when you do something because you love it; one surrenders completely to the moment, and time means nothing.

2. **Extrinsic motivation** is when your motivation to see and to succeed is controlled externally. It includes doing something to avoid getting into trouble or working hard to earn more money. This type of motivation is short-lived. A good extrinsic motivation is when you are practising to get better and you still need to be a student or have a teacher to validate your efforts.

The other two types of motivation are introjected and identified.

3. **Introjected motivation** is similar to intrinsic in that it is internalised. The distinctive aspect of this is that if it is not done, then a person feels tension and guilt.

4. **Identified motivation** is when a person knows that something needs doing but has not yet decided to do anything about it.

If you have a lack of motivation and you are not achieving what you want check:
- Is your intention clear?

- If your why is strong enough.
- What are you focusing on?
- Are your energy levels low?
- Is your environment supporting you?
- Are you living a balanced lifestyle?

> I AM HIGHLY MOTIVATED TO ACHIEVE AND SUCCEED IN EVERYTHING THAT I DO.

Understanding your why
THE RULE: KNOW WHY YOU DO THE THINGS YOU DO.

"When your why is big enough, you will find your how."
Unknown

Your why in life gives you a reason to do what you do, a direction that provides confidence so that when you make decisions, you are not confused and it feels right. It helps keep you focused on what you want. You will be better equipped to avoid distractions and concentrate. To stay focused, the action – whatever it is – must be important to you, so you won't waste time on other stuff and stay motivated to achieve your desired outcome.

When you know why you want what you want, your goal becomes fuelled by your passion. It also helps you become more resilient when you experience setbacks or challenges. It allows you to live with integrity and be true to yourself.

Your why is twofold:

1. Your why as your motivation. If your why is strong you can achieve anything.

2. Your why as a tool of self-discovery. Getting to the root cause of any disharmony or challenge you may have in your life.

THE JOURNEY HANDBOOK

When you ask the why question the key is to be honest with yourself. You might be surprised by the answers you get and that's okay, because you will have learnt something about yourself.

YOUR WHY VERSUS SURVIVAL

I was talking to a friend recently; she is an extraordinarily positive person who has been through so much. I asked her what she did in the face of adversity and what her why was initially, ie, why she did the things she did. She said it was initially for survival. She set goals and took baby steps to move away from the situation, so she could survive one day at a time. These baby steps and goals helped her move through each day, until she became more confident, she then allowed herself to dream again.

Her story inspired me. You see Your WHY is relevant to any level of achievement and success one step at a time. When your why is strong enough you can achieve anything. How exciting is that!

> I HAVE FIRE IN MY BELLY AND I AM
> PASSIONATE AND EMPOWERED TO LIVE
> MY BEST LIFE.

> "Such happiness as life is capable of comes from the full participation of all our powers in the endeavour to wrest from each changing situation of experience, its own full and unique experience."
> **John Dewey**

Participation
THE RULE: PARTICIPATE IN YOUR LIFE LIKE YOU MEAN IT.

The action of taking part in something is incredibly powerful. We all have busy lives and things to do, but when you can't be bothered to show up, what does that mean? Everyone says they want to live a great life, have healthy relationships and look and feel their best, but how many of us are willing to put in the work every day to actually achieve this? Be engaged, connect with those around you, remove negative thoughts and distractions. Focus on the positives and get involved.

Challenge yourself and discover the joys in life through participation. Get involved in your life. Follow your passion, connect with friends, and your family. It does not matter what it is – it might be through exercise, knitting, running, cooking, being creative, writing, painting, and playing. Join a group of likeminded people, get excited, and experience everything. If you don't have a go, you will never, ever know how amazing your life could be.

> I WHOLEHEARTEDLY PARTICIPATE IN LIFE EVERY DAY.

Gratitude
THE RULE: DEVELOP AN ATTITUDE OF GRATITUDE: ADD IT TO YOUR DAILY ROUTINE.

"When we focus on our gratitude, the tide of disappointment goes out and the tide of love rushes in."
Kristen Armstrong

An attitude of gratitude is so important. The concept of gratitude is directly related to the idea of positive thinking, or focusing on what we do have as opposed to what we don't have. Yes, we all have stressful and negative things in our lives. We could let them overwhelm us. But everyone has reasons to be thankful too. If we train ourselves to become more aware of the good things, we will start to find our life changing, maybe not on the outside but on the inside, where it really counts. Appreciating what is right in our lives is a habit well worth the effort.

Being thankful is a choice. Even in all our busyness, we can take a few minutes each day to intentionally focus on the reasons we have to be grateful. This can take some practice. Often, we feel too tired, too distressed, too sad, too mad, too frustrated or too overwhelmed by our lives, and it's easy to get lost in these feelings. The load is too heavy. But that is exactly when we need an attitude of gratitude the most. The surprising thing about choosing to be grateful is that it changes our focus and, ultimately, our life. Gratitude lifts your energy and vibration. The first step can also be the hardest.

Start a gratitude journal. Write three things you are grateful for each day before bed. Connect to the positive feelings and see how good you feel when you wake up in the morning. Write and connect to the feelings you experience; be specific.

For example: *I am grateful for all the things my mother does for me, because it makes me feel loved and cared for.*

List and connect with three to five things you are grateful for today. And explain what you feel for each one.

1. Today, I am grateful for: ....
   because it makes me feel ....

2. Today, I am grateful for: ....
   because it makes me feel ....

3. ....

4. ....

5. ....

Be specific and mindfully connect to the feeling that each gratitude gives you.

PART TWO

> I EXPERIENCE GRATITUDE FOR EVERYTHING
> I HAVE IN MY LIFE.

The power of kindness
THE RULE: BE KIND TO YOURSELF AND OTHERS AND LET GO OF WHAT DOES NOT SERVE YOU.

"There is no need for temples; no need for complicated philosophy. Our brain, our own heart is our temple; the philosophy is kindness."
Dalai Lama

Kindness is a quality or state of being kind, and treating yourself and others with care and compassion. Extend kindness to everyone around you, including yourself. You know those kind words you say to others? Say them to yourself as well, along with that moment of mindful listening, being present and courteous. Tell yourself why you are a wonderful person, and if you repeat it enough, you will believe it. Think kind, positive thoughts about yourself and others, rather than focusing on negatives.

Kindness and forgiveness go together. Sometimes, to forgive is to let go and not linger on that which does not serve you. Let go of the past, as it has already gone, and forgive yourself, because whatever you did then was the best you could do at that point in time. Forgive yourself for your mistakes – they might have been driven by negative emotions, take your learnings and move on and open yourself up to new possibilities.

> I CARRY NOTHING BUT KINDNESS AND
> LOVE IN MY HEART FOR MYSELF
> AND OTHERS.

Potholes of judgement
THE RULE: REFRAIN FROM JUDGING OTHERS; YOU HAVE NOT WALKED IN THEIR SHOES.

> *"Learn to experience yourself without judging yourself."*
> **Bryant McGill**

A judgement is a conclusion or opinion. We all judge others, and they judge us. Sometimes, we judge with positive or harmless intentions. Unfortunately, our judgement often comes from a negative place, with darker intent. Judging is when you don't give someone a chance. If you want to grow as a person and become wiser, you should learn how to respect other people, including your enemies.

Yes, your enemies. They are different to you, and they think differently. You have not walked in their shoes. We all need to accept what is different, and if they truly don't align with who we are, then find the wisdom to walk away and accept them for who they are. We judge our enemies and try to make their lives miserable, but often end up ruining our own lives instead. Let's stop judging, and just focus on making ourselves happy. We don't have the right to judge others, so why do we do it?

Below the surface, people tend to judge others based on their own fears. When we look at someone for the first time, we see a reflection of our past experiences and associations. It could be based on their body language, the way they dress, or their behaviour. If we don't know a person well enough yet, often we cannot identify with their belief system, values or behaviour. That person somehow threatens how we perceive ourselves. Maybe we are insecure, scared, lonely, seeking change or wanting our lives to be different. We are not only judging others, but also ourselves.

When you judge, you hurt others, bring yourself down, create negativity and perpetuate stereotypes in the world. So, stop it! Your life is more valuable than you can imagine. Focus on your life so that you can live your best life! Monitor your thoughts, look for the positive, and stop judging yourself; avoid stereotyping and remember how it feels to be judged. What other people do is none of your business. Allow yourself to enjoy your life.

> *"Do not judge me by my successes, judge me by how many times I fell down and got back up again."*
> **Nelson Mandela**

THE JUDGEMENT AUDIT

"Do unto others, as you would have them do unto you." Take time to consider your behaviour when it comes to judgement. Do you judge others on a regular basis? If so, have you worked out why? What do you achieve in doing so?

Judgement + criticism = self-doubt + paralysis	Appreciation + affirmation = belief + action

> I RESPECT, LOVE AND APPRECIATE WHO I AM.

Habits: they can make or break you
THE RULE: ONLY NURTURE GOOD HABITS AND RECOGNISE THE DIFFERENCE.

A habit is defined as an automatic response to a specific situation that is usually acquired as a result of repetition and learning. When a behaviour is developed to the extent that it is automatic, it is called a habit. Habits can be divided into four categories:

- **Instigating habits:** these are the life processes we establish to help guide us in the project of living life, such as going to the gym, reading, making time for friends.

- **Avoidance habits:** these habits are the ones we try to break, such as drinking, smoking, gossiping, and procrastinating.

- **Regimental habits:** doing an activity the same way each time, leaving no room for serendipity, such as showering, cleaning our teeth, parking in the same place.

> *"We are what we repeatedly do. Excellence, then, is not an act, but a habit."*
> **Aristotle**

- **Unconscious habits:** the biggest category, such as frowning, picking your nails, picking your nose, speeding.

These can then be seen as either good or bad habits: the key is to know the difference.

✓ **Good habits:** these are behaviours that are beneficial to one's physical or mental health; they are often linked to a high level of discipline and self-control. Examples of good habits are regular exercise, minimising alcohol use, and a balanced diet.

✗ **Bad habits:** bad habits appear when one is faced with challenges such as stress due to school, work or family issues. We tend to fall back on reliable crutches such as food, alcohol, procrastination, avoidance, overreacting, arguing or even nail-biting, even though we know they are likely to make us feel worse in the long run.

Bad habits can generally be triggered by stress and can actually be caused by our thoughts and our negative self-talk, not the situation itself. The key to changing our habits is to shift our self-talk from negative messages to realistic, positive assessments of the situation. Changing a habit is possible and can be a struggle, persistence is the key, small lapses shouldn't make you feel doomed. Remember to be kind to yourself, you're always learning.

One popular method to build new habits is called the 21/90 rule. The rule is simple enough: commit to a personal or professional goal or new habit for 21 straight days. After this three-week period, the pursuit

PART TWO

of that goal should have become a habit. Once you've established that habit, you continue to do it for another 90 days.

Check out the handy monthly habit tracker in the Toolbox at the back of the book.

> EVERY DAY I AM DEVELOPING NEW AND POSITIVE HABITS. MY MIND ALTERS MY THOUGHTS, AND MY THOUGHTS ALTER MY HABITS.

Time out
THE RULE: GIVE YOURSELF A BREAK.

Life does seem to be speeding up and becoming busier, we are often bombarded by outside influences telling you what you should be doing when and why. The reality though, is if you don't take time out you can get lost in the humdrum of life, who you are and what you really want to achieve in life. How hard can it be to take some time out, relax, catch up with a friend or family? Reconnect with yourself, your partner, your children and your inner voice. Find your balance and be empowered to live your best life.

> *"The truth is we all need a time out, timeout to re-evaluate, find balance, heal, detox, and time to breathe!"*
> **Michael Baisden**

> I VALUE MY TIME OUT AND PLAN IT INTO MY DAILY, WEEKLY, MONTHLY ROUTINE.

"You may not be able to control every situation and its outcome, but you can control your attitude and how you deal with it."
Unknown

6. The road to success

Know your outcome

The result of something or the consequence of it, is the outcome, final product or end result. No matter what you're doing, you will always get a better result if you know exactly what you are aiming for. So be clear about what you want. Is it a dream house or that seven-figure income? Create a vision board and a road map (a U C A N B S M A R T goal) to get you to your destination and keep you motivated. You don't have to do it all at once. Take one step at a time. Know your outcome, create your vision, and live your best life!

Most importantly of all, do you have the physical and emotional resources to maximise your effectiveness to achieve your outcome, as well as the everyday activities of your balanced life?

Excuses be gone; make time to find a routine that works for you. You don't have to do it all at once. Take one step at a time. Know your outcome, create your vision, and live your best life!

> I RECOGNISE EVERY NEW CHALLENGE
> AS AN OPPORTUNITY.
> I HAVE THE POWER TO CREATE ALL THE
> SUCCESS AND PROSPERITY I DESIRE.

Make a commitment to yourself

Commitment is dedication in action; it is the state or quality of being dedicated to a cause or activity. A commitment means you are obligated to do something. Committed people constantly make new goals and are always striving to push the boundaries and achieve more. They work hard out of habit and loyalty. They have a unique endurance that allows them to find success and achieve their dreams.

"Motivation is what gets you started. Commitment is what keeps you going."
Jim Rohn

PART TWO

Whenever you commit to an outcome and do everything you need to do to get there you will inevitably achieve success. This includes ensuring you have a supportive environment to support you along the way. You can take the next step because you're capable, and it feels good.

> I AM COMMITTED TO LIVING MY BEST LIFE
> AND ACHIEVING MY DREAMS.
> I AM CONFIDENT AND COMMITTED TO
> LIVING A PASSIONATE LIFE.

Take action

We write our own destiny. If you don't take action, nothing will change. Action means getting something done. An action is the *doing*; the act is the result of the doing. Taking action often depends on the motivation to complete a task. Sometimes, we just aren't motivated or inspired, and we tend to avoid the task instead of taking action. It all comes back to how strong your why is. So, find your motivation, show commitment, and take it one step at a time if you have to.

"Your talent determines what you can do. Your motivation determines how much you are willing to do. Your attitude determines how well you do it."
Lou Holtz

If you want to work out, start with a short 10-minute routine. If you have to write a paper, tell yourself that you'll write 200 words today and 300 words tomorrow and keep increasing the number. Make whatever it is doable, because you can do it. If it's not working, stop, take a break, review, renew, and start again. Ask for help if you need it. Constantly keep your eyes on the benefits of the outcome, the light at the end of the tunnel, swap negative thoughts for positive ones, and celebrate each step along the way. You are in control.

> I TAKE ACTION AND BRING MORE POSITIVE
> RESULTS INTO MY LIFE.

THE JOURNEY HANDBOOK

Dare to dream!

Dreams make us wonder, and open us up to endless possibilities as well as making us believe

"Nothing is impossible, the word itself says 'I'm possible'!"
Audrey Hepburn

in a better future. What would you do if you knew your dreams could come true, if there is no risk or failure? Free up your mind; think about what it would be like to live your life to your full potential, a life full of infinite possibilities, a life you would love.

Be clear on what you really, really want and dare to dream. Nothing is impossible if you put your mind to it. Don't limit yourself by what you think or the roadblocks that may or may not pop up, put them aside and begin dreaming.

Create a vision/dream board and visualise, use your active imagination and feel the feelings of what you can see and hear as if it has already happened. Then take that first step and make it happen.

> I AM FREE TO BREAK FREE.
> IF I CAN IMAGINE IT, I CAN ACHIEVE IT.

"Hope lies in dreams, in imagination and in the courage of those who dare to make dreams into reality."
Jonas Salk

ADVENTURE CALLS

In reality, it can be a dilemma, a catch-22 situation. When you are feeling low, you don't feel like doing what makes you feel happy and good. It is a choice. The high road to happiness and a fulfilled life or the low road to despair; the choice is yours. No matter what is happening in your life right now, you are beginning to understand what makes you feel good and what you need to focus on to get to where you want to be.

You have the power, and the choice. You have made the decision; the opportunity to change is now within your grasp. From the very first chapter, you may have realised that all is not quite right and that you need to change something in your life, even if you don't have total clarity about what that is yet. Embrace who you truly are, now you have your list of skills, celebrate and accept that there may be more within you to discover. Open yourself up to the boundless opportunities of the future and upgrade your knowledge and develop your skills – because you can.

Get excited, be curious, and positively charge your emotions for the adventure ahead. The fact of the matter is that our journey takes effort. Whatever it is, be courageous, and the result may be closer than you think. While we are each a work in progress, it's important to know that through support and the acknowledgement of self, you will discover what you have, what you need and how to take action. All you have to do is take the next step.

Before we move on to creating your road map, let's just do a check on where you are right now with your mindset qualities for success.

Your Success Circle Map

Success encourages you to develop eight invaluable qualities within yourself to take your life to the next level. In order to go somewhere and make a change, you need to be very clear on where you are right now in each section. Let me explain a little more about these.

Eight invaluable mindset qualities for success

Quality 1:
I take responsibility for the choices I make.

To take responsibility for the choices you make, you need to be honest with yourself and understand that every thought you have and your behaviour stem from your experience and programming. Understand this and act on it when necessary.

Quality 2:
I can be honest with myself.

One of the hardest things is to be honest with yourself, to look within and align yourself with your reality. Ask yourself: *Am I honouring my personal circumstances? Am I honouring who I am? Am I making decisions to take the appropriate action out of fear or love? What matters most to me?*

Quality 3:
I take action when I need to.

If you don't take action, nothing will change. Be aware that all actions have consequences. Our lives are complex, and a change will ripple out, like when a stone is dropped into a still pool of water. Some ripples disappear; some become waves, and some become tidal waves. Check internally and externally if the actions you are taking are the right ones for you. Think about whether your actions are pushing you in the right direction towards the outcomes you desire.

Quality 4:
I can see outside the box.

The box represents your comfort zone. Understand that where there is a will, there is a way. Can you take that first step, whether it is on your own or with assistance, it doesn't matter. Just do it! A fulfilled life awaits you.

Quality 5:
I have an attitude of gratitude.

To be grateful is to raise your energy, connect that energy to yourself and allow yourself to feel the gratitude, not just see it. Focus on gratitude for everything in life. Notice the little things. You may be surprised by what you find. Do you connect with and really feel your attitude of gratitude?

PART TWO

Quality 6:
I am willing to experiment.

Are you willing to do what it takes to get to where you want to go, take a risk, have some fun along the way, be flexible, try all sorts of things and enjoy the experience? If what you are doing is not working, then try something else. The more strategies you have to reach your outcome, the greater your chances are of achieving it. Learn your lessons and keep going.

Quality 7:
I trust my own intuition.

Are you able to go within to find the answers? Are you connecting with your body and listening to what it is telling you? Can you find that peace within you that truly shows who you are?

Quality 8:
I believe I can do anything.

Do you truly believe you can achieve anything you desire? Do you believe in yourself? Understand you already have the resources you need to overcome anything. Self-belief empowers us to love, accept and appreciate who we are, to stand strong and overcome everything that comes our way.

Creating your Success Circle Map

Now with the knowledge of what your Success Circle is made of, you are ready to evaluate what mindset qualities you have in your life right now! On your Success Circle Map there are eight lines radiating from the centre, each one representing a mindset quality.

1. On each line, mark a dot and number it from 1 - 10:
   Zero being the centre and 10 landing on the inner circle.
   1 represents the least amount of confidence you have in the quality and 10 represents the best it can possibly be.

THE JOURNEY HANDBOOK

2. Join the dots and this will create the map of where you are now and it represents where your starting point is.

3. When completed, pick three sections as explained on the next page, fill in the appropriate score and ask yourself the questions that follow.

Be honest with yourself. Join the dots until you have a complete shape within your Success Circle Map.

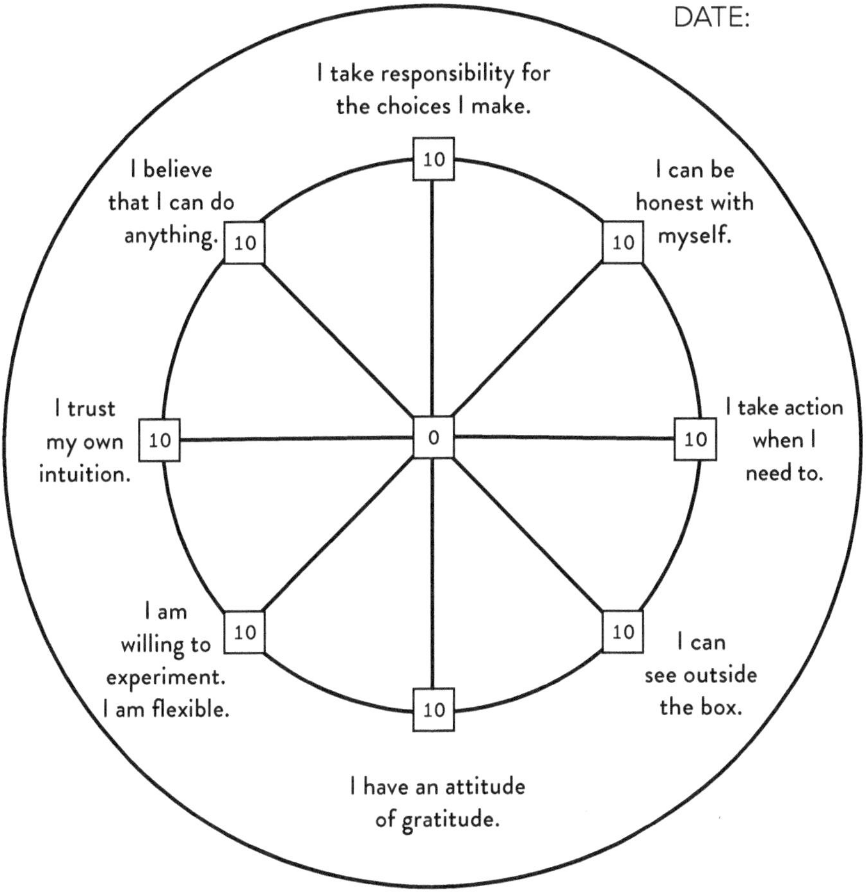

DATE:

- I take responsibility for the choices I make.
- I can be honest with myself.
- I take action when I need to.
- I can see outside the box.
- I have an attitude of gratitude.
- I am willing to experiment. I am flexible.
- I trust my own intuition.
- I believe that I can do anything.

PART TWO

Time to reflect

Step 1: First, choose your lowest-scoring section.
The lowest-scoring area in my Success Circle is:

Area 1: ....

Currently rated: /10

Step 2: Now, choose the area of your Success Circle that you feel most challenged with right now.
The most challenging area in my Success Circle is:

Area: ....

Currently rated: /10

Step 3: For each focus section, answer the following questions:

1. How, specifically, is this mindset a challenge for you?

2. How long has it been a challenge?

3. What is this challenge stopping you from doing?

4. Is there anyone else involved in this challenge?

5. What do you do instead when you *(don't/can't/are not)*..........
(Insert..........mindset here)?

6. What do you think you need to change?

7. What WILL you achieve if you changed the way you think about..........
(what you feel you need to change)?

8. What WON'T you achieve if you don't change anything?

THE JOURNEY HANDBOOK

Step 4: What did you learn?

Once you have finished answering the questions in both sections, write down what you have learnt about yourself in regard to what is working and what is not working in your life right now.

....

....

....

....

....

....

....

....

....

....

....

Please Note: don't be too hard on yourself, this is just an exercise of discovery to support you and set you on the right path and get you into the driver's seat. In the next chapter, we are going to be a little more specific about what we want and how to create your road map. Take the handbrake off – and let's go!

You're still sitting at the bus stop waiting for permission to get on the bus.

You sit in quandary for a moment. A cloud goes across the sun, and it sends a chill over your body.

After reading the Journey Handbook you realise that you already have some of the tools and knowledge you need to succeed. You understand there may be some potholes and roadblocks along the way yet you still question yourself.

"But am I ready now?" Your thoughts dive down a little. You may be feeling a little overwhelmed as there is so much to learn and understand.

You know what you want and you have more clarity around your destination, but is your dream big enough or your desire clear enough?

You have come this far, what would be the point of giving up now?

The clouds move on, the sun warms your face and your body. You start to feel relaxed and excited for what is to come next.

You actually start to feel goosebumps spreading all over your body.

The Handbook is on the seat beside you; you have completed the Success Circle. You ARE ready.

You close your eyes and take a deep breath, you start to relax even more, and you can still feel the warmth of the sun on your cheeks. You intuitively imagine yourself drifting into the future and it feels so good.

When you finally open your eyes you are surprised to see that the sun is setting and it's getting dark. You move around a little on the seat and as you go to stand up, you feel the clipboard that the young man had given you earlier fall to the ground. You pick it up and see that there are some forms on it, a check list, the road map instructions and your itinerary that needs to be filled in before you start the journey and get onto the bus.

You quickly read over them and as there is no sign of the bus and there is a chill in the air, you decide to go home as you are feeling a little tired.

PART THREE

THE ROAD MAP

"

Understanding your traits, feelings and behaviours, both good and bad, is vital if you want to build better relationships, achieve your goals and lead a contented life. It takes bravery but the payoffs are worth it.
Nikki Williamson[4]

"

PART THREE

The reality of life

You never know what's round the corner

As a child, I experienced flow. As an only child brought up on a dairy farm, I was in that zone for the majority of my childhood. I spent a lot of time on my own, experiencing everything to the fullest extent. And as a child, it was easy, no directions, no distractions, and nothing to worry about. I remember being on a swing under the pine trees on the farm for hours on end. I was in that zone, though I may not have realised it at the time.

Have you ever just watched a young child in their own little world, the look of wonder as they encounter a new experience, a smell, a flower, life and nature, blowing bubbles, all the wonders and the magic that exist in our world? From childhood to adulthood, what happens? What changes? We can no longer bathe in the innocence of childhood. We take on the responsibility of survival – a roof over our heads, food on the table. We can get swept up with the ups and downs life throws at us. We can experience natural disasters, illness, bullying, abuse, drugs and alcohol abuse, robbery and the invasion of personal privacy, war, pain, grief and more.

My point here is that we can't get caught up in the doom and gloom life throws at us. We have to consciously make the effort to become resilient until it becomes a habit and realise that our life can become easier. We need to believe that we can be, do and have whatever we want in life; the key here is that whatever you need to do, do it for the right reasons. Understanding your authentic self gives you strength and courage to keep on track. You never know what's around the corner.

Recently, I found out I had breast cancer. It's scary to be faced with such a challenge, but I didn't want to sit in fear and hurt and anger. I decided to focus on the positives instead and get help where I needed it and then get back on track with my learnings from the experience. Creating a new and slightly different pathway to where I wanted to be. The quickest way to freedom and success is setting a goal big or small; it doesn't matter, align it with who you are, take action, create a road map and take over the driver's seat for the rest of your journey.

Dare to dream

Take the handbrake off and let's go

I want you to simply close your eyes and take a big breath in and out 3 times. Now breathe in for six, hold for three, and out for nine. Repeat until you feel relaxed and a sense of calm comes over you and you have created some thinking space for yourself.

When you are ready, I want you to ask yourself this question: **If you could see the future, what would your life be like and feel like 10 years from now?**

Use your active imagination and take yourself to this day, 10 years from now. You already know what you want, and you have achieved it. What have you achieved? What is happening on that day? What do you see, hear and feel around you? Allow your thoughts to flow and create every little detail of this day. Connect completely to it.

There is a big, white screen in front of you. Create a moving picture of this day, from the time you get up to the time you go to bed. Feel it, see it, as if it is happening. Now, when you're ready, I want you to open your eyes, grab your journal and just start writing. Write down everything that happened throughout that future day. What did you do? Who did you see? What did you hear? What did you feel? Remember to include every detail. You could start it off like this:

On this day.......(month).......(year)......., the birds were singing. I roused myself sleepily from my bed to get ready for the day. I stretched my arms as if I could touch the sky and......

You sit back when you have finished, and you realise you are smiling. It feels good to write it, because it makes you feel that your dreams and desires are truly achievable. You can accomplish anything you want. If it felt good, you are probably aligned with your dream and it is congruent with who you are. You are now well and truly ready for the next step, and that is to create your road map to your goal, your dream, no matter how big or small this goal is.

It's not until you actually get into the driver's seat and start your journey that you get the realisations and learnings along the way. Something might need to change. Don't let the bumps of life allow you to veer off course. They are part of the journey. Just gently take the steering wheel again and make a small turn towards your 'happy place'.

The road map to your destination

> *"There's no doubt that setting goals gives you focus. Achieving goals feels fantastic."*
> **Carol Dweck**

Why create a road map to your goals?

Life isn't just about finding yourself; life is also about creating yourself, and your goals help you do both. Something wonderful happens when you put pen to paper and write down your goals. They inspire you to live with intention and start every day with the knowledge that you can do anything if you set your mind to it. A goal creates a pathway, a focus point, a means to an end, the light at the end of the tunnel. We may go off track every now and again, and that's okay. Realistically however, so many people never reach their goals – there is a difference between setting a goal and achieving a goal. How many times have you made a New Year's resolution that didn't happen?

A goal has to have some specific guidelines to be achievable. Setting a goal in the right way helps us to make our outcome achievable because it:

- Forces us to be specific.

- Gives us a plan or course of action.

- Helps us prioritise and organise.

- Gives us focus and clarity.

- Keeps us accountable.

- Helps us avoid procrastination.

- Breaks our steps down into smaller achievable chunks.

- Allows us to celebrate successes and milestones.

- Allows us to measure our progress.

- Builds confidence and gives us a sense of accomplishment.

- Provides motivation.

- Triggers new behaviours.

- Provides a pathway to our dreams.

Are you getting excited about what will happen next? Your goals create a pathway to an outstanding life. You may not have all of the answers yet, but you have a direction and you know where you want to be in ten years' time. Now, you can focus on mapping out how you are going to get there. The purpose of your road map is to realise what you have to do or change to reach your dream and break it down into doable steps. I use a ten-step strategy that helps to create greater clarity and connection when setting a personal goal. I have used this myself on so many occasions and I can assure you that it works. The strategy towards your goal has turned into a helpful analogy:

PART THREE

U Understanding the process

During my depression, I went to a bookshop in a nearby town. I was looking for something to read, so I asked for some suggestions from the owner. The book she recommended was *Food, Sex and Money* by Liz Byrski[5], a book highlighting that age is no barrier to the good things in life. Little did I know that that book was going to be the beginning of my journey away from depression. I started to believe I could change my life. I just needed to find out how.

The first thing I had to do was to realise I had to do something. The second was to find out what I needed to do. It was not until I asked myself deep questions that I knew what I had to do next. I went searching for the answer, and it came when I said yes to undertake a personal development program. It changed my life. You see, I had made the decision to do something, but I did not know what. My why was big enough; I just wanted to be happy, and that still remains my big why today. Today, I know what fills my cup and what makes me happy. I just needed to take action and ask the right questions. My thirst for knowledge about how I could change my life was the beginning.

Deciding what you want is the first step and deciding to read this book means you have begun the process – well done! When we do make the effort, often we don't know what we want. We could always be very general, complacent and unspecific and claim everything is okay; but is it? When things are not quite right, we can get sick and feel angry, unhappy and unfulfilled. Sometimes, we don't even know what's happening, and then the shit hits the fan.

There are four important aspects of creating a successful outcome that need to be considered when forming a goal.

> *"The only impossible journey is the one you never begin."*
> **Tony Robbins**

1. THE DECISION
The decision to do something will inevitably lead to a goal (a desired outcome).

Decide what you want: the advantage of goal setting is that it makes us decide what kind of life we want, rather than leave it to chance or live by someone else's rules. For example paying your bills on time or shedding some kilos can realistically be the first step to maybe owning your own house one day, having that dream job as a fashion model, taking the kids away on that dream holiday or just living a happy and fulfilling life. Get excited!! You can do this, allow yourself to dream and believe anything is possible!

- In which area of your life do you want to improve?
- What is it you specifically want?

2. WHY DO YOU WANT IT?

Understand why you want it: make sure your why is strong enough to keep you motivated and on track. Knowing your why gives you direction and provides you with the confidence to make the right decisions.

- Is your why strong enough?

3. ALIGN YOUR GOAL WITH YOUR VALUES

Understand that when your goals are value-driven, the more likely you are to achieve success, and your foundation is strong. A lot of the time, we give up too easily because there are times in our life when circumstances beyond our control get in the way of our perceived outcome. Don't beat yourself up if you are diverted by a roadblock. Remember that the light at the end of the tunnel will always be there to guide you. Your ability to be flexible is invaluable. If it's not working, do something else. As long as your values foundation is strong you will get there.

Never ever give up! Don't be hard on yourself, remember where there is a will there is a way.

- Are your core values aligned with what you want?

Please note: be mindful you have the core values of what you live by, then realise that in each area of Your Life Circle your values may be different.

If you are not sure what your core values are in the area you have chosen, please return to part 2 and reacquaint yourself with your core Values

Exercise. It might even be a good idea to redo this exercise in the area you have chosen as you may be seeing more clarity now.

EXERCISE

Whatever you are focusing upon, it could be career, family, relationships, health, fitness, fun or finances, either go back to your list of 10 values you did previously in the area of life you want to work in and pick out of your top 5 values, or redo the exercise.

Even if you can't think of anything, keep asking the question, and you may strike gold. (If you are stuck for words there is a Values List in the Toolbox at the back of the book.)

The area of my Life Circle I have chosen to work on is ....

Ask yourself: *What is important to me in this area?*

My top 10 values in this area are..

From your list of 10 pick out your top 5 values and order them from the top, most important to least.

My top 5 most important values in this area are ....

| **Value 1** | **Value 2** | **Value 3** | **Value 4** | **Value 5** |

When you have your top 5, I want you to answer these questions about each value:

Why is it important for you to be...........?

How do you feel when you have/are/act...........?

What do you need to do to be...........?

Do you/are you...........of others?

EXAMPLE: VALUE 1: RESPECT

Why is it important for you to be respected?
It is important for me to be respected as it acknowledges me for who I am, what I do and what I have achieved.
How do you feel when you are respected?
When I am respected, I feel that I belong, that I am useful and appreciated.
What do you need to do to be respected?
I need to be true to myself, honest and trustworthy and live my life to my fullest potential.
Do you respect/are you respectful of others?
I respect others for who they are without judgement.

Remember: You will have ups and downs, don't be hard on yourself as your values are your guide out of any challenge you may have, they are there to support you, give you clarity and confidence and open you up to your full potential. How exciting! Your light will start to shine brightly, and everyone will want to know your secret.

I recommend taking a break now. Leave this for a while, sleep on it, and, in a couple of days, continue on with the process and ask yourself these questions:

> *How are you feeling right now?*
>
> *What have you learnt about yourself?*
>
> *Are your values aligned with what you want in the area you have chosen to work on? If not, what do you need to change?*

Remember that this book is taking you on a journey.

4. THE POWER OF INTENTION

Script your goal statement with the power of intention and an attitude of positive purpose.

Firstly, you need to move and develop an attitude of positive purpose. Are you moving *towards* or *away from* what you want?

For example; a goal centred around moving '**AWAY FROM**' negative motivation is "I don't want to be fat", the negative being don't.

A goal with '**A TOWARDS**' motivation would be; "In 12 months, I will have lost 10kgs, will be able to fit into size 14 jeans and feel comfortable and free to be me." Focusing on the result, what you want.

Can you see the difference?

Secondly, we need to talk about intention. An intention is an idea or a determination to carry out a specific thing. It's something you mean to do, whether you pull it off or not. Knowing what you want and why leads to having a clear intention. You might say,

> *"I want to be fit and healthy, lose weight and have a toned body."*

An example of a powerful intention for this area of your life could be the following:

"I live my life in radiant health, filled with all of the boundless energy and vitality I need to enjoy my life and time with my loved ones to the fullest."

This statement includes a strong why and thus creates a stronger intention. Feel the energy that this intention carries. It's positive, uplifting, empowering and inspiring, and it describes the future you want to step into! Your intention is really the big, overarching why behind any goals you set for yourself. It's a long-term vision that you have for your future; an energetic statement that describes what success looks and feels like in any particular area of your life. If you don't set a clear, energised intention that includes your strong why, you may find that:

- You set goals that are all over the place and experience a lack of meaning or direction.
- You get discouraged or perhaps even give up when the going gets tough, because you don't feel super connected to the future you're trying to create.
- You achieve some results, but not the ones that make you feel truly happy and fulfilled.

By connecting to this process around our desired outcome/goal, we are forced to reassess and focus on what we specifically need to do to reach our desired outcome, keep the light shining at the end of the tunnel and stay motivated.

C Commitment

As mentioned previously, commitment is the state or quality of being dedicated to a cause or activity and the importance of making a commitment can't be overstated. If we don't commit, we will not achieve our outcome. We can get easily distracted and lose our way. But you know what? It doesn't matter because if you just stay committed, you will find your way back and get back on track.

Deal with the roadblocks you may have encountered along the way. Be flexible, and transform your identity, brain and environment to ensure you get what you want. Become laser-focused and stop getting distracted by what you don't want. Stay committed, take action, and change or do the things you need to do to reach your desired outcome.

Prior preparation prevents poor performance so you won't give up.

> *"Self-discovery is a process, a journey.
> Knowing yourself is the beginning of wisdom."*
> **Aristotle**

 Awareness

By now you will be familiar with this concept of awareness, opening up and becoming conscious of something, going within to get the answers often with all your senses and emotions. Self-awareness is a journey of discovering who you are, what you stand for and how your thoughts affect everything you do. It allows you to reorganise if something is not working, and to connect and go within to find the answers, to ask yourself if it's not working, why not? It's a place where you can connect deeply and meaningfully to your vision, your values and your principles or standards of behaviour and gain insight into what's important in your life.

Some tips on how to practise connecting are:

! Learn to listen to your inner voice about what suits you and acknowledge what that gut feeling is telling you. What is your greatest desire? What kind of aspirations do you have? Is it right or wrong for me?

! Prepare yourself mentally to overcome any roadblocks you encounter.

! Build an environment that is going to support you; surround yourself with people that you know well, love and trust.

! Journal your thoughts, actions, outcomes, failures, learnings and 'ah-ha' moments so that you can reflect and maybe, at a later time meditate on them.

! Reflect on your vision and edit it until it resonates with who you are. Know yourself.

N Nurturing

Do you love who you are and nurture yourself on a regular basis? Nurturing is all about nourishing and caring for yourself; the act of self-care is to protect and support you to understand your own needs, while you are growing and achieving your outcomes. Your aim is to thrive emotionally, physically and mentally and recognise balance in your life. It will take time; so don't be hard on yourself.

> *"It's not selfish to love yourself, take care of yourself, and to make your happiness a priority. It's necessary."*
> **Mandy Hale**

Nurturing yourself is not selfish. It is essential self-preservation, so that you can be the best you can be, not only for yourself but also for all those around you. Nurturing yourself must be a priority if your foundation is going to be strong enough to take you on the journey to reach your dreams.

B Believe you can

If anyone wants to succeed in life, they must believe in themselves. We have to believe in our abilities because our inner faith will create our external results.

> *"No one can make you feel inferior without your consent."*
> **Eleanor Roosevelt**

Our world is becoming more competitive. Everything can become too hard. People easily lose faith in themselves when encountering the roadblocks life throws at them; feelings of failure and fear creep in, and we slowly lose confidence in ourselves. Sometimes, it's easier to just give up on our dreams. Instead of giving into the fear, we need to be confident and trust in our own abilities, capacity and judgement.

You can achieve anything you put your mind to if you truly want it. Our world is full of possibilities; you just need to see them. Once you become aware of who you are and your needs and wants, you gain confidence in yourself. During Covid-19 in 2020/21, I doubted myself and allowed what was happening externally to engulf me as I wrote this book. So many people have written self-help books, what was the point of me doing the same? Instead of giving into these thoughts, I delved deep and asked myself if I was going to let those thoughts and what I was feeling stop me.

No, I wasn't. I love working with my clients; this is my genius zone. I want to help and support people to be empowered to live their best life, because I know I can. I have the experience and the knowledge to help, and no one else has walked in my shoes or experienced my depression as I have. Sometimes we just need to remind ourselves that when we believe in ourselves, the possibilities are endless.

- Do you believe you can achieve anything you want? If not, why not?

S Specific and simple

Your goal statement must be clearly defined, identified, detailed and exact. Say it exactly how you want it. Specific information refers to exact, precise facts. To be specific, you need to answer these 'W' questions:

Who: *who is involved?*

What: *what do you want to accomplish?*

Where: *where is the location?*

When: *what is the time frame?*

Which: *what are the requirements and constraints?*

Why: *why do you want it? What are the specific reasons for and purposes or benefits of accomplishing the goal?*

A general goal would be, "I want to get into shape". A specific goal would be, "I will join a health club and workout three days a week so that I can tone my body and look and feel great."

Go for specific goals, make the steps clear, manageable, process and progress oriented.

M   Measurable and meaningful

Measurable: create a timeline to establish a stepping-stone process to get to your destination. When you break your journey down into specific steps of achievement, it makes it easier to stay motivated and celebrate your achievements along the way.

1. What do you need to do to achieve your goal?
2. How many steps do you need to reach the outcome?
3. How will you know when you have reached the goal?

Meaningful:
1. Is your goal meaningful to you?
2. Is your why big enough?
3. Does it light you up when you think about it?

A   Achievable

To achieve something, it is important to know that it is attainable and can be brought about or reached successfully. Remember to break your goal down to achievable chunks and celebrate each one, one step at a time. Reflect on the following:

> *"Every day, do something that will inch you closer to a better tomorrow."*
> **Doug Firebaugh**

- Do you have a supportive environment around you, or is it just you?
- Is your why strong enough?

- What are the limitations around what you need to do to achieve it?
- How can you accomplish the goal? Do you have the skills you need to reach your goal?
- What do you need to do/change to make sure you can achieve this goal?

R Relevant, realistic and responsible (and a little risky)

Here are some important questions on the points you need to consider when setting a goal with the purpose of keeping you motivated and interested in achieving your desired outcome.

RELEVANT

- This goal needs to be relevant to the situation in which it is being developed.
- Is this goal for work or is it personal?
- Is your focus relevant to each step you need to take?
- Is the goal relevant to what you want to portray and achieve in regard to your overall outcome?
- Does it seem worthwhile?
- Are you aligned with the outcome and the right person to achieve this?

REALISTIC

- Do you have a plan as to how you can achieve your goal in the time you have set aside to work on it?
- Is the end outcome realistic/achievable?

RESPONSIBLE

- Can you fit this goal into your life and still maintain a balanced lifestyle?
- Are you committed to and accountable for your results?

RISKY

- Your goal needs to be stimulating, adventurous and challenging to a certain degree to keep it alive.
- Are you willing to do what you need to do to achieve the desired outcome?

T Time-bound, towards what you want, and tangible

Time-bound: this refers to the time allocated to reach your goal. Whether it is a work goal or a personal goal, you must take into consideration your circumstances; there should be clear start and end dates. Please note: a time bound goal can keep you accountable and don't stress as roadblocks can pop up along the way as long as you are not making excuses and you are doing the best that you can at any one point in time, you know you can reset and follow that light at the end of the tunnel.

> *"You will never find time for anything. If you want time, you must make it."*
> **Charles Buxton**

Ask yourself: is the goal or task measured or restricted by time? Is time allocated for each step along the way?

A work-related goal will have strict time restraints. Time restrictions on a personal goal are more related to the endpoint giving you something to work towards and making you accountable.

Towards what you want: it is important to be moving towards and not away from your outcome. Each step you take must be towards the outcome with the end in mind. Instead of thinking, "I don't want to be fat", your statement and thinking should be what the result of not being fat would be, e.g. "I want to be fit and healthy". Can you see the difference? The way you think about your outcome can determine the success of your goal. Which way are you facing – forward or backward?

Tangible: how will you know you have achieved it, what evidence will you have to show that you have achieved your goal?

PART THREE

Release the handbrake

The key to living your best life, a life you can love is to keep moving forward, take on your learnings and release the handbrake. This book is intended as a reference point that helps you find the answers to your questions along the way to wherever you are going. A lot of the content you may already know. Yet the journey can still be a little overwhelming at first, as there is so much to learn and understand. Don't allow yourself to get stuck.

> *"Life is a journey, not a destination."*
> **Ralph Waldo Emerson**

To put it simply, the three main aims set out in this book are:

1. Become aware of what you want and why you do not have it yet.
2. Create a goal and a road map to show you the way.
3. Take the actions you need to reach your destination (because if you don't take action, nothing will change).

Our experiences and our failures are very important for our growth; there is no doubt about that, you never know what's around the corner. Without a target, a plan, a goal or a road map, our experiences become meaningless, because we don't learn and grow. It is difficult to become motivated if you are not facing forward towards new possibilities and achievements and expanding into your full potential. Travel, relax and enjoy the moment by all means, but do so with a destination in mind.

A dream: Visualise and connect with your dreams

A plan: A road map on how to get there

A goal: A clear picture of your desired outcome

= Your future of endless possibilities

> *"Your goals are the road maps that guide you and show you what is possible in your life."*
> **Les Brown**

5 steps to creating a road map/goal

STEP 1. WRITE OUT YOUR WELL-DEFINED GOAL STATEMENT.

At the beginning of this chapter, you wrote about where you want to be in ten years. Now it's time to create some goals and a road map to get you there. Revisit the area of your Life Circle you want to work on, and write a well-defined goal statement as if it has already happened.

CHOSEN AREA:

What is your intention, the understanding of what you want to improve in the chosen area?

Goal Statement:

On (date):..........

STEP 2. NOW IT'S TIME TO REVIEW IT AND GO THROUGH THE CHECKLIST BEFORE YOU TAKE THE NEXT STEP.

Part A: Review it by answering the following questions to get clear on your why.

- For what purpose do you want to achieve this goal?
- What will you gain if you have it?
- What will you lose if you don't have it?
- What will your life be like if you get it?
- What will your life be like if you don't get it?
- What will you miss out on if you don't get it?

How do you feel about your goal statement now?

Part B: Checklist

Complete this checklist and review your goal statement.

	Y/N		Y/N
Are you clear about what you specifically want?		Is your goal statement clearly defined?	
Is your why strong enough?		Is your goal achievable?	
Is your outcome important to you?		Is your goal measurable?	
Are your core values aligned with what you want?		Is your goal risky?	
Are you prepared to be aware, go within and nurture yourself on your journey to achieving this goal?		Is your goal relevant?	
Does your intention include a strong enough why to keep you motivated?		Is your goal realistic?	
Are you committed to achieving this goal?		Has your goal got an end date?	
Are you aware of what you need to do to achieve this goal?		Are you moving towards your outcome?	
Are you committed to doing the things you need to do to achieve the goal?		Is it self-initiated or self-maintained?	
Do you believe you can achieve your goal?		Is it only for you?	
Is your goal specifically about what you want?		Is your goal ecological?	

> *Make a list of your No answers.*
>
> *Is there anything you need to change in your goal statement? If so, what?*

Part C: Rewrite your goal statement if you need to.

STEP 3. VISUALISE AND EMBODY IT.

Embody your goal, connect with it and see how it feels. Please make sure you do this before you start on the road map. I call it the Active Imagination Visualisation Exercise, which you can find in the Toolbox at the end of the book.

STEP 4. GET TO WORK AND CREATE YOUR ROAD MAP.

When is your end date? How many months/weeks/days are there till you reach your destination? For example, if your end date is 12 months from now, you need to work backwards from your arrival time at your destination.

a. Work out what needs to be done when.

b. Work back to the present moment by monthly increments: what are the specific tasks that you need to do to accomplish your outcome each month?

c. Then, at the beginning of each month, work out specifically what you need to do each week, i.e. steps that will get you closer to where you want to be. For example, if you want to have $10,000 in your bank account within 12 months, how much money do you need to put away each month? "I would need to put away $833 a month, approximately $209 a week, $29 a day." Is that possible? Yes!

d. Next, you need to work out where that money is coming from. Is it from your clients? Something you sell? Extra money from your savings?

e. You can make a plan. Depending on what you want, you just need to work out what you have to do to get it. It's amazing what you can do by just putting $10 a day away, that's just coffee and cake or lunch money.

Ask yourself how you can do it differently.

> Here is an example of how it could work if you're dreaming of a holiday to Japan. Let's work backwards:
> 12th month: depart for Japan!
> 11th month: pack my suitcase.
> 10th month: plan work and home responsibilities for while you're away.
> 9th month: buy a new suitcase
> 8th month: prepare passport and visa.
> 7th month: put down a deposit on my trip.
> 6th month: practise my Japanese phrases and etiquette.
> 5th month: book accommodation and tours.
> 4th month: research destinations in Japan.
> 3rd month: forgo a few little luxuries and put that money aside as daily spending money in Japan.
> 2nd month: set up a new budget based on a realistic financial situation.
> 1st month: set up a new savings account that I can't touch, with a good interest rate.

Every day, think about what you can do to get you closer to your goal. If you are planning a holiday, you just do what you have to do. So why should it be any different with your life goals? Start taking daily actions, no matter how big or small, towards making your goals happen! A goal gives us a focus point, a reason to keep moving and growing and a reason to be motivated to do what we have to do to get there.

STEP 5.
   a. Create a Vision Board for your dream, frame it and hang it somewhere that you can see it on a daily basis and connect with the emotions it stirs up. (See the Bonus Content to learn how to create a Vision Board.)

   b. Download a road map from the Bonus Content and fill it in.

Remember, each day, you can achieve something! The hardest thing is taking the first step. If you break it down and start with baby steps, everything seems much easier than you thought.

ARE YOU EXCITED? I AM!

This whole process creates a pathway to your dreams. You can do this.

Gillian is sharing more in her BONUS CONTENT.

See exclusive downloads, videos, and more.

DOWNLOAD it now at
www.deanpublishing.com/gilliangorrie

> *Optimism is the faith that leads to achievement.*
> *Nothing can be done without hope and confidence.*
> **Helen Keller**

The next morning you return to your seat at the bus stop to wait for your bus. You feel the warmth of the sun on your face. You close your eyes and just enjoy the moment.

You have your road map, your goal and your lists that you completed the night before. You are well and truly ready. You have done your preparation, you are feeling good. Whatever could go wrong?

You hear a noise, and you open your eyes. It's the bus you saw in the beginning, the one with your name on it. You feel a tingle of excitement creep all over your body. You stand up and take a step towards the bus. As it pulls up right in front of you, the doors open.

As you step up into the bus, you feel a strange feeling of calm come over you. There is no one else on the bus, and all the seats are empty. The seat covers are colourful, and you choose a seat in the middle on the left-hand side. It's calling out to you, 'sit here, sit here'. You take your seat. The engine of the bus starts, and the bus moves slowly away from the curb.

You know from experience roadblocks will come up in your journey – you might hit a speed bump, or get lost along the way. You smile because you know that whatever happens, it's going to be okay. You now know what you need for your journey, you have your tool kit and if something is missing you know where to find it. The most important thing is you will never give up. You deserve to be happy and empowered to live the life of your dreams, because you can. You are in control.

Get ready and enjoy your journey.

PART FOUR

ROADBLOCKS

"

The truth of the matter is every roadblock is an opportunity to achieve success, when you understand how it was created.
Gillian Gorrie

"

PART FOUR

Diversions and distractions are part of the journey

It's not about the destination; it's the journey you take to get there that's important.

I would like to tell you about a story that a friend and I were discussing recently. It was from a book we had both read when we were children. The author, Frances Hodgson Burnett wrote and published *The Secret Garden* more than one hundred years ago. It was about a little girl called Mary: an obnoxious, spoiled, selfish little girl who found her way to love the life she had and was empowered to help others along the way.

You see, you never know what is around the corner, or what challenges you may face in the future, to me this book, *The Secret Garden* illustrates that even after a century our challenges in life have not really changed. When we dig deep and think outside the box, ask the right questions and believe in ourselves, miracles can happen. My mum always used to say, "Where there is a will, there is a way" and I believe this is true – if you want something badly enough you will find a way no matter what's happening around you.

Mary had been orphaned at a young age in India and was sent to live with her rich uncle in the English countryside. She was lonely and had no one to play with. And because she had nothing to do and no distractions, she learnt to go within, learnt how to skip and wandered around her uncle's garden looking for secrets. Her curiosity and continual questions led her to new discoveries. She became aware that there was a secret garden, then she found its secret door and with the help of a little robin she found the key to the garden. The garden had been locked for a decade.

Each day, she visited the secret garden. As Mary connected with nature and her newfound friends, her journey led her to discover new things about herself and she developed an even deeper understanding of the complexities of life and growth. Mary also discovered that she had a cousin she did not even know about. His name was Colin. He was a little boy the same age as Mary, and just as unpleasant as she was, who had been hidden away in the depths of the inner chambers of her uncle's home (a mansion so to speak).

They soon bonded, and together they went on a journey: from the impossible to the possible.

Their journey towards personal knowledge had begun with the unlocked door to the secret garden. The secret garden became an important key to personal knowledge, growth, and the understanding that one could live a happy, fulfilled life. With Mary's new skills, the skills of her new friends and the many secrets that unfolded within the secret garden, Mary's life was transformed. For Colin, it was the miracle of being physically disabled to walking again, while for Mary her reserve and rude detachment blossomed into an active interest in the world around her. By filling their minds up with beautiful thoughts, it left no room for disagreeable thoughts, and resulted in positive mindsets and a choice to be happy.

The journey was a discovery of life's treasures. Mary and her friends explored a limitless wonderland with a sense of amazement, adventure and curiosity, unlocking secrets from the past, which revealed a whole new life of hope and friendship. They lived in a supportive environment that allowed them to be their best selves. The garden held the secret, and once they had the key, the whole world opened up for them.

The point is you just need to be flexible and open to new opportunities. Imagine if you could do the same. Mary's strength and willfulness enabled life and limitless hope to unfold.

What are the chances you have experienced a roadblock or have one lurking in the background? A roadblock is something that blocks progress or prevents accomplishment of an object, idea, dream or goal and is predominantly negative.

- Are you feeling stuck?
- What are the challenges you are experiencing in your life right now?
- Do you want to get more out of life?
- Do you feel things are okay but could be better?
- Are you unhappy?
- Are you feeling stressed?
- Are you suffering physically or emotionally, overwhelmed, angry, frustrated or out of control?

PART FOUR

- If you were to know, do you know why you feel this way?
- How long have you been feeling this way?

Your roadblocks don't always stop you, but they can be big enough to distract you from reaching your destination and living your best life. They can stop you from being happy. Nine times out of ten a roadblock is a form of self-sabotage

On your journey, daily setbacks and failures are inevitable because shit happens, we have our ups and downs, and we don't really know what's going to be around the corner. Roadblocks both physical and mental, come in all shapes and sizes and they often come out of nowhere. When something is not working and you are finding it difficult to make progress, it's usually because you are stuck at a roadblock. You may have always lived with a roadblock unconsciously and it might only rear its ugly head when you want to change something in your life that is out of your comfort zone and brings in a lot of uncertainty.

Sure, you might be nervous about whatever is to come, but it's time to take stock of what you are leaving behind and look ahead, when one door closes and another opens. When you change your direction and discover a new way, you will find your confidence.

Distractions and diversions

Distractions and diversional thinking can create any roadblock you may have. To recognise your roadblocks, you need to understand a roadblock is only a challenge. If you want to be more or do more, it's a process of taking deliberate action, and creating that U CAN B SMART goal. Being prepared, being flexible and always having a backup plan which will help when you encounter a roadblock.

> "Challenges are gifts that force us to search for a new centre of gravity. Don't fight them. Just find a new way to stand."
> **Oprah Winfrey**

The key is to get to the bottom of the issue, become aware and work out why the roadblock has appeared, discover the root cause, then take action, learn your lessons and get back on track. Remember: it's a journey, so get excited. Do not let the roadblocks get you down. Ask yourself the right questions, be honest with yourself, get directions, ask for help if you need it, and keep moving forward, no matter how long it takes. The key to understanding your roadblocks and making your journey easier is to STOP at the traffic lights when you have reached a roadblock, and never ever give up.

Red: STOP! When things don't quite feel right or are not working STOP! Realise what is stopping you. Ask yourself: *Why am I stuck? Why am I not moving forward? Why am I unhappy* etc.

Amber: THINK! Ask yourself: *What do I really want? What have I been doing that is working really well? What is not working? What do I need to change?* Make a plan. *What new actions do I need to take to help me achieve my desired outcome?*

Green: FLICK THE SWITCH! Flick from negative to positive. Take action and do what you have to do to achieve your desired outcome.

Refer to the Stop, Think and Flick the Switch exercise in the Toolbox at the back of the book and take your understanding to a deeper level.

 PART FOUR

How do roadblocks show up?

The journey is about discovering your roadblocks; becoming aware of them, navigating through them and taking the appropriate action when you need to. You are the only one who can drive your bus and determine your journey and destination. You just need to make the right choices that are aligned with your goals, your values and who you are and what you stand for.

Let's explore more about how our roadblocks manifest, keep in mind that roadblocks are predominantly negative. The five major elements progress in the order below.

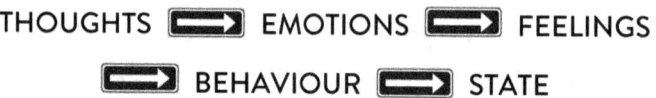

DO YOUR ROADBLOCKS SHOW UP AS ONE OR MORE OF THE FOLLOWING?

1. **A thought**
   A Limiting belief

2. **Emotions**
   Negative emotions (anger, sadness, fear, hurt or guilt)

3. **A feeling**
   Frustrated
   Lost
   Unhappy
   The language we use (internal and external)

4. **Behaviour**
   A Distraction
   An Avoidance strategy
   An Excuse
   A Habit

5. **Physical disease/state**
   Depression
   Anxiety etc

Understanding your roadblocks

Creating your flow in life requires you to understand your roadblocks so you can live your life to your fullest potential. If you don't stop, reassess and take action, nothing will change. Our responses originate from our neuro-linguistic

"You have the power over your mind – not outside events. Realise this, and you will find strength."
Marcus Aurelius

processes. The way we each uniquely process information from the filters of our programming from childhood, our life experiences and memories that are stored in our unconscious mind.

Most times, we are not even aware of how or why we are reacting in a certain way. We are more aware of the outcome; we wonder why we behaved the way we did or said the things we said. You may even avoid a situation or a consequence of your behaviour and just keep going without dealing with it. Your levels of reactive behaviour can then worsen and eventually affect you mentally, or physically and create an even bigger roadblock.

My studies around neuro-linguistic programming took me a step closer to understanding myself. It gave me the confidence that I could change my life by changing the way I think. On my own personal journey, I just wanted to know more. I now know I have the tools to support myself on my journey whenever anything pops up to challenge me, and I know these tools work. I will never go back to the depression that held me back for so long.

Understanding my particular roadblocks on my journey created my biggest 'ah-ha' moments where everything just seemed to make sense. I finally understood what I was dealing with and how to overcome each challenge that came my way. It's just like going to the doctor; they diagnose the problem and tell you how to deal with it, and you walk out of the surgery feeling better because you know what to do next. You then realise you have a

PART FOUR

choice: you can put a Band-Aid on, or discover the root cause and act on that.

One of my biggest challenges was realising that once you start peeling the layers off the onion there is always another layer underneath that in a weird way is related to the layer you just released, so be prepared because once you start the journey through your roadblocks and use the tools you have picked up on the way, you can never go back, the only way is the way forward and your life can become an adventure. And that for me was exciting.

Now let's dive a little deeper into understanding why we do what we do. Starting off with a recap of how our mind works.

OUR BRAIN
RECAP IN A NUTSHELL

We touched base in The Journey Handbook about how the brain works in the "Our internal wiring" section. In simple terms the brain interprets information from the outside world and embodies the essence of the mind. It is an amazing organ that controls all functions of the body, as well as being the primary receiver, organiser and distributor of information. It attains knowledge from our experiences and stores it in our unconscious mind, where the information affects our thought processes and decision-making abilities and our behaviour.

If you DON'T understand how your brain works, then it will take charge of you. This is what we need to work through together. Become aware of how you react to certain situations and make the changes you need to in order to achieve what you want, because you can. Everyone is uniquely different, what may work for one person may not work for you.

We need to consider three main points together when delving into how our thought processes evolve:

1. The first is understanding the conscious versus unconscious mind.
2. The second is understanding where the information comes from (the process of 'delete distort and generalise' that create our NLP Meta programs).
3. The third is understanding the other filters involved.

The filters

Apart from the fact that we distort, generalise and delete information, we also need to understand our Meta programs: the language we use along with the other filters. These programs act at deeper levels that originate from our programming since birth.

NLP Meta programs

Our programming from birth is created from our Memories, Values and Beliefs, which in turn creates our NLP Meta programs. They represent how you uniquely process information, form your internal representations that direct your behaviour. They are not good or bad, they are just the way you handle information and make sense of your world. They help us decide what to pay attention to and then we delete, distort and generalise the rest. (To understand our Meta programs at a deeper level is for another time.)

Our values

Our Values are essentially an evaluation filter. They are the principles and beliefs that guide us. They determine whether our actions are good or bad, right or wrong, and how we feel at any one point in time. They are basically a deep, unconscious belief system around what's important, and they can change over time.

Our beliefs

Beliefs are essentially our on/off switches. It's important to discover what Beliefs we have and how they affect and shape what we do. A positive belief system will support you, a negative belief system will feed your roadblocks. Note: everyone is different and we all process information differently.

PART FOUR

Our memories

As we get older, our reactions in the present are increasingly affected by collections of past memories that can create triggers from past life experiences and programming either good or bad.

Decisions

This filter consists of the decisions that we have consciously made in the past. The problem with many decisions is that they were made at a very early age and forgotten, but the effect is still filed away as a trigger in our memories. Once we understand our triggers, we can then make the changes we need to, to keep moving forward and create a positive mindset.

ARE YOU CONFUSED?

Filters determine how we internally represent an event that is occurring now, and this internal representation puts us in a certain state and creates a certain physiological response, our behaviour. The state in which we find ourselves will determine our behaviour.

Our unique past life experiences, programming and traumas are stored in our unconscious memory bank. You may experience a trigger that is based on your past experience, (it can be negative or positive), and a thought, emotion or feeling thus creating a response in the form of a behaviour that, if not addressed, can form a distraction/roadblock.

Simply put, when a situation arises, we have thoughts about the facts of that situation. Those thoughts trigger feelings and emotions (either consciously or unconsciously) and based on those feelings, we engage in behaviours that impact the situation (either positively or negatively) and the cycle continues.

At the root of all our roadblocks are our:
- Thoughts
- Feelings
- Negative emotions
- Limiting beliefs

From our original responses, behaviours are then created in the form of:

1. Avoidance strategies/distractions
2. Habits
3. Excuses
4. The language we use (internal and external)
5. Physical disease

> *"The mind is its own place and in itself, can make a heaven of hell, or a hell of heaven."*
> **John Milton**

OUR THOUGHTS

> *"We are what we think. All that we are arises with our thoughts. With our thoughts we make the world."*
> **Buddha**

A thought is an idea or opinion produced by thinking. Thinking helps us define and organise experiences, plan, learn, reflect and make decisions that eventually guide our behaviours. The conditions and circumstances of your life are a result of your thoughts and beliefs. Thought power is the key to creating your reality.

There are four types of thinking skills:

1. **Convergent or analytical thinking** (breaking complex problems into their component parts).
2. **Divergent thinking** (exploring many possible solutions).
3. **Critical thinking** (thinking clearly and rationally).
4. **Creative thinking** (looking at problems from a fresh perspective; a way of developing unorthodox solutions; thinking outside the box).

But sometimes our thinking is created from our filtered experiences and interpretations that paint us in a negative light. These thoughts, if left

 PART FOUR

unchecked and unquestioned, can have a negative impact on our wellbeing. Our thoughts create our mindset and growth, positive and negative. *What type of thinker are you?*

OUR EMOTIONS

An emotion is the experiential, chemical and neurophysiological response we have to stimuli. It is a feeling deriving from one's circumstances, moods or relationships with others. In fact, different people have varied emotional responses to the same stimulus. Emotions can manifest consciously or subconsciously and are more powerful than thoughts.

> *"Your emotions are the slaves to your thoughts, and you are the slave to your emotions."*
> **Elizabeth Gilbert**

When we become emotional, either positively or negatively, our clarity of thought can disappear and create an emotion-based roadblock keeping us from thinking creatively and moving forward. When we hit emotional roadblocks, we can get side-tracked and we can become confused.

Negative emotions generally become roadblocks.

A negative emotion can be described as any feeling that causes you to be sad. These emotions make you dislike yourself and others, and decrease your happiness and confidence. Negative emotions can dampen our enthusiasm for life, depending on how long we let them affect us.

The five major **negative emotions** (anger, sadness, fear, hurt and guilt) can be a major cause of roadblocks.

1. **Anger** is a strong feeling of annoyance, displeasure or hostility toward something or someone you feel has deliberately done you wrong. Excessive anger can cause problems physically and mentally, and make it difficult to think straight. (*It is difficult to feel or experience peace when experiencing the emotion of anger.*)

2. **Sadness** is emotional pain associated with feelings of disadvantage, loss, despair, grief, helplessness, disappointment and sorrow. Sadness prevents you from enjoying all the good things you have in your life, especially if you allow yourself to become too nostalgic and live in the past. *(It is difficult to feel or experience happiness when experiencing the emotion of sadness.)*

3. **Fear** is an unpleasant emotion caused by the threat of danger, pain or harm. Its primary aim is not to distress you but to help you. Fear warns you about possible danger, illuminating the real situation and making you aware of difficulties so that you are ready to face them. In the context of a roadblock, this could be the fear of success or failure. Fear is 'false evidence appearing real'; fear creates images of unpleasant surprises and unexpected obstacles, failures and accidents with the power of thought. *(It is difficult to feel or experience safety and certainty when experiencing the emotion of fear.)*

4. **Hurt** is unhappiness or sadness caused by words, actions, or unfortunate events. The hurt can cause mental pain. *(It is difficult to feel or experience love and acceptance when experiencing the emotion of hurt.)*

5. **Guilt** is a form of self-punishment that often affects over-thinkers and deeply sensitive people. Guilt can make you feel unhappy because you think that you have done something wrong or have failed to do something that you should have done. *(It is difficult to feel or experience self-worth when experiencing the emotion of guilt.)*

What negative emotions do you experience on a regular basis?
Do you know what triggers them?

PART FOUR

> "Triggers are like little psychic explosions that crash through avoidance and bring the dissociated, avoided trauma suddenly unexpectedly back into consciousness."
> **Carolyn Spring**[6]

Emotional triggers

The meanings we give to current and past events trigger our emotional roadblocks. You know the feeling when someone makes a 'jokingly' mean comment that might not be a huge deal to another person, but totally destabilises you for the rest of the day? Suddenly, you find yourself feeling off-centre and thrust into a bout of negative emotions, anxiety, guilt or shame. We all have emotional triggers. It can be challenging to identify what exactly those triggers are, but the process of getting to know and understand them can help us heal and learn how to better cope when we're faced with situations that trigger us.

Why do we all have triggers? In short, we have triggers because we were all children once. When we were growing up, we inevitably experienced pain or suffering that we could not acknowledge and/or deal with sufficiently at the time. So, as adults we typically become triggered by experiences that are reminiscent of these old, painful feelings. As a result, we typically turn to a habitual or addictive way of trying to manage the painful feelings.

These painful feelings innately become roadblocks.

Your emotional triggers often emerge as a form of behaviour, a feeling, an unexplained reaction, a mindset, a strategy, the language you use or even a physical or mental illness.

Some examples of common emotional triggers are as follows:
- Someone rejecting you.
- Someone leaving you (or the threat of them leaving).
- Helplessness over painful situations.
- Someone discounting or ignoring you.
- Someone being unavailable to you.
- Someone giving you a disapproving look.
- Someone blaming or shaming you.

- Someone being judgemental or critical of you.
- Someone being too busy to make time for you.
- Someone not appearing to be happy to see you.
- Someone trying to control you.
- Someone being needy or trying to smother you.
- A negative word or an action from someone you care about.

Here is an example of how a trigger affected me a couple of years ago.

One day I was in my home office with a client. My sons were in the backyard, arguing. We could hear every word of the colourful language they were using. My older son was going overseas in a couple of days and he had so much work to do before he left; he was extremely stressed. My younger son was helping him get things done, but their differences had sparked the argument. All of a sudden, tears started rolling down my face. Somewhere in the depths of my unconscious mind was an emotional experience I had not dealt with, that had been triggered by my boys' argument in the backyard.

My client and I looked at each other in disbelief. I got my act together and we finished the session a little earlier than expected. When I calmed down, I was left sitting there, bewildered about my reaction. I avoided my boys until the next day, but still found it difficult to talk to them. With my training and experience, I knew what I had to do. I had to go within and ask the right questions.

You see, I had a choice to let it go and get over it, or to delve deeper to find the root cause of my trigger and release it. What I found was that the emotions came up from an experience I had had with an ex-boyfriend years before, where I had been used and disrespected and brushed aside. I had a past emotional association to that memory that was triggered when my boys were arguing. Although for readers, the association may not be obvious without all the gory details; but in my mind, after I discovered the cause of the emotional impact, I worked through the process, released the emotions from the past, and was able to enjoy the last couple of days with my son before he went overseas.

PART FOUR

Something to keep in mind here is the fact that I had done a lot of work on myself. I totally trust my unconscious mind. Once you start to recognise and release your triggers, everything becomes so much easier.

Whenever I become aware I have been triggered my key go-to question is:
Why am I allowing this to bother me?

And ask it several times to get to the root cause.
Have you been triggered lately?
If so, why are you allowing it to bother you?

OUR LIMITING BELIEFS

A limiting belief is a false belief that a person acquires as a result of making an incorrect conclusion about something they have experienced in the past. Limiting beliefs constrain us in some way, just because we believe them, and can keep you stuck in a negative state of mind. They could be about yourself, your interactions with other people, or the world and how it works. They can keep you from making good choices, taking on new opportunities or reaching your potential.

> *"You are only as limited as your beliefs."*
> **Jennifer Ho-Dougatz**

Upbringing

Limiting beliefs originate from your family morals, values and life experience while growing up, beliefs and ideas about how both you and the world should be, the career path to take, how to behave and how to engage with others. For example, if your parents reinforced a belief that authority should never be challenged, you may believe that unfair treatment from people in positions of authority should be accepted not challenged, and you may not even be able to recognise this behaviour.

Education

Education plays a major role in forming limiting beliefs. When you're learning from authorities you respect, you are inclined to conclude that the things they tell you are true. Whether you're learning from family members, teachers or friends, they all have an impact on what you adopt as the truth.

Life experiences

When you make decisions about life experiences, it is common for you to draw conclusions afterwards that can be either positive or negative. If, for example, you fall in love and it ends in heartbreak, you might conclude that love always ends in pain. You may have been bullied in school and thus believe you are not good enough. These sorts of negative experiences can strongly shape your limiting beliefs.

It's important to remember that the conclusions you make from past experiences are only temporarily valid. You can always work on and break down your limiting beliefs.

Do you have any limiting beliefs?

The language we use (internal and external)

The language I am referring to here is primarily your self-talk, that little itty-bitty-shitty committee that whispers in your ear. What you say to yourself and the meaning you apply to it can come across as negative and if you constantly repeat this self-talk, your mind actually begins to believe it. It can become a roadblock, especially when we want to change, improve or get through a new challenge in life. This is why affirmations are invaluable when you want to change something in your life.

Negative self-talk can create limiting beliefs. For example, telling yourself, *I can't do this; I'm not good enough; I'm stupid; I'm too slow; I'll never be able to do it; I hate myself; Nobody likes me*, will intensify limiting beliefs. There are so many, I am sure you

> *"Language shapes the way we think and determines what we can think about."*
> **Benjamin Lee Whorf**

 PART FOUR

can think of other negative examples of things you have told yourself. When we use the words 'should', 'could', 'would' and 'but' in our self-talk or in our conversations with others, our words become an excuse. They limit us. Think about words you say on a regular basis. Particularly those that disempower us.

There are two statements in particular that I would like to bring to your attention;
- I don't know (which is an excuse); and
- I tried (which is disempowering).

Depending on the context in which you use them, they can disempower you.

Let me explain: I was tutoring a young girl in Maths and English. She would arrive at each session, and as usual I would start a conversation:

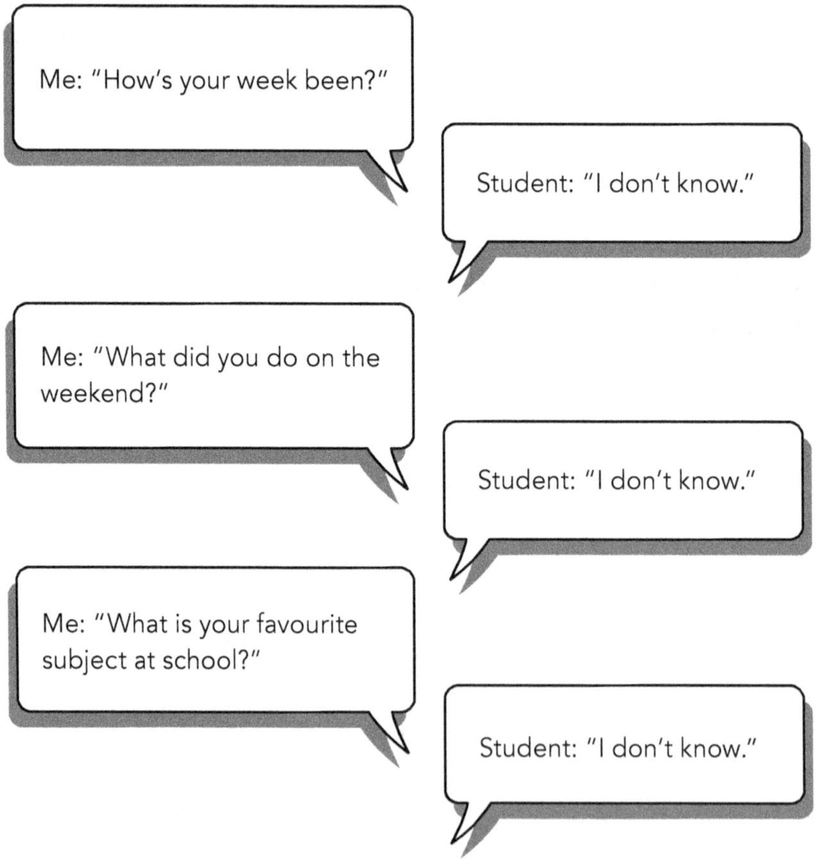

Me: "How's your week been?"

Student: "I don't know."

Me: "What did you do on the weekend?"

Student: "I don't know."

Me: "What is your favourite subject at school?"

Student: "I don't know."

And so it went on and on. She was using the phrase "I don't know" as an excuse to not think, to avoid getting into a conversation and to remain in her comfort zone. This was not healthy. She needed to take responsibility for her thoughts and understand that "I don't know" is an excuse to not think.

Another example is the use of the word 'try'. For example, if I ask you to take a pencil out of my hand, you have a decision to make – you either do it or you don't do it either way is okay. Can you 'try' and take the pencil out of my hand? How much more empowering is it if you tell your child to go and do their best and have a good time as opposed to go and 'try' to have a good time? Instead of saying you can 'try', say you can 'do' it and they actually do it, no matter what the outcome is.

Negative phrasing and language often have the following characteristics:
- It tells the recipient what cannot be done.
- It has a tone of blame, as if the person you're talking to is at fault.

Be wary of derogatory statements about yourself, as they don't support who you want to be. What you say is often a reflection of who you are and what you think. You can look at unhelpful language at a deeper level in the Bonus Content.

Do you have any negative self-talk that pops up every now and then?

OUR FEELINGS

In psychology, a feeling can be defined as a person's response to the emotion that comes from their perception of a situation. The response depends on their prior life experience. For example, the sight of tigers in a zoo might trigger admiration and awe in some, but others will feel anger and bitterness at the sight of caged animals. In this situation, the stimulus is the same, but the reaction is quite different.

"Feelings are much like waves, we can't stop them from coming, but we can choose which one to surf."
Jonatan Mårtensson

A fundamental difference between feelings and emotions is that feelings are experienced consciously, while emotions manifest either consciously or subconsciously. Some people may spend years or even their lifetime not understanding the depths of their emotions.

When we become more self-aware we become more mindful of what we are feeling, good or bad, and why. We can then put the feelings/emotions into the right context and delve in a little deeper if what we experience/feel has become a roadblock. When we discover the root cause we can change the way we think/act and keep moving through any roadblock/challenge that comes our way. How exciting is that!

What are you feeling right now?
Why are you feeling the way you do? Is feeling this way bothering you?
Why are you allowing this feeling to bother you?

OUR BEHAVIOUR

Human behaviour is a complex interplay of three main areas: actions, cognition/thoughts and emotions/feelings. It is influenced by our internal dialogue, biology (genetics) and environmental stimulation. Environmental stimulation encompasses consequences of what goes on in your immediate surroundings throughout your childhood and adulthood (programming).

> *"Once your mindset changes, everything on the outside will change along with it."*
> **Steve Maraboli**

Putting it simply, one's behaviour is the way in which a person behaves in response to a particular situation or stimulus, either internal or external. Becoming self-aware is the key to why we do what we do.

Mindset

Your **mindset** is a set of beliefs that shape how you make sense of the world (the way we think creates our thoughts, feelings and behaviour). As explained previously, there are three types of mindsets: a positive mindset, a fixed/negative mindset and a growth mindset. Your attitude and mindset have significant effects on the behaviour you exhibit in specific situations. Several types of behaviour to be aware of when delving into our roadblocks are discussed below.

Distractions

Your distractions can be either internal or external.

An internal distraction results from your own internal drives, your obsessive thoughts and your conflicts. Worry, stress, anxiety, depression, sickness, hunger, pain, daydreams and anticipation of upcoming events, are examples of internal distractors that reduce your level of concentration.

An external distraction results from something outside of yourself. These might include loud noises, other people speaking, music, smells, heat/cold and text messages/phone calls. External distractions also include factors such as visual triggers and social interactions, bushfires, floods and any other natural disaster you can think of.

How do you generally get distracted?

An avoidance strategy

Avoidance is escape coping. It is a form of behaviour that inhibits your ability to adjust to situations and involves changing your behaviour to try to avoid thinking about or feeling things that are uncomfortable. In other words, avoidance coping involves trying to avoid stressors or challenges instead of dealing with them. There are three main types of avoidance:

"Avoiding problems you need to face is avoiding the life you need to live."
Paulo Coelho

- Procrastination
- Passive-aggressive behaviour
- Rumination

Procrastination

Procrastination is the act of delaying or postponing something. People often procrastinate because they are afraid of failing at tasks they need to complete; thus, they either avoid starting or finishing the tasks. Over time, chronic procrastination not only affects our productivity, but also is detrimental to our physical and mental health, creating stress-related illnesses such as hypertension, depression, anxiety, low self-esteem and low life satisfaction.

PART FOUR

> *"A year from now you will wish you had started today."*
> **Karen Lamb**

Some reasons why we procrastinate include:
- Not knowing what needs to be done.
- Not knowing how to do something.
- Not wanting to do something.
- Not caring if something gets done or not.
- Not caring when something gets done.
- Not being in the mood to do something.
- Habitually waiting until the last minute to do something.
- Believing that you work better under pressure.
- Lacking the initiative to get started.
- Forgetting.
- Blaming sickness or poor health.
- Waiting for the right moment.
- Needing time to think about the task.
- Delaying one task in favour of working on another.
- Thinking that you can finish something at the last minute.

We often come up with a number of excuses or rationalisations to justify our procrastinating behaviour.
Do you procrastinate?

Passive-aggressive behaviour

Passive-aggression is a type of behaviour or personality trait characterised by indirect resistance to the demands of others in avoidance of direct confrontation. Instead of communicating openly, people who engage in this type of behaviour share their negative feelings through actions. For example, a person might repeatedly make excuses to avoid certain people as a way of expressing their dislike or anger towards those individuals, instead of openly communicating.

Recognising your own passive-aggressive behaviour:
- Do you often find yourself sulking when you are unhappy with someone?
- Do you avoid people with whom you are upset?
- Do you ever stop talking to people when you are angry at them?
- Do you put off doing things as a way to punish others?
- Do you sometimes use sarcasm to avoid engaging in meaningful conversations?
- Do you have any passive-aggressive behaviours? If so, what are they?

Rumination

Ruminating is endlessly going over a thought or a problem. It refers to the tendency to repetitively think about the causes, situational factors and consequences of one's negative emotional experiences. In short, if you find yourself constantly replaying something in your mind, dwelling on the injustice of it all and thinking about what you should have said or done without taking any corresponding actions, you're making yourself feel more stressed by ruminating.

An excuse

An excuse is a reason or explanation given to justify a behaviour, or lessen the blame of a fault or an offence. We must be mindful of excuses, because an excuse that lets you off the hook doesn't serve you.

> *"The only thing standing between you and your goal is the bullshit story you keep telling yourself as to why you can't achieve it."*
> **Jordan Belfort**

Making excuses is normal. It's important that we have narratives that help us make sense of our lives and our worlds. However, it causes problems when your excuses take up too much airtime in your life and you start believing them. That is when roadblocks appear, and you lose clarity around what you are doing. If you feel stuck, it could be that an excuse you're telling yourself is holding you back.

Do you make a lot of excuses?

PART FOUR

A habit

A habit is a behaviour that becomes automatic or habitual through regular repetition. They are settled or regular tendencies or practices that are hard to give up. Every habit starts with a psychological pattern called a habit loop, a three-part process that includes a cue or trigger that tells your brain to go into automatic mode, a reward and, finally, a behaviour. The behaviour becomes routine.

Neuroscientists have traced our habit-making behaviours to a part of the brain called the basal ganglia, which also plays a key role in the development of emotions, memories and pattern recognition. Decisions, on the other hand, are made in a different part of the brain called the prefrontal cortex. As soon as a behaviour becomes automatic, the decision-making part of your brain goes into a kind of sleep mode.

We all have our own personal habits; some are longstanding, while others are more recently acquired. Some are good for us, and some negatively affect us. They help define us as individuals. We have our own ways of living our lives, and our habits have their place in helping us along. Unfortunately, our bad habits can turn into roadblocks.

> "If your habits don't line up with your dreams, then you need to either change your habits or change your dreams."
>
> **John Maxwell**

Here is a list of habits, just to give you an idea of the extent to which a habit can develop in different areas of your life:

- **Being with people who don't appreciate you:** being in bad relationships or depending on somebody too much. Haven't all of us been in this situation before, trying to please people who don't appreciate us and bending over backwards to be there for people when they are never there for us?

- **Any kind of addiction:** taking drugs, drinking excessively and smoking; emotional, comfort and stress eating; physical habits such as biting your fingernails, biting your lips, picking your nose and tapping your foot.

- **Lazy habits:** watching too much TV; talking while eating; staring at mobile and computer screens for too long without taking regular breaks; texting or talking on your mobile phone while driving; being late; leaving things to the last minute; not taking care of your health.

- **Eating habits:** eating too much sugar and salt; skipping a main meal of the day.

- **Living in Effect:** unnecessarily blaming others for nothing; levying baseless allegations against others; lying; insulting others; cheating on others; being judgemental. Living in a victim mindset.

- **Irresponsible habits:** not wearing a helmet while riding a bike; not putting on your seatbelt when in a car; not taking responsibility for your actions; breaking promises made to others; getting angry very easily; purposely creating misunderstandings between people; judging others instead of accepting them; living on borrowed money.

- **Self-debilitating habits:** criticising yourself and others; focusing on the negatives; having unrealistically high expectations; always complaining about something; making a mountain out of a molehill, thinking too much.

Do you have any habits that could be a roadblock on your journey?

STATE

A state is a condition, behaviour, pattern or way of being that exists at a particular time. When you are in a particular state, it is important to question your thoughts, your feelings and your emotions and ask yourself why the state exists and in which direction the state is taking you.

PART FOUR

States that may exist for you, both good and bad, include:

Anxious	Arrogant	Moody
Depressed	Presumptuous	Irritable
Stressed	Conceited	Focused
Lazy	Unrealistic	Motivated
Confused	Disappointed with life	Excited
Overwhelmed	Irresponsible	Happy
Impulsive	Objectionable	
Pretentious	Joyful	

All states and behaviours happen either consciously or unconsciously. In a nutshell, we determine our own behaviours and distractions through the choices we make. And we do have a choice.

Our emotions can be the result of repressed behaviour that leads to triggers, which leads to internal/external habits, limiting beliefs and negative emotions. Practised consistently, these habits or behaviours can create dis-ease and negative states, and thus sabotage our goals, dreams and desires. On the flip side, of course, our positive states will support us once we get through the roadblocks.

> *"Stress is a mental and physical state resulting from the perception that the demands on oneself are greater than one's ability to meet the demands."*
> **Pamela Edwards**[7]

Physical disadvantage

How we show up physically can be determined by how we live our life. Our body is our home, and we need to look after it. Sometimes, life sucks and creates distractions. It comes with responsibilities and challenges regarding family, work and so much more. How you deal with these challenges affects your quality of life. Yes, we need to be flexible, and we may need to take a different path to either survive or achieve our dreams. As long as we deal with our challenges along the way, we won't become stuck at roadblocks.

> *"Health is like money, we never have a true idea of its value until we lose it."*
> **Josh Billings**

We may become unwell and face physical roadblocks, and when we do, this is our body telling us we need to change something. The most common physical signs are headaches, depression, stress, anxiety and obesity.

Are you suffering from any mild illness at the moment?

Do you listen to your body and what it is telling you on a regular basis?

Discovering your roadblocks

Now you can start to recognise how roadblocks can turn up specifically in the form of a thought, an emotion, a feeling, a limiting decision or limiting belief, a behaviour/state or illness.

> *"They aren't roadblocks. They are sign posts."*
> **Richie Norton**

And roadblocks can come in the form of stress, ill health, anxiety, depression, procrastination, overwhelm, excuses, not enough time, and many other struggles we face internally or externally.

How is your roadblock showing up for you?

This is the juicy bit where we get real and discover why you feel the way you do. We are taking the band aid off and will in turn take a deeper look and find the key to unlocking each challenge/roadblock until we get to the root cause.

There are three main checkpoints you need to pass to discover your roadblock.

PART FOUR

Checkpoint 1

Check you have clarity around what you want and that the road to your destination/desired outcome is clear.

a) CHECK your goals (if you have one in the area you are working on).

- **Destination:** is your destination/outcome clear?

- **Your why:** is your why strong enough? Are you committed/motivated and inspired to achieve the desired outcome?

- **Timescale:** is your timeline realistic for each step?

- **Your action plan:** is your plan of action specific enough? Are you taking baby steps towards your goal? Is your progress visible? Is something actually happening?

- **Achievable outcome:** do you have the skills and resources needed to reach your outcome?

- **Support:** have you got people around you who will support you on your journey?

- **Review:** are you reviewing and celebrating each step as you get closer to your goal?

Remember a goal is not just a pathway to a destination; it is the light at the end of the tunnel that will inspire you and keep you motivated.

b) If you don't have any goals yet **CHECK that what you want is aligned with your core values** in the area you are working on.
What did you learn?

Checkpoint 2

Discover your roadblocks and ask the right questions.

Let's dive deeper and discover what else might be holding you back.

Once you have clarity around what you want and are satisfied that you have the right goal in place, you might realise that something else is still not quite right. If this is the case, dive deeper and contemplate what other types of roadblocks you could be facing. Let's be brutally honest. Answer the following questions in the tables with a yes or no. Follow the directions below each table and write your answers down in your journal or on a separate piece of paper. Don't allow yourself to get overwhelmed as you can learn so much by asking the right questions.

Remember this is a process of discovery; be as honest as you can.

Are you often?	Y/N
Are you baffled by a problem?	
Are you scared of taking action?	
Are you being lazy?	
Are you waiting for perfection?	
Are you worried about the risks of taking action?	
Are you worried about what others think?	
Are your moods or emotions holding you back?	
Are you distracted?	

Write down a list of your YES answers.

I am often ....

....

....

Do you make ANY of the following excuses?	Y/N	Do you make ANY of the following excuses?	Y/N
I'm not educated enough		I'm not motivated enough	
I don't know		I'm not destined to succeed	
I'm afraid of what others might think		I'm just not confident enough to do this	
I don't have the support		People are holding me back	
I can't handle failure		I fear failure would crush me	
I fear the unknown		I am not good enough	
I'm not smart enough		I don't know the right people	
I'm not talented enough		I don't have enough money	
I'm too old to start		I don't have enough experience	
It's just too risky		I've tried, and it just can't be done	
I'm too easily distracted by other things		I just can't deal with all these problems	
I don't believe I can do it		I'm not creative enough	
Nobody believes in me		I wasn't born in the right area	
It all seems too hard		I am not lucky enough	
It isn't the right time		I don't know where to begin	
I don't have enough time to discover what I like		My family and friends don't think I'm capable	
I don't have enough time		I don't know if I will succeed	
I'm just not ready yet		I didn't have the right teachers	
I tried (and failed)		I come from a poor background	
I just don't have any luck		I'm afraid of making a mistake	
It's just too difficult		I will start tomorrow	

ROADBLOCKS

Make a list of all the **YES** excuses you make on a regular basis at home, socially or at work.

I regularly make the following excuses at home: ....

I regularly make the following excuses socially: ....

I regularly make the following excuses at work: ....

Are you feeling ANY of the following right now?	Y/N	Are you feeling ANY of the following right now?	Y/N
Disappointed in life		Angry	
Presumptuous		Guilty	
Pretentious, assuming		Judged	
Neglected		Hurt	
Unfocused		Fearful	
Depressed		Irritable	
Focused		Moody	
Objectionable		Irresponsible	
Sad		Lost	
Anxious		Lazy	
Overwhelmed		Left out	
Impulsive		Arrogant	
Conceited		Responsible	

Write a list of all your **YES** answers

I am feeling..........right now

PART FOUR

Do you think you lack?	Socially	At home	At work	Y/N
Knowledge				
Understanding				
Confidence				
Support				
Motivation				
Inspiration				
Commitment				
Communication				

Complete the following sentences with your YES answers.

I lack..........socially around ....

I lack..........at work around ....

I lack..........at home around ....

Which of these relate to you?	Y/N
Do you compare yourself to others?	
Do you blame others for your misfortune?	
Do you focus on your weaknesses?	
Do you learn from your mistakes?	
Do you take appropriate action when needed?	
Are you a positive thinker?	
Are you a pessimist?	
Are you an optimist?	

Make a list of your YES answers

I ....

ROADBLOCKS

Which of these relate to you?	Y/N
Do you live a balanced lifestyle?	
Do you get enough sleep?	
Do you have a balanced nutritious diet?	
Do you exercise regularly?	
Do you love and care for yourself?	
Do you believe in yourself?	
Is what you are doing right now pushing you towards your outcome?	
Are you on the right road?	

Make a list of your NO answers.

I don't ....

Whatever you are feeling right now is okay. You know there is a flip side. **The important question here is**: do you have a better understanding around your roadblocks?

> "Never give in, never give in, never, never, never ..."
> **Winston Churchill**

 PART FOUR

Checkpoint 3
REVIEW: WHAT DID YOU LEARN?

Review the lists and answer the following questions.

It is important to recognise what you have just uncovered about yourself. Write down a list of what you think your main roadblocks are and what you have learnt.

I learnt that on the positive side of things I have/I am: ....

....

....

....

If you were to know, what do you think the main roadblocks are? ....

....

....

....

In which areas of your Life Circle are your roadblocks showing up? ....

....

....

....

Roadblock awareness

At the beginning of this chapter, you thought about possible personal behaviours that could turn into roadblocks for you on this journey towards living your best life.

What did you learn about yourself?

....

....

....

What specifically are your roadblocks and in which area of your Life Circle do they show up?

....

....

....

If you were to know, what is the specific trigger to each roadblock you experience?

....

....

....

> "Our life is not determined by our roadblocks.
> If you want to change the view you can and become empowered to live your best life, a life you can love."
> **Gillian Gorrie**

> *If you make your internal life a priority,
> then everything else you need on the outside will be given
> to you and it will be extremely clear what the next step is*
>
> **Gabrielle Bernstein**

You are just looking out the window of the bus, you are feeling a bit uncomfortable in the tummy, your phone rings, a friend you haven't seen for a while begs you to meet up for a coffee and chat, she has some important news to share, you think for a minute, you can get started on the first part of your new plan tomorrow. If you get off at the next stop you can meet her in thirty minutes. Yes decision made, mmmmm.

A couple of days later you are sitting at the bus stop just staring into a void. Buses come and go; you become aware of a child crying and you look at your watch, the bus should be here by now, you turn and ask the person leaning on the corner of the bus shelter, "Has the 10 o' clock bus to the city arrived yet?" The young man nods his head while answering, "Yes, five minutes ago." You look at your watch in disbelief; you had missed the bus again. It's the seventh time this month you have missed it, a little shiver goes down your spine as you become aware that it is becoming a bit of a bad habit.

As you get closer to home you realise there is something bulging out of your letter box and as you get closer you realise it is another book. You pull it out of the mailbox and see that it is the HANDBOOK FOR ACTION AND EMPOWERMENT.

How does the universe know what I need at this point in time? Mmmm.

You hurry inside to find that comfy chair and make a cuppa and settle in as you are excited to see what words of wisdom will appear to push you into the next stage of your journey.

You open the book and there it is, "Feeling stuck? Start the process."

You grab your journal in preparation for what is to come next.

PART FIVE

YOUR GUIDE TO ACTION AND EMPOWERMENT
Navigating Your Roadblocks

"

*Success is not final, failure is not fatal:
it is the courage to continue that counts.*
Winston Churchill

"

Contents

Introduction to the Handbook............ 153

THE SECRETS TO SUCCESS 154

1. Develop a positive/growth mindset 154

Tips to start your journey to positivity 154

2. Make journalling a habit 155

3. Develop an attitude of gratitude ... 156

4. Breathe and have self-compassion 156

5. Commit and be consistent 157

6. Take action 157

7. Be flexible, set and refresh your goals when required 157

8. Ask for help if you need it 158

9. Don't get too stuck with the process/questions 158

Feeling stuck? Start the process.......... 160

THE PROCESS.................................. 160

YOUR GUIDE TO ACTION AND EMPOWERMENT................. 169

THE FOUR KEYS 171

1. Good health.. 172

2. Stuck awareness 180

3. Honesty.. 187

4. Good Communication..................... 190

STATE 198

Stressed 198

Depressed.. 211

Anxious 222

BEHAVIOUR 231

Procrastination 231

Perfectionism 240

Habits.. 246

Victim mindset......................................256

Distractions 264

Excuses 268

FEELINGS 274

Unhappy..274

Scared 284

Confused 288

Overwhelmed..292

NEGATIVE EMOTIONS.................300

1. Anger 303

2. Sadness... 307

3. Fear 312

4. Hurt 316

5. Guilt.. 319

THOUGHTS 325

Low self-esteem/lacking confidence .325

Limiting beliefs/decisions 341

YOUR GUIDE TO ACTION AND EMPOWERMENT

Introduction to navigating your roadblocks

The intention now is to give you strategies and tools to navigate through your ups and downs, your roadblocks and move from resistance to resilience. Decide whether you want to take the high road that offers rewards and opportunities for growth or the low, easy road in your comfort zone with exactly the same view. Let's face it: life sucks. Sometimes we can get lost and there will always be a new challenge around the corner. Our challenges may take us in different directions for one reason or another. If we are not achieving what we want along the way, it probably means we have come up against another roadblock.

Knowing what's happening and why is the key to navigating through your roadblocks. Your life from this day forward is not about creating a fantasy or having that perfect life, and it's definitely not about living someone else's life. It's about growth. It's about becoming something more, not something else. It's about progress, not perfection. Above all, it's about connecting with your unique potential, taking time to imagine how you want your future to look, feel and be for you and your loved ones, and then taking the action to create it.

Learn to use the tools you pick up along the way and develop a greater understanding of who you are and what you want. Once you have clarity about what you want and are willing to do whatever it takes to get there, you can get excited. Stay focused and always keep the destination in mind – it's the light at the end of the tunnel that will keep you on track.

Don't stress on the things you can't change and focus on the ones you can. Where there is a will there's a way. Is your why big enough? Take responsibility for the choices you make. Don't allow yourself to become overwhelmed, ASK for help if you need it and take one step at a time. You just need to follow the road rules, enjoy the

> "Understand that the right to choose your own path is a sacred privilege. Use it. Dwell in possibility."
>
> **Oprah Winfrey**

PART FIVE

journey, focus on the positive, believe in yourself and know that you can achieve anything you put your mind to. And most importantly, take action! In the previous chapter, you may have discovered some of your roadblocks. This is your life – you need to be in the driver's seat. Strap on your seat belt and let's go!

There are two parts that are important to navigating through your roadblocks: the secrets to success and the process.

THE SECRETS TO SUCCESS

To move forward from your roadblocks there are nine secrets to success relevant to the process of navigating your roadblocks.

1. Develop a positive/growth mindset

As we've explored earlier, having a positive mindset allows you to be more flexible and enables you to see the opportunities that can help you move forward easily. Let's expand the principles about positivity and growth mindsets that I outlined in your Journey Handbook.

TIPS TO START YOUR JOURNEY TO POSITIVITY

! Identify areas of your life where you usually think negatively whether these are work or home related, your daily commute or a relationship.

! Evaluate what you're thinking periodically during the day.

! Live a healthy lifestyle. Exercise can positively affect your mood and reduce stress. Follow a healthy diet to fuel your mind and body and learn techniques to manage stress.

! Surround yourself with positive, like-minded, supportive people who you can depend on to give helpful advice and feedback and be there when you need them.

! Practise positive self-talk. Start by following one simple rule: don't say anything to yourself that you wouldn't say to anyone else.

2. Make journalling a habit

Writing, especially self-exploratory writing done on a regular basis has been linked to emotional wellbeing and a strong sense of self-knowledge and self-trust. Many people find that writing is therapeutic. Just getting your thoughts out of your head helps to release tension, and it can even be used as a form of meditation. Writing gives insight and perspective, it's a problem-solving technique, and it can serve as an outlet for bottled-up emotions, unresolved trauma or creative expression.

Go within. Take ownership of your life and recognise your thoughts and what they create. Just getting your what, how and why out of your head can give you clarity and make it easier for you to move forward. Don't worry or stress about it, journal your behaviour patterns so that you will be able to differentiate between valid and invalid excuses. Pay attention to your thoughts and emotions; become aware of what you are feeling throughout the day instead of just reacting blindly.

Please note there is a list of journalling prompts in the Toolbox at the back of the book.

Write lists

List writing is always a go-to when you need some clarity around a certain topic/roadblock. Lists put everything into perspective, creating a clear pathway to the outcome you desire. Focus on your strengths and don't compare yourself to others. To start off with, write some lists about yourself (you may already have done this).

- What you love about yourself (the colour of your eyes, your smile, your intelligence, etc).
- What you love doing (cooking, walking along the beach, etc).
- Your favourite things (your cat, ice cream, chocolate, etc).

PART FIVE

- Your strengths, the skills you possess, the things you do well (a good communicator, honest, trustworthy, etc).

Now, in each area of your Life Circle write a list of:
- Your strengths (internal). What is great? What is working?
- What skills do you have that are relevant to the area you are working on?
- Your weaknesses (internal). What needs work? What do you need to learn?
- Opportunities (external). What opportunities do you need to look out for? Examples include networking and a supportive environment.
- Threats (external). Is there anything that will get in the way or stop you from reaching your goal? What roadblocks could hinder you?

3. Develop an attitude of gratitude

Working on an attitude of gratitude is the first thing I ask anyone I work with to do, as it trains us to focus on the positives in life. Noticing the little and positive things from both positive and negative life experiences and connecting to the feelings you get from being grateful can raise your energy, improve the way you feel about yourself and support personal growth.

For example, a negative life experience or a broken relationship can be more challenging to find the gratitude in. When you focus on your learnings from the experience you realise that if you hadn't had that relationship you wouldn't have those learnings.

For more information around gratitude, refer to the Toolbox.

4. Breathe and have self-compassion

Sometimes you just need to stop and breathe, relax and release any stress or tension that may have been building up in your body, feel it, become aware of it and let the tension go. Go easy on yourself, after all, you're doing the best you can at that moment in time.

Don't have unrealistic expectations, because you will only be disappointed if they don't come to fruition. Don't dwell on your mistakes; look at them as opportunities. Learn to be more open and flexible. Change is one of the natural flows of life that occurs often, even when we don't want it to. Acknowledge that it takes courage to make the changes and take the steps you need to create your best life. This is courageous and commendable.

5. Commit and be consistent

Be consistent and don't give up. Find an accountability partner. Check that your why is strong enough and realise that you have the power to change. You can only do your best at any one point in time, and as long as you know you are doing your best, nothing else matters. Use the tools and strategies set out in this book. I constantly refer to them when a roadblock is triggered. I know that they work. No excuses just enjoy the journey.

6. Take action

It's your choice. It is up to you whether you take the high road to success or the low road, where nothing will ever change unless you take action. When will enough be enough? Know that whichever road you choose is okay; understanding the reasons why you made the choice is empowering within itself. And when you take responsibility for the choices you make you are in control, you are in the driver's seat.

Create a daily routine and take action every day.

7. Be flexible, set and refresh your goals when required

Remember that when you set a goal, a new road map to your desired outcome, there will always be a detour and that's okay. Be flexible,

PART FIVE

review and get back on track. Each step is a significant achievement. Acknowledge it and get excited. Celebrate! It's your journey, and how long it takes is no one else's business.

Create a bucket list; it can help you identify what you want to be, do, experience and have in life. Once you have started your lists, keep them available to you so you can revisit them, create a vision board and use them to regain some motivation and inspiration when things are not going so well. If needed, you can take your bucket list and turn it into short-term, mid-term and long-term goals.

8. Ask for help if you need it

It's okay to ask for help. If you are feeling overwhelmed, emotional or stuck, if whatever you are doing is not working and you don't know what to do next. Don't accept that things are okay and that it is what it is. Whatever the situation, if you need support, it's okay to ask for help. If it's not good enough, take action. Don't allow yourself to wallow in inaction.

A coach offers outside intervention to ensure you are accountable, providing the reality check you need to embrace reality with productive action and get the results you need to keep moving forward. No matter what your issues are, mental or physical, I recommend you ask for help if you feel you need it. There are a lot of health practitioners, coaches and mentors out there to support you on your journey.

> "How long can I sit here not doing the things I want to do."
> **Deborah Landau**

9. Don't get too stuck with the process/questions

Becoming unstuck is about finding your life's purpose so that you can move on. Your life's purpose is not only your job, your responsibility or your goal; it's what makes you feel alive. These are the things you are passionate about and will fight for. Once you realise what is keeping you stuck, you can let it go.

YOUR GUIDE TO ACTION AND EMPOWERMENT

Keep the purpose of the exercise up front and have some fun and realise your 'ah ha!' moments are paved with gold. Then celebrate!

"Not until we are lost do we begin to find ourselves."
Henry David Thoreau

A couple of days later on your walk home from the bus stop you are considering your thoughts around why you missed the bus again.

What is it specifically you need to change?
Do you need to be more organised next time?
Are you too easily distracted?
Is something unconsciously stopping you from moving forward?
Are you living at **CAUSE or EFFECT***?*
Are you making excuses?

Maybe you need to get up earlier, take a shorter route to the bus stop or make sure you have an updated timetable.

You realise you need to take control.

You have a little more clarity around your roadblocks now so maybe it's time to delve in a little deeper as to why this is happening.

You know you are ready, LET'S DO IT!

Feeling stuck, start the process, become aware and navigate yourself to success.

First understand The Process, then take Action!

"There are two primary choices in life: to accept conditions as they exist, or accept the responsibility for changing them."
Denis Waitley

PART FIVE

FEELING STUCK? START THE PROCESS

To be stuck means to be trapped in something; you can't move forward and can't go back. Sometimes, you don't even realise you are stuck – you just keep doing what you need to do to get on with the day. It's not until we stop that we realise that something is not quite right. You are unhappy, stressed, tired, and anxious. You make the decision that enough is enough and that something must change. Change is scary and painful, but it's also necessary for becoming unstuck.

Once you have made the decision, opportunities remarkably open up. How exciting is that? The truth is that we're all lucky to have choices; we just have to be brave enough to make them.

In the previous chapter you will have identified your roadblock and how it is showing up for you. Whichever category your roadblock eventuated from (thoughts, emotions or behaviours), it will inevitably have been triggered by a negative life event or experience. Getting to the root cause of your roadblock, finding clarity and getting your learnings is the primary aim of the process. You will have a better understanding of why you do what you do and what you need to change to keep moving forward. As you progress through this process you will see that asking the right questions is paramount to navigating through to your success and completing your journey with a full toolbox.

THE PROCESS

When there is a need to go a little deeper, ask some more questions: be honest and be specific.

YOUR GUIDE TO ACTION AND EMPOWERMENT

1. AWARENESS: Recognise/identify your roadblock

Engage your self-awareness

Pay attention to your thoughts and emotions throughout the day instead of just reacting blindly. Feel where your roadblock is sitting and pay attention to what your body is telling you. Take a deep breath in and a deep breath out. Pinpoint the thoughts, feelings and sensations your body is experiencing and allow yourself to simply feel them without resistance or judgement.

Your solution could be as simple as going for a walk. For example, if you're stressed at work, your response could be a tension headache. You need to take a break and go for a walk, stretch, breathe and relax so that you can return to work feeling relaxed and energised. Realise where the stress is coming from and deal with the situation.

To gain clarity through self-awareness around our roadblock we need to identify the event, your response and the outcome and then ask the right questions. It's a matter of being really honest with yourself when a roadblock appears. It's not so easy, but it is important. Every outcome you experience in life is the result of how you responded to an event or experience in your past.

Event: What's happening/not happening?
- What specifically is the challenge?
- Why is it a challenge?
- What part of the challenge triggered a reaction?

> *"Only I can change my life – no one can do it for me."*
> **Carol Burnett**

Response: How did you react?
- What specifically was your reaction?
- Was it a thought, an emotion or a behaviour?

Outcome: What is the result of the way you reacted to the event?
- Is it internal or external? A limiting decision, a negative emotion, a habit, an avoidance strategy, etc.

PART FIVE

- Was it a physical reaction ie, a headache, an ache, pain or did you just remove yourself from the situation?
- Has the outcome become a roadblock?
- If you were to know, what is it stopping you from doing?

2. TAKE OWNERSHIP

After conducting self-examination and taking ownership, your resilient mind is open and prepared to learn some valuable information regarding the roadblock/setback. The hardest part is often identifying your roadblock, and you have already done that. Once you name your roadblock, it becomes much easier to switch perspectives and identify what you need to do to move through it. We can't change some of life's circumstances or how other people behave towards us, but we can control our responses to these things to change the outcome. Dealing with your issues makes you stronger and brings you closer to your flow state and living your best life.

Take ownership of your roadblock – it's yours. Take responsibility for your thoughts and your actions. Live at cause. If something feels wrong, where did that feeling come from? How was that feeling created? Question yourself.

- Are you blaming others?
- Why are you allowing yourself to feel the way you do?
- Are you taking responsibility for your choices, your thoughts and your reactions? If not, why not?
- Are you living at cause? If not, why not?
- What is it you have to do to take ownership?

Be accountable. Make an active and enthusiastic commitment to who you are. Don't play the blame game.

YOUR GUIDE TO ACTION AND EMPOWERMENT

3. JOURNAL IT OUT

Ask the right questions
Dive in a little deeper to discover the root cause

If you are not getting the results you want or that roadblock is more persistent, you need to change your focus. Understand and connect to your why, why you do what you do. The more you practise the easier it becomes. As you move through to the next section, *Your Guide to Action and Empowerment*, you will find the key to changing or coming out of each roadblock is to ask the right questions. Don't wallow or get stuck in the process. See it as an opportunity to find more clarity and purpose in your life. Just be honest with yourself and get things out of your head. Get excited!

- What are you feeling about the event now?

Breathe: make space for your thoughts.

- Breathe in for six, hold for three, and breathe out for nine, until you feel a sense of calm come over you.
- Allow the answers to your questions to bubble up.

Ask the right questions

- Then ask: Is my reaction, roadblock/setback at this point a feeling, an emotion, a thought or a behaviour?
- What specifically triggered your reaction?
- What was the first thing you did? How did you react?
- Why are you allowing your reaction to bother you?
- For example, if you started to cry and you didn't want to cry: Why are you crying?
- You are allowing yourself to cry because..........
- Write down the answer: *I am allowing (my reaction, the answer to the previous question..........) to bother me because..........*
- Ask the question again and again relating to the answer of the previous question each time. Keep asking the question until you find it hard to answer.

PART FIVE

For example: I am allowing myself to cry *(bother me)* because he hurt my feelings; I am allowing him to hurt my feelings because he said I was weak; I am allowing myself to feel weak because I know I am not good enough. That is deep enough; I now know I have a limiting decision. Proceed to the section on limiting decisions and continue the process.

At the end of any journalling exercise, list five things you are grateful for and how they make you feel. Close your eyes and connect to those feelings that you have discovered. Smile and allow those warm feelings to grow from the tips of your toes up to the very top of your head. Breathe in for six, hold for three, and breathe out for nine. Repeat three more times if you need, until you feel relaxed, calm and ready for what comes next.

4. DISCOVER THE ROOT CAUSE:
Find the solution

- What are you feeling now? *I am feeling weak.*
- Is this feeling important to you? If so, why?
- *The answer to the question is important to me because..........*
- Keep asking the question until you find it hard to answer.
  For Example;
  Why is NOT feeling weak important to me? *When I don't feel weak, I feel strong.*
  Why is feeling strong important to me? *Feeling strong is important to me because it means I can achieve anything I want.*
  Why is achieving anything I want important to me? *Knowing I can achieve anything I want will make me happy.*
  Why is being happy important to me? *I just want to be happy.*

YOUR GUIDE TO ACTION AND EMPOWERMENT

So what do you need to do to bring more of what you want into your life? (In the above example, you just want to be happy.) Do you need to do or change something right now? If so, what? What did you learn?

5. MOVE AWAY FROM RESISTANCE

At first it will be natural to want to resist your roadblock, to ignore or reject it as not happening or denying its importance to you. However, resistance to change (or in this case acknowledging the roadblock) will keep you in your comfort zone. While this is a place that is familiar and easy, it can also ruin your life by limiting your potential and your growth. And growth is vital in a fulfilling human experience.

The worst thing that can happen is that you get so distracted and out of control that you lose sight of the light at the end of the tunnel, you lose sight of your short or long-term goal and every challenge you have, if you don't deal with it in a positive way, it can lead to disharmony, unhappiness and illness.

These are some of the signs that show us that we are in a state of resistance:

Chaos and anger: this resistance comes in the form of stubbornness, digging your heels in and arguing to stay in your comfort zone.

Trapped in patterns: this includes good or bad habits that make life more challenging.

Low self-esteem: you might be stuck in a negative mindset. An "I am not good enough" attitude that can keep you from having a go, meeting new people and learning new things.

Drinking and other addictive behaviours: resistance to change often makes people turn to alcohol or drugs to avoid reality or taking responsibility for life experiences.

PART FIVE

Staying in bad relationships: they say the devil you know is better than the one you don't know, but there comes a time when enough is enough and you need to find a new way forward.

Making excuses: your mind generates resistance by creating excuses for why you can't or shouldn't do something.

Developing resilience is the ability to accept and then recover quickly and easily from the stresses, upsets and setbacks of your roadblocks. Be mindful and let go of physical tension in the body and relax. The key is to recognise you are in a state of RESISTANCE. And more importantly move toward RESILIENCE. Focus on what you want, because what you focus on is what you get, right? So be careful what you focus on. Create focus and balance your priorities. In doing so, you will create a mental space where you can differentiate between your thoughts, beliefs and stories about the world and look on them objectivity in order to get clarity.

It all comes down to how badly you want to get to that light at the end of the tunnel and get to your destination. The constant questions you need to ask are:

- Is everything I do getting me closer to my desired outcome, a life I will love living?
- How would my life be if I didn't get there, didn't reach my destination/outcome?
- What would happen if I did get it/get there?

6. REFRAME: FLIP FROM NEGATIVE TO POSITIVE

Generally, with every roadblock there is some form of negativity. Check in with yourself and the language you use, flip that negative thought to a positive, and you will discover the solution to the challenge. The hard bit is to find out how to get there. Below are some examples of the negative roadblocks/challenges that can present themselves and the positive outcomes/solutions you will experience when you have discovered the root cause and progressed through the roadblock.

Challenge	Solution
Unaware	Honesty, self-awareness
Stuck	Discover your flow Live life on purpose
Poor communication	Good communication, results, clarity, understanding
Self-neglect Unhealthy	You become a VIP in your life. Diet, exercise, time out, self-awareness and connection to your true authentic self.
Self-sabotage	Self-care, self-support, self-respect, self-love

State	Solution
Stressed	Relaxed
Depressed	Free
Unhappy	Happy
Unconfident	Confident
Anxious	Calm
Scared	Strong, focused
Confused	Clarity
Overwhelmed	Focus, balance, clarity
Bad habits/behaviour	Good habits
Victim mindset	Results, responsibility, choices and flexibility
Excuses	Relief, strength and potential
Distractions	Focus

PART FIVE

Procrastination	Action
Perfectionism	Flexibility, self-confidence
Negative mindset	Positive and growth mindset

Flip from negative thoughts to positive thoughts

Change your thoughts: change your outcome. Once you identify your negative self-talk, draw up two columns. Write the negative self-talk down in the first column and then flip it positively in the second:

Negative self-talk	Positive thinking
I've never done it before	It's an opportunity to learn something new
There's no way it will work	How can I do it differently?
I can't do it	I can do it
No one bothers to communicate with me	Who can I talk to that is a good communicator?

- What is the positive feeling opposite to the feeling you have around this challenge?
- What could you do differently to feel this positive feeling?

7. WHAT DID YOU LEARN?

Acknowledge your learnings and how far you have come; take action towards empowerment that will enable you to live your best life.

8. TAKE ACTION

Life is only as difficult as you make it. It's your choice; if you don't take action nothing will change. Break your goal up into doable baby steps.

YOUR GUIDE TO ACTION AND EMPOWERMENT

Create a new routine one step at a time and get excited for and celebrate each step along the way. Work out when you do your best work.

- Are you a morning person or an afternoon person? Do your work when your willpower is strongest. Show up and be accountable. Schedule 1–2-hour blocks of time where no one can interrupt you.
- Eliminate your distractions by creating a plan. Create a morning routine: meditate, exercise, drink coffee and make to-do lists to get yourself on track.
- Check on your daily habits. What is the purpose of them? Are they aligned with what you want or need to achieve? Where there is a will there is a way! RIGHT!

Here, I want to point out that our reactions are triggered unconsciously. It's not until we recognise our reactions consciously that we can start to clear and let go of what is holding us back. As you become more familiar with the process, you will find the answers to your questions come more easily and you will really start to trust your unconscious mind.

Your guide to action and empowerment

This section is your guide to flicking the switch from your specific roadblock to empowerment, finding the key to unlock each part, driving the bus and living a life you can love!

We have arrived at a major checkpoint in the journey. In this section I will break down each of the more common road-blocks many of us face. I'll talk about how

"Everything is on the way, not in the way."

Dr John Demartini

challenging emotions, beliefs, habits or states of being can limit our potential and really hold us back. Some of them we don't even realise hold us back until we are challenged in a certain way. The reality is many of us underestimate the value of reflecting on these challenges as a roadblock and if left unchecked they can develop from a simple

PART FIVE

thought to a behaviour that will eventually be harder to move through. And a learnt behaviour is more complex and getting to the root cause can be challenging.

My biggest 'ah-ha' moment was when I realised I could change my life by changing the way I think and take action. My biggest empowering moment was when I realised that I always have a choice and that when I took responsibility for the choices I made I was in control of my life and the direction it was taking. How exciting is that! The key to finding solutions to my roadblocks was to ask the right questions and use the tools in my toolbox.

As you move through the solutions and changes you can implement from this section, you will see there are different sets of tools for each roadblock and as you get closer to the root cause of the roadblock you get closer to the core of your true authentic self. You may find that as you go deeper within, your triggers may create a more intense reaction especially from those events that come upon you unexpectedly and that's okay, remember you have the tools. It's how you deal with your challenges in life that's important, take your learnings and keep moving forward to the front of the bus.

Having read the previous sections you realise that our thoughts create our emotions that in turn are expressed by our feelings and thus create our behaviours, habits and state, whether they are either positive or negative.

Each roadblock discussed below will challenge you to move from stuck to empowerment, from negative to positive. I have covered as many types of roadblocks as possible and I will support you to develop your own toolbox that will help you to move through any challenge/roadblock you will have in the future. This part of the book can be a go-to section at any time in your life. Enjoy!

Doing your best at any one point in time is about being aware of what is happening around you; clear focused communication, and being able to be honest with yourself and others. Everything you do from now on needs to have meaning and be aligned with your true authentic self and where you are going (what you want to achieve in life).

YOUR GUIDE TO ACTION AND EMPOWERMENT

THE FOUR KEYS

The four important keys to master on your journey through your roadblocks are:

1. **Good health**, living a healthy balanced lifestyle. Are you a VIP in your life? Do you make time for a healthy diet, exercise and time out? Do you have a positive attitude around self-care, self-awareness, self-support, self-respect, self-love and connection to your true authentic self?

2. **Stuck awareness**, what is happening? What is not happening? What's working, what's not working? Get unstuck. Discover your flow, live your life on purpose, a life you can love.

3. **Honesty**, a quality of being honest, living your truth with self and others. Honesty implies you are honourable, you have integrity, you are loyal, trustworthy, fair, sincere and are authentic.

4. **Good communication.** Good communication equals results, clarity and an understanding of self and others.

When one or all four of these keys become a roadblock, this is where you need to start. How we process our thoughts consciously or unconsciously is the interesting part and we have a choice to focus on a negative or positive pathway. When our thoughts, feelings, emotions and behaviours are negative they can turn into a roadblock.

We are all unique and have our own unique system of survival programmed from birth from our life experience. And this is okay but if it

PART FIVE

gets in the way of achieving our dreams and living to our fullest potential then it's not okay. So now you are at the point of discovery.

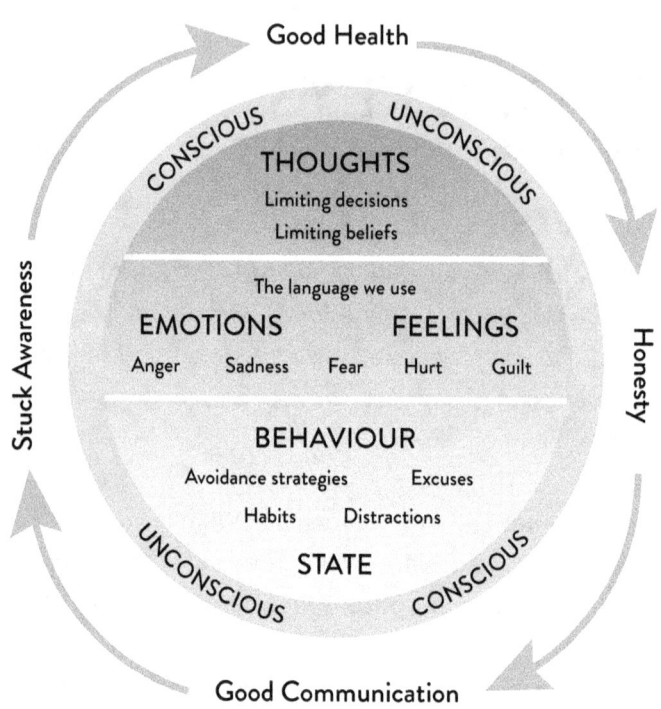

1. Good health

The challenge here is to be healthy, a state of complete physical, mental and social wellbeing. Being fit and having a healthy, balanced lifestyle is so important

"Being fit and healthy isn't a fad or a trend, it's a lifestyle."

Anonymous

to your health and wellbeing, creating a quality of life that should be approached in a holistic way that takes into account your physical, mental and emotional health.

If you have been working through this book, you will understand that the main catalyst in life is to be happy and live a balanced lifestyle, in

YOUR GUIDE TO ACTION AND EMPOWERMENT

turn building a strong foundation. Having a strong foundation will set you up to overcome any challenge that may come your way, empowering you to live a life that you can love.

THERE ARE TWO ELEMENTS TO BEING FIT AND HEALTHY

- **Physical health:** your body needs the right fuel and regular movement to stimulate your organs to function properly, and be fit and healthy enough to do the things you love.
- **Mental health:** your mind, like your body, needs to be stimulated. Mental health includes our emotional, psychological and social wellbeing; it affects how we think, feel and act.

> *"Our greatest wealth is our health."*
> **Virgil**

Your physical health is the first step to creating a strong foundation. If you are eating a healthy, balanced diet, getting regular exercise, staying hydrated by drinking water and getting enough sleep, you immediately start to feel good – and when you feel good, it's easier to maintain a positive mindset.

UNHEALTHY

Your challenge here is to understand that being fit and healthy mentally and physically is so important to the quality of life you live and when you get the balance right it empowers you to live your best life. If you choose to change nothing, the consequences of your inaction over a period of time are self-sabotage and self-neglect.

UNHEALTHY AS A ROADBLOCK

When you are unhealthy, life can become a challenge, creating roadblocks along the way. To understand when you are unhealthy is a tricky one, because there are so many different roadblocks that can lead to an unhealthy lifestyle. Everyone is different

> *"Self-care is how you take your power back."*
> **Unknown**

PART FIVE

and experiences different levels of unease before they realise the consequences of their actions and question why things are not quite right. Being aware is the key, and motivation is the answer to make the changes you need to get back on track.

IDENTIFY YOUR ROADBLOCK

When you are not feeling 100% it's important to identify why you feel the way you do. There are so many components of your health that can show up as a roadblock. When you don't identify whatever you are negatively feeling, seeing, experiencing at any one point in time as a possible roadblock, ill health may rear its ugly head.

The first signs that you may be stuck in an unhealthy state are physical signs:

- Are you having trouble sleeping? If so, why?
- Are you always tired and experiencing a lack of energy? If so, why?
- Do you experience heart palpitations on a regular basis?
- Do you constantly run out of breath?
- Do you have swelling in the legs?
- Is your urine a dark colour? Find out why.
- Do you snore?
- Is your skin itchy?
- Do you catch every cold/flu going round?
- Are your lips cracked?
- Is your skin breaking out?
- Do you have blurred vision?
- Do you urinate too often?
- Do you have bad breath?

Take note – these are generally signs that your body is trying to tell you something; it could simply be that you may need to readjust something in your diet or your daily routine. Or it could be a reaction to an experience or lack of something you need at a deeper level of your existence. **If the symptoms don't go away, please see a medical practitioner.**

AWARENESS: WHAT'S HAPPENING/NOT HAPPENING?
- What specifically is the challenge?
- Why is it a challenge?
- Do you have any symptoms telling you that you may be living an unhealthy lifestyle? If so, what are they?
- Is your physical health a roadblock on this journey? If so, in what way?
- Is your mental health a roadblock on this journey? If so, in what way?
- Is your emotional health a roadblock on this journey? If so, in what way?

WHAT IS THE RESULT?
- Is it internal or external? A limiting decision, a negative emotion, a habit, an avoidance strategy, etc.
- Was it a physical reaction i.e. a headache, an ache, pain or did you just remove yourself from the situation?
- Has the outcome become a roadblock?
- If you were to know, what is it stopping you from doing what you need to do to overcome this challenge?

What did you learn?

TAKE OWNERSHIP
1. Are you blaming others for the way you feel?
2. If you are not feeling 100%, do you know why are you feeling the way you do?

Let's start with the basics. Are your basic needs being met?

PART FIVE

MASLOW'S HIERARCHY OF NEEDS

Going back to Maslow's hierarchy of needs gives me a simple framework to work from, starting off at the foundation level one: physiological needs and the environment. This hierarchy is something you can refer to any time to just check in if things don't feel right and you don't know where to start. If you don't get the answers you need, keep going up the levels. Refer to the diagram in the Journey Handbook/To understand your life balance.

Level 1. Basic needs
Physiological/the environment you live in.

- **Food:**
  Are you eating a balanced diet? If not, why not?
  (I am not eating a balanced diet because..........)

- **Water:**
  How much water should you be drinking? Find out.
  Are you drinking enough water? If not, why not?

- **Personal hygiene habits:**
  Do you care for your body in a healthy way?
  Do you shower regularly? If not, why not?

- **Warmth:**
  Do you have warm clothes and a roof over your head?
  If not, why not?

- **Rest:**
  Do you get enough rest, sleep well, etc? If not, why not?
  Do you take time out on a regular basis?

- **Safety:**
  Are you living in a safe environment?
  Do you feel safe? If not, why not?

YOUR GUIDE TO ACTION AND EMPOWERMENT

- **Security:**
  Do you feel you have security in your life? If not, why not?
  Do you have people around you that support you? If not, why not?

What did you learn?
Are you taking responsibility for your choices, your thoughts and reactions around health?
If not, why not?
Is there anything you need to change?

"Each new day is a new opportunity to improve yourself. Take it. And make the most of it."
Anonymous

JOURNAL IT OUT

DISCOVERING THE ROOT CAUSE

Make a list of your learnings from the questions above. And now let's dive in a little deeper.

Breathe
1. Breathe in for six, hold for three, and breathe out for nine, until you feel a sense of calm come over you.
2. Allow the answers to the following questions to bubble up.

NOTE: I need you to be really honest with yourself as you answer the questions.

ASK THE RIGHT QUESTIONS

- How do you feel now?
- So, what do you need to do to bring more of what you want into your life?
- Do you need to do or change something right now? If so, what?

MOVE AWAY FROM RESISTANCE

- Is everything you do getting you closer to living a healthy life, a life you will love living?

PART FIVE

- If you were to know what specifically do you want?
- How would your life be if you DIDN'T get fit and healthy and live a balanced lifestyle, a life you can love?
- What would happen if you DID start to become fit and healthy and live a balanced lifestyle, a life you can love?

Sometimes, it's just hard to break away from that which does not serve you. You know it's NOT good for you, but you just keep doing it. Don't let your health become a roadblock to what you truly want in life.

- Write a list of 10 activities you enjoy that bring fun and laughter into your life.
- Write a list of 10 creative activities you enjoy doing.
- Write down 10 things/activities that would go onto your bucket list (ie, things you would like to do before you die).
- Write down at least 5 things that you do or would like to do that have some element of risk involved.

WHAT DID YOU LEARN?

TAKE ACTION AROUND YOUR HEALTH

- Create a plan, and write a list of the changes you would like to make where your health is concerned. Prioritise your list from most important to least important. Create a U CAN B SMART goal. Break it up into small, achievable steps.
- What action are you going to do today to get closer to your desired outcome?

TIPS FOR STAYING HEALTHY AND LIVING A HEALTHY LIFESTYLE

! Eat a well-balanced diet, including lots of fruits, vegetables and grains. Choose a diet that's low in saturated fat and cholesterol and moderate in sugar.

YOUR GUIDE TO ACTION AND EMPOWERMENT

! Be physically active for at least 30 minutes a day. Break it up into 10-minute sessions when pressed for time. Suggested activities for healthy movement include yoga, Tai Chi, walking, stretching, sports, dancing, running, going to the gym and other activities you enjoy.

! Get plenty of rest and sleep well. Take time out – rest and recuperate when you need to.

! Stay hydrated.

! Become aware of what your body is telling you, and find out why.

! Navigate through your roadblocks.

! Recognise your stress levels, take action and learn to relax. Journal it out, meditate and do what works for you to release stress. Refer to **Stressed** in this Handbook.

! Understand your triggers and your comfort zone.

! Avoid negative people, as they can bring you down.

! Maintain a positive mindset; choose to be happy.

! Be flexible and open to positive opportunities.

! Drink alcohol in moderation.

! Avoid addiction of any kind and stop smoking. If you have an addiction of any kind, understand why you started, find the root cause and change what you have to in order to create a new positive habit.

 PART FIVE

- ! Brush your teeth morning and night and floss daily. Maintain oral health and go to the dentist regularly.

- ! Stay out of the sun in the hottest part of the day (10 am to 3 pm) and use sunscreen.

- ! Take baby steps. If you need to change a habit that does not serve you, make it manageable.

"When you feel like quitting, think about why you started."
Anonymous

Maintain a healthy body and lifestyle. Nobody is perfect – we all need a little kick in the bum sometimes. Never, ever, give up on yourself. You are unique and deserve to be able to live your best life. Our greatest wealth is our health. Remember it's your choice and whatever you choose is okay.

> I AM FIT AND HEALTHY;
> I DO MY BEST AT ANY ONE POINT IN TIME.
> I LOVE MY LIFE!

2. Stuck awareness

STUCK AS A ROADBLOCK

Stuck is not moving forward or being able to go back. Whatever is keeping you stuck could be a thought, an emotion, a feeling, a state or behaviour. You may need to delve in a little deeper ie, it could be you are stressed or depressed, you may be making excuses or holding on very tightly to a limiting belief or experience, or you could be experiencing a negative emotion on a regular basis.

The challenge here is to acknowledge you're stuck, find the root cause, flick the switch and never ever give up. Once you realise what is keeping you stuck, you can let it go. Being unstuck is about finding your life's purpose so that you can move on. Your life's purpose is what makes you feel alive, it's what you are passionate about, what you are willing to fight for. It's more than your job, your responsibilities or your goals.

Let's get started.

AWARENESS: Identify your roadblock

Event: What's happening?
- How do you know that you are stuck?
- What do you think is keeping you stuck?
- What is your challenge around being stuck?

Response
- How specifically do you 'do' stuck?
- Is it a thought, an emotion or a behaviour?

Outcome
- Is it internal or external? A limiting decision, a negative emotion, a habit, an avoidance strategy, etc.
- Was it a physical reaction ie, a headache, an ache, pain or did you just remove yourself from the situation?
- Has the outcome become a roadblock?
- If you were to know, what is it stopping you from becoming unstuck?

TAKE OWNERSHIP
- Are you blaming others?

PART FIVE

- Are you taking responsibility for your choices, your thoughts and your reactions? If not, why not?
- Are you living at cause? If not, why not?
- What is it you have to do to take ownership?

What did you learn?

JOURNAL IT OUT, so you can dive in a little deeper

- What are you feeling about being stuck now?

Breathe
1. Breathe in for six, hold for three, and breathe out for nine, until you feel a sense of calm come over you.
2. Allow the answers to your questions to bubble up.

Ask the right questions
- Why am I feeling stuck?
- Then ask: Is my reaction, roadblock/setback at this point a feeling, an emotion, a thought or a behaviour, etc?
- If you were to know, what is triggering your reaction? (What is keeping you stuck?)

DISCOVER THE ROOT CAUSE
- How do you feel when you are stuck?
- Then ask yourself: Why am I allowing myself to feel this way? *I am allowing myself to feel (the answer to the question above)..........because..........*
- Ask the question again and again relating to the answer to the previous answer. Keep asking the question until you find it hard to answer.
- Is the final answer a limiting decision, a negative emotion, an avoidance strategy etc or a physical reaction/state?
- Proceed to the relevant section and continue the process.

YOUR GUIDE TO ACTION AND EMPOWERMENT

FIND THE SOLUTION
- What are you feeling now?
- Is this feeling important to you? If so, why?
  The answer to the previous question is important to me because..........
- Keep asking the question until you find it hard to answer.
- So what do you need to do to bring more of what you want into your life?
- Do you need to do or change something right now? If so, what?
- What did you learn?

MOVE AWAY FROM RESISTANCE
- Is everything you do getting you closer to living a life unstuck, a life you will love living?
- What would happen if you DIDN'T get unstuck? What is your stuck keeping you from doing?
- What would happen if you DID get unstuck?

WHAT DID YOU LEARN?
- Do you have any clarity around what is keeping you stuck?

TAKE ACTION
- What actions are you going to do to get unstuck? (Create a plan/goal)
- What action are you going to do today to get closer to being unstuck?

You may find you have a smile on your face because now you know you don't need to feel this way and you know what you need to do next. Once you have gained some clarity, you can give yourself some space to look at the situation, change your perspective, make a plan and open yourself up to new ideas and people. Start with small changes and de-clutter. Develop a new routine, change your habits, and remember to take one step at a time.

PART FIVE

TIPS FOR BECOMING UNSTUCK

CONNECT to who you are. Rediscover your flow and find out what you are passionate about. What are the things that float your boat and make you feel good? Allow yourself to dream and then align your life with who you are. Answer the following questions and really connect with your true authentic self:

! What makes me happy? Why do these things make me happy?

! What were my favourite things to do in the past? Make a list of at least 20 of your favourite things you did in the past.

! What are my favourite things to do now? Make a list of at least 10 of your favourite things you do now.

! When do you enjoy an activity so much or become so committed to something that you lose track of time? Make a list of at least five things that make you lose track of time when doing them.

! Make a list of at least three people who inspire you the most. Why do these people inspire you?

! What makes you feel good about yourself and when do you feel good?

! Make a list of at least 50 things you like/love about yourself.

! What are you good at? Make a list of at least 20 things you are good at.

! Make a list of at least 5 skills you have in each area of your Life Circle.

What did you learn?

BELIEVE in yourself. Trust that you can reach your expectations and get out of your comfort zone. You have the power within to achieve anything you desire.
- Do you believe you can achieve anything you desire? If not, why not?
- With all the knowledge you have now, what do you need to do to really and truly believe that you can?

Take action: if you don't, nothing will change.
What action can you take today to begin your journey to freedom and becoming unstuck? Set up a regular routine that will inspire you to move forward and continue your journey.

CHOOSE an area from your Life Circle where you feel stuck. Work out what you need to do to become unstuck, something that aligns with who you are: study a new skill, go back to university, e.g. welding, watercolour painting, accounting or counselling. Exercise, walk, or join a club or choir. It's up to you – whatever it is, make sure it gets you excited and gives meaning to your existence and become unstuck!

> "Wait a minute," you might say. "I can't do that yet."
> Why not?
> "I'm working on it."
> What specifically are you doing? Is it truly aligned with the outcome you desire?
> "I don't know how."
> What specifically don't you know how to do?
> Learn to reframe any blocks in your thinking that may appear. Become aware of them and take action! Okay? Good.

ACKNOWLEDGE YOUR LEARINGS SO FAR

Now, it's time to write the letter. You are writing the letter to tell your

PART FIVE

future self about your newfound purpose in life, what you want to achieve in the future and how you want to live your life. .

1. Find some special paper and an envelope.

2. Give yourself time; don't rush.

3. Close your eyes. Breathe in for six, hold for three, and breathe out for nine. Repeat at least five times until you feel a wave of calm come over you.

4. Relax and open your eyes.

5. Start writing:

> *Dear (your name),*
> *Today, I am writing a letter to tell you how much I have learnt about you today.*
> *I found that..........*
> *I love to..........*
> *I feel good when..........*
> *My favourite things mean so much to me because..........*
> *When I am.........., I know I can..........*
> *I have all..........*
> *Finish off with a positive affirmation* (Refer to Affirmations in the Toolbox.)
> *Signed, (your name and date)*

Once you have written your letter put it somewhere safe and open it up when you feel the stuck creeping back into your life. You are worthy, you are unique, and you are special. Believe in yourself because you can do this.

GET HELP

Feeling stuck is not okay if it is stopping you from being who you want to be or reaching your goals. ASK FOR HELP. A coach or a mentor can offer a different point of view, provide clarity around a situation, keep you accountable and support you to take productive action to get you back on track, moving in the right direction to living a life you can love.

"Some people believe holding on and hanging in there are signs of great strength. However, there are times when it takes much more strength to know when to let go and then do it."

Ann Landers

I MOVE THROUGH LIFE EASILY AND EFFORTLESSLY

3. Honesty

"Be honest with yourself and never settle for a life that is not true to who you are."

ATGW

The challenge here is to be authentic. This may be the biggest challenge you have had yet. I remember a previous boyfriend of mine said to me, "The hardest thing in your life is being honest with yourself." I am so grateful for the part he played in my growth.

When you are honest, you speak the truth. More broadly you present yourself in a genuine sincere way. It's a quality of being fair and truthful. When you have a strong sense of self, live in your truth and feel like you are worthy, it doesn't matter what other people think, say or do. It is none of your business. You don't feel the need to judge or gossip about others because you are secure within yourself.

HONESTY AS A ROADBLOCK

As a child, we want to fit in and be liked; we do what we think is normal. But during this process, we can lose ourselves. We suffer from insecurities, and we don't accept who we are. The thoughts we repeat eventually affect our behaviour and create corresponding changes. We self-sabotage ourselves through addictions and other behaviours, and we don't get what we truly want because we can't be honest with ourselves and take responsibility for our thoughts and actions in everything we do. We create roadblocks.

When you take responsibility for your thoughts, actions and everything you do, you are in control, you have more clarity and any changes you need to make are not seen to be impossible.

AWARENESS

What's happening/what's not happening? Choose an area in your life where honesty has been a challenge.

JOURNAL IT OUT

Breathe
1. Breathe in for six, hold for three, and breathe out for nine, until you feel a sense of calm come over you.
2. Allow the answers to your questions to bubble up.

Ask the right questions
- Can you be honest with yourself and speak your truth?
- If not, why not?
- What does honesty mean to you?
- How important is honesty in your life?
- In what ways is honesty important in your life?
- What are the results in your life if you are dishonest?
- What are the results in your life if others are dishonest?
- Do you take responsibility for your thoughts/actions and everything you do?
- If not, why not?
- Ask a couple of friends to tell you your good points, make a list.
- Now ask them to tell you your bad points, make a list.
- How do you feel about your lists?

WHAT DID YOU LEARN?

HERE ARE EIGHT KEY WAYS YOU CAN BECOME MORE HONEST WITH YOURSELF

- Practise honesty and develop trust with self and others.
- Take time to reflect. Mindful meditation.
- Admit when you make mistakes.
- Pay attention to your feelings.
- Find someone you trust to be open with you and give you feedback.
- Be straightforward – don't over analyse.
- Learn what you don't know.
- Acknowledge both the good and bad in your life and let go of that which does not serve you.

To my mind living your truth is living your authentic life in accordance with fact or your reality that is aligned with your values that guide you, who you are, what you do and why you do it.

What action can you take today to begin your journey to living an honest life and living your truth?

> I AM ALWAYS OPEN, HONEST AND SINCERE WITH MYSELF AND OTHERS; I LIVE IN MY TRUTH.

PART FIVE

4. Good communication

Communication is the imparting or exchanging of information not only in the spoken form. People communicate with one another to share ideas, express thoughts and feelings, resolve problems, express wants and needs, develop social relationships and talk about ideas, thoughts and emotions. Getting the intended message across to another person is what communication is all about. The challenge here is to be a good communicator and connect with yourself and others in a positive way.

Good communication is an essential part of everyday life; it helps us understand people, situations and experiences both internal and external. To communicate effectively is an essential skill in every area of your life. It is generally a two-way activity. If you are talking, you need to be clear; if you are listening, you need to be a good listener. You need to be aware of the other person's reality, communicate at their level and show empathy and compassion when needed.

> *"To effectively communicate, we must realise that we are all different in the way we perceive the world and use this understanding as a guide to our communication with others."*
> **Tony Robbins**

When you are a good communicator, you:
- ✓ Build trust; you are easy to talk to; you speak clearly; you are authentic; you care; and you are reliable and sincere.
- ✓ Can prevent problems or resolve problems.
- ✓ Can provide clarity and direction.
- ✓ Can create better relationships.
- ✓ Can increase engagement.
- ✓ Are interesting to be around and people listen to you.
- ✓ Can improve productivity by giving clear, precise instructions.

✓ Can promote team building by understanding and communicating on the level of those you are speaking to and becoming aware of their personal needs, wants and desires.

COMMUNICATION AS A ROADBLOCK

A lack of communication between people can cause roadblocks, especially when a communicated message is not given or received. You feel like you don't have a voice, you can't get your point across or say what you need to say to release stress or find out how the other person is feeling about a certain thing.

When you have a lack of communication in your personal and work life, it's like you haven't put the blinker on to change lanes. Have you ever been driving and experienced someone stopping in front of you suddenly or turning a corner with no blinker? It is so annoying and it may cause an accident/misunderstanding. When you put your blinker on, you know where you are going, the other person driving knows where you are going and it shows that you know what is going on around you. Using your blinker (communication skills) is an important part of communication.

Whichever form of communication you choose, communication is a skill that can always be improved upon. Keeping in mind that conversations are a two-way street. You have the right to be heard and what you want/need to say is worthy of listening to as well. Before we get started, answer these reflective questions to get you on track with communication.

AWARENESS: What's happening/not happening?

Identify a situation where you feel you need to improve your communication.

JOURNAL IT OUT

Event
- What specifically is the issue?
- Is it personal (with your children, family member, partner or friend)?

PART FIVE

- Is it work-related?
- Why is a lack of communication in this area a challenge?
- What is it you need to say?
- Why do you need to say it?
- What is the desired outcome?
- Is the desired outcome important to you?
- If so, why is the desired outcome important to you?
- What are your personal boundaries and values related to this issue?
- What is the real reason you need your desired outcome?

Response: How did you react?
- Is it going to be difficult to get your point across? If so, why?
- What specifically happens when you don't communicate effectively?
- Was it a thought, an emotion or a behaviour?
- What part of the issue triggered your reaction?

Outcome: What is the result of the way you reacted?
- Is it internal or external? A limiting decision, a negative emotion, a habit, an avoidance strategy, etc.
- Was it a physical reaction ie, a headache, an ache, pain or did you just remove yourself from the situation?
- Has the outcome of your reaction become a roadblock?
- If you were to know, why is it stopping you from communicating well in this situation?

TAKE OWNERSHIP
- Are you blaming others?
- Are you taking responsibility for your choices, your thoughts and your reactions? If not, why not?
- What is it you have to do to take ownership?

Let's dive in a little deeper.

YOUR GUIDE TO ACTION AND EMPOWERMENT

Breathe
1. Breathe in for six, hold for three, and breathe out for nine, until you feel a sense of calm come over you.
2. Allow the answers to your questions to bubble up.

- What are you feeling now?
- Is this feeling important to you? If so, why?
  The answer to the previous question is important to me because……….
- Keep asking the question until you find it hard to answer.
- Repeat the last answer you had.
  ……………is important to me because……………
- How do you feel now? What did you learn?
- So, what do you need to do to bring more of *(your last answer, what you want)* into your life?
- Do you need to do or change something right now? If so, what?

MOVE AWAY FROM RESISTANCE
Acknowledge the skills you have.
- What are your personal strengths around communication? Make a list.
- What communication skills do you feel you need to improve? Make a list.

WHAT DID YOU LEARN?
- What is it around this situation you need to accept that you cannot change?
- What is it around this situation you can change?
- Are you willing to compromise? If so, how much?
- Specifically, what is it you need to do differently next time?

TAKE ACTION
- What are you going to do next?
- How are you going to get your point across?

- When and where are you going to have that conversation?
- What are the important things you need to keep in mind when talking to this other person/group etc?
- What action can you take today to improve your communications skills?

TIPS TO BETTER COMMUNICATION WHEN COMMUNICATION BECOMES A ROADBLOCK

! **Be a good listener:** understand where they are coming from and ask good open-ended questions. Active listening is the key; it involves hearing and understanding what someone is saying to you. It's all about being respectful: other people will be more likely to engage in communication with you if you respect them and their ideas.

! **Ask questions and find common ground:** develop understanding; give and receive feedback. You are not a mind-reader and have not walked in their shoes, so never assume you know what someone is going to say. Ask good open-ended questions, because this allows others to have an opinion and change the energy around a conversation. They can create rapport and you can show that you are interested and want to know more.

! **Be prepared:** and it won't be so scary. Once you understand yourself better and understand where your feelings are coming from, and you know what the outcome is that you want, your confidence to speak up can be rewarding. You may need to compromise, but hey, it feels good to talk about it, right?

! **Be clear and concise:** whether in person, on the phone, or in a message or email, convey your message clearly. Be concise and direct. If you start rambling, the listener may either lose focus or be unsure about what you want.

- **Be open-minded and honest:** be present. Allow yourself to speak up and be honest. You don't have to pretend or lie as that leads to more issues and miscommunication. Always engage in active listening, and be sure to demonstrate empathy by acknowledging you understand what the other person's point of view is.

- **Pay attention to body language:** build rapport. Build a connection by paying attention to tone of voice, nonverbal cues and signals. Be confident; make eye contact, use a firm but friendly tone, smile and ask questions.

- **Consider:** the way you speak to someone and the way they speak to you. Are they listening? Have you gone off track? Are they on a time schedule? Do they need to be somewhere? Is what you are saying interesting to them? What are they doing while the words are coming out of your mouth? Have they got their arms crossed? Are they tapping their feet? Are you speaking too loudly or in a monotone? Pay attention to what's happening and adjust your conversation appropriately. Allow them to speak; they need to be listened to as much as you.

- **Set up your boundaries:** set time aside to talk. Whether for work or personal communication, you need to be aware that there is a right time to communicate. Choose when you have the conversation. Be flexible and patient, and make sure you have that conversation. I take my husband out for coffee or a friend/workmate out for lunch if I have something important to discuss. In a different environment they can't get distracted, and in a more relaxed atmosphere it's easier to get your point across.

- **Don't be afraid of a little silence:** in the right place, it can give a sense of understanding. Allow the energy of the conversation to regain its momentum and flow.

PART FIVE

Communication tools

1. **Communication sandwich** (refer to number seven in the Toolbox) I totally see it as a freedom tool. It allows you to say what you need to say with the purpose of getting them to listen, get your point across and release any stress that you may have accumulated around the topic, at the same time as sharing the love and keeping the energy around a situation positive.

    The purpose of the communication sandwich is two-fold.

    a) To communicate in a positive way what you need to say to the other person as you have their attention and they will be more inclined to listen to you if you keep it positive.

    b) Saying what you need to say to get it out of your head so you are not dwelling on the negatives in your mind.

2. **Reality check** (refer to number six in the Toolbox) is for the purpose of understanding what is happening prior to effective communication so you can gain the right sort of communication starter, etc. No matter what is happening in your life at any one point in time if we get emotional or are triggered, we can't see clearly, we need to Stop, Think and Flick the Switch. Whatever it is – is it yours, or is it someone else's challenge – that has created a situation, ask the question, "R U OK?" The reality of the situation might have nothing to do with you.

> I AM A GOOD LISTENER,
> AND I COMMUNICATE MY MESSAGE WELL.

YOUR GUIDE TO ACTION AND EMPOWERMENT

So, what's next?

For me, my starting point was the depression I was diagnosed with. The realisation that enough was enough was my decision and so my journey back to me began.

Even though we have to go in deeper to get to the root cause, the intensity when left unattended is heavy and resides at the bottom of the stairs. Once you arrive at the root cause the intensity lifts and we are able to release, let go and celebrate. Please note, depending where you are situated on the stairs will depict how much work you will have to do to release your roadblock.

THE JOURNEY TO RELEASE YOUR ROADBLOCK and CELEBRATE!

ROOT CAUSE ESTABLISHED

THOUGHTS
Limiting beliefs
Limiting decisions
Low self-esteem
Low self-worth

EMOTIONS
Anger
Sadness
Fear
Hurt
Guilt

MAJOR ROADBLOCKS

FEELINGS
Lost
Confused
Frustrated

BEHAVIOUR
Habits
Excuses
Distractions
Avoidance
The language we use

STATE
Stressed
Depression
Anxiety
Scared
Confused
Unhappy
Physical disease

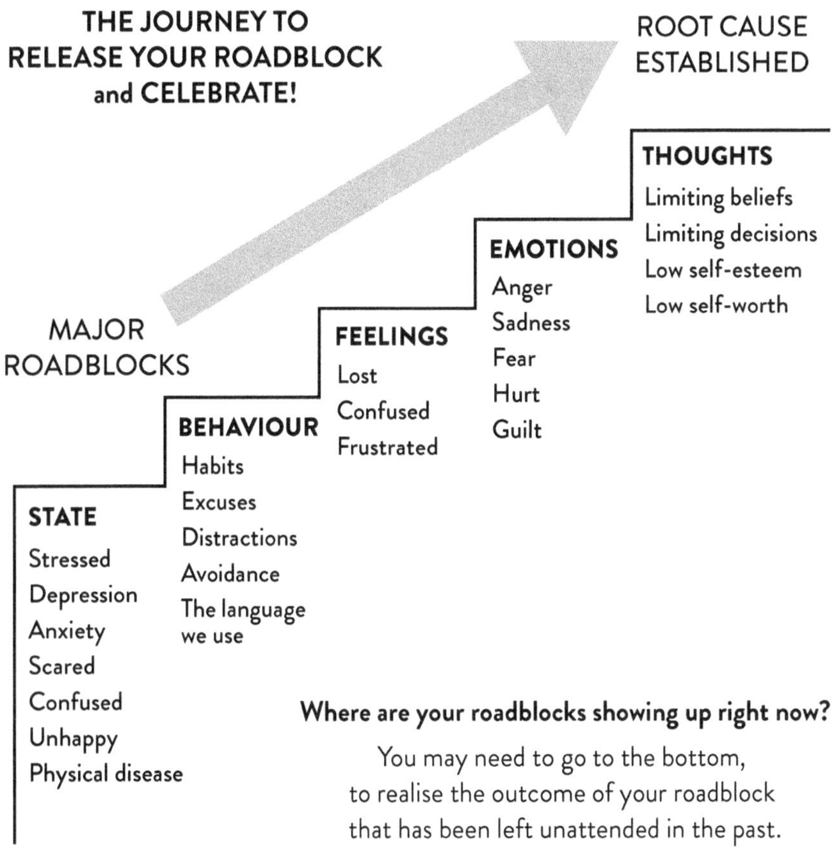

Where are your roadblocks showing up right now?
You may need to go to the bottom,
to realise the outcome of your roadblock
that has been left unattended in the past.

PART FIVE

State

A state is a particular condition that someone or something is in at a specific time.

> *"You can't always control what goes on outside, but you can always control what goes on in the inside."*
> **Wayne Dyer**

STRESSED

The challenge here is to recognise when you are stressed, discover your stressors and take action to release the tension in your body and get it under control.

- Are you feeling stressed right now?
- Are you feeling over-extended, lonely or unbearably tense?
- Are you upset by conflicts with others, worn out, burned out and often angry or irritated?

Stress is the body's response to physical, mental or emotional pressure and can affect your body, thoughts, feelings and behaviour. When you sense danger, whether it's real or imagined, the body's defences kick into gear in a rapid, automatic process known as the fight-or-flight reaction or stress response. The stress response is the body's way of protecting you.

For many people, stress is so commonplace that it has become a way of life. Stress isn't always bad. In fact, in small doses, it can help you perform under pressure and motivate you to do your best. But beyond a certain point, stress stops being helpful and starts causing major damage to your health, mood, productivity, relationships and quality of life. When working properly, the fight-or-flight response is the body's way of protecting you. It helps you stay focused, energetic and alert. When you feel threatened, your nervous system responds by releasing a flood of stress hormones, including adrenaline and cortisol, which arouses the body for an emergency reaction. Your heart beats faster. Muscles tighten, blood pressure rises, breath quickens and your senses become sharper. In emergency situations, stress can save your life by giving you extra strength to defend yourself by spurring you to slam on the brakes to avoid an accident.

However, stress that's left unchecked can contribute to many health problems. Modern life is full of hassles, deadlines, frustrations and demands. I can't promise that you can live a life without stress. But once you become aware of what stresses you out and the long-term effects stress can have on your body and mind, you are ready to take control. The key is to understand your stressors and then take the appropriate action to get them under control.

During my journey, depression became a big part of my existence. I eventually realised I was overly emotional, not coping, constantly in survival mode yet I hadn't even realised I was stressed and had been for a long time. I saw my doctor, and the first thing he did was put me on some antidepressants. I did some counselling with him, and that allowed me to talk about it.

Unfortunately, talking did not solve my issues. I needed strategies to manage my stress. He just gave me a stronger dose of antidepressants. Sometimes, we just keep on keeping on because we know we must. We go into survival mode until everything falls into a heap.

That was when I made a decision that there must be more to life than the misery I was feeling – and so I started my journey to who I am now. I am not the person I used to be, I don't think the way I used to and now I see my life as an adventure. How exciting is that!

As you can imagine, when you are constantly running in emergency mode, your mind and body pay the price. By just understanding and becoming aware of how stress affects you, you can change your life by changing the way you think and start to enjoy every element of your life.

There are three main types of stress:
1. **Acute stress**: fight-or-flight as the body prepares to defend itself. It takes about 90 minutes for the metabolism to return to normal when the response is over. Internally, we all respond to the fight-or-flight stress response the same way; our blood pressure rises, our heart pumps faster, and our muscles constrict.

   Externally, however, people tend to respond to stress in different ways:

PART FIVE

In **'fight'** mode, you may appear overexcited or become angry, agitated, keyed up, overly emotional or unable to sit still.

In **'flight'** mode, you can appear under-excited, pull away, space out, show very little energy or emotion or become depressed.

In the **'frozen'** stress response, your external appearance may also be very different from what's going on inside. On the surface, you look paralysed but inside, you're extremely agitated and feel 'stuck', unable to do anything to help yourself.

2. **Chronic stress**: this can come from the costs of daily living, bills, kids and jobs. This is the stress we tend to ignore or push down. Left uncontrolled, this stress affects your health, your body and your immune system.

3. **Eustress**: this is stress in daily life that has positive connotations. Still, oftentimes, it can feel like we're powerless to stressors and we have no choice but to get bothered by traffic, the flu, responsibilities, taxes or bills. The key is to take action.

Stress can be caused by external and internal situations. Eight **external** stressors that could relate to you are:
1. The death of a loved one.
2. Divorce.
3. Loss of job/income.
4. Increase in financial obligations.
5. Getting married.
6. Moving to a new home/new job.
7. Negative work environment.
8. Negative home environment.

Eight **internal** stressors that could relate to you are:
1. Simply worrying.
2. The way we think, attitudes and perceptions, optimistic as opposed to pessimistic.

3. Fear and uncertainty around global disasters or that which is closer to home: finishing a project on time, enough money to pay the bills.
4. Unrealistic expectations, no one is perfect.
5. Change of any kind.
6. Chronic illness.
7. Emotional problems (depression, anxiety, anger, grief, guilt and low self-esteem).
8. Any major life changes.

Symptoms of stress can come in the form of different behaviours

Be aware! Stress usually shows up in our body in the form of a physical reaction, a behaviour, an emotional outburst, a strategy of avoidance or a thought process. Sometimes, we don't recognise our body's reaction is caused by a stressful situation, the symptoms show up before we realise that we are actually stressed, in turn we don't acknowledge what our body is telling us. Sometimes, we just need to connect with our body when something just does not feel right and acknowledge the reaction and do something about it.

For example, one participant who attended a 'Stress Less' workshop I was running explained her stressful work situation to me. She had already taken action and spoken to her boss as she was doing the work of two people and something needed to change and it soon would. Her situation did not change immediately and she said she was stressed. I asked her how she knew she was stressed, she replied she was feeling overwhelmed and was super tired and had no energy by the time she got home. I then asked her if she had any symptoms of stress while she was working.

She thought about it for a moment and said that while working at her computer, she sighs a lot.

Then I asked, "So, what do you do about it? What do you do next?"

"Nothing. I just keep on working," she replied. Can you imagine how she would be feeling by the end of the day? We came to the realisation that when she felt stressed in front of the computer, her sighing was her

PART FIVE

body telling her she needed to do something different. The solution was to get up, have a break at regular intervals, move to release the tension that was building in her body, go for a short walk, and allow her body to relax before getting back to her work.

There are four distinctive areas where symptoms of stress can affect us:
1. **Behavioural symptoms:** habits and behaviours.
2. **Cognitive symptoms:** cognition is the way we process knowledge.
3. **Emotional symptoms:** strong feelings derived from circumstances.
4. **Physical symptoms:** how our body is affected by our thoughts, emotions and behaviours.

Behavioural symptoms	Cognitive symptoms
Eating more or less	Memory problems
Sleeping too much or too little	Inability to concentrate
Isolating yourself from others	Poor judgement
Procrastinating or neglecting responsibilities	Seeing only the negative
Using alcohol, cigarettes or drugs to relax	Anxious or racing thoughts
Nervous habits (eg, nail biting and pacing)	

Emotional Symptoms	Physical Symptoms
Moodiness	Aches and pains
Irritability or short temper	Diarrhoea or constipation
Agitation/inability to relax	Nausea/dizziness
Feeling overwhelmed	Chest pain/rapid heartbeat
Sense of loneliness and isolation	Frequent colds
Constant worrying	Loss of sex drive
Depression and general unhappiness	

YOUR GUIDE TO ACTION AND EMPOWERMENT

IDENTIFY YOUR SYMPTOMS OF STRESS

The first step is to listen to what our body is telling us.

A body scan

One way to identify any symptoms that may be showing up in your body is to do a body scan. Find a quiet space.

Breathe: in for six, hold for three, breathe out for nine. Repeat at least five times until you feel a wave of calm come over you.

- Close your eyes. Focus on your breath. Now, mindfully scan your body for sensations of pain, tension, or anything out of the ordinary, from the top of your head to the tip of your toes. Recognise your points of stress/tension and sit with it for a moment and allow your thoughts to bubble up.
- Ask yourself, "What is my body telling me?"
- How is the stress showing up in my body?
- Can you see or recognise any of the above symptoms in yourself?
- Are you feeling anxious or finding it difficult to focus/concentrate?
- Are you feeling moody, irritated or overwhelmed?
- Are you procrastinating, overeating or not eating enough?
- Do you have diarrhoea, constipation, heart pain or a rapid heartbeat?
- What did you learn?

HOW YOU DEAL WITH YOUR STRESSORS

But just how much stress is too much? It differs from person to person; we're all unique. Some people can roll with the punches, while others seem to crumble in the face of far smaller obstacles or frustrations. Some people even seem to thrive on the excitement and challenge of a high-stress lifestyle. Your ability to tolerate stress depends on many factors.

Ask the right questions and you will find your way.

PART FIVE

Here are five major areas that may influence your stress levels.

	Positive	Negative
Your support network	Supportive friends and family members.	The lonelier and more isolated you are, the greater your vulnerability to stress.
Your sense of control	If you have confidence in yourself and your ability. It's easier to persevere through your challenges.	When things are out of your control, you're likely to have less tolerance for stress.
Your attitude and outlook	Positive mindset. Optimistic people are often more stress-hardy. Life is easier when you're happier.	Negative mindset. Everything can become a challenge. And you can live in a victim mindset.
Your ability to deal with your emotions	Self-awareness gives you the ability to bring your emotions into balance and bounce back from adversity.	You're extremely vulnerable and don't know how to calm and soothe yourself, allowing yourself to feel sad, angry or overwhelmed.
Your knowledge and preparation	When you know more about a possibly stressful situation, how long it will last and what to expect it makes it easier to cope with e.g. major surgery.	When the unexpected happens and you are not prepared you can feel stressed, anxious, become angry and overwhelmed. If you don't plan, you plan to fail.

- Do any of the above situations relate to you?
- What did you learn?

AWARENESS: Stress as a roadblock

We have worked out how stress is showing up in your body, now let's dive in a little deeper. Ask the following questions to find out why you are feeling stressed.

YOUR GUIDE TO ACTION AND EMPOWERMENT

Event: What's happening/not happening?
- Choose a stressful situation you are experiencing right now.
- How specifically is the stress showing up in my body and where? (tension, an ache, a pain, an action, etc).
- What specific situation do you believe created your stress? Work, family, friendship, relationship, financial situation.
- Is your stressor internal or external or a bit of both?

Response: How did you react?
- What is the specific trigger that set off your reaction?
- What specifically was your reaction? (Was it a thought, a physical, emotional or behavioural reaction?)
- What specifically is the challenge around your reaction?
- Why is it a challenge?

Outcome: What is the result of the way you reacted to the event?
- Is it internal or external? A limiting decision, a negative emotion, a habit, an avoidance strategy, etc.
- Was it a physical reaction ie, a headache, an ache, pain or did you just remove yourself from the situation?
- Has the outcome of your stress become a roadblock?
- If you were to know, how will it affect you in the future if you don't do something about it?

TAKE OWNERSHIP
- Are you blaming others for feeling the way you do?
- Are you taking responsibility for your choices, your thoughts and your reactions? If not, why not?
- Are you living at cause? If not, why not?
- What is it you have to do to take ownership?

JOURNAL IT OUT: Let's dive in a little deeper
- What are you feeling about the event now?

PART FIVE

Breathe
1. Close your eyes. Breathe in for six, hold for three, and breathe out for nine. Repeat until you feel a sense of calm come over you.
2. Allow the answers to your questions to bubble up.

Ask the right questions
- Then ask yourself: why am I feeling stressed about……….?
- How does feeling stressed about……….make me feel?
- Why am I allowing myself to feel……….about this situation?
  I am allowing myself to feel this way because……….
- Ask the question again and again relating to the answer to the previous question. Keep asking the question until you find it hard to answer.
- How do you react when you feel this way?
- Is my reaction, roadblock/setback at this point a feeling, an emotion, a thought or a behaviour?

DISCOVER THE ROOT CAUSE: Find the solution
- What are you feeling now? (ie, *I am feeling weak.*)
- Is this feeling important to you? If so, why?
  The answer to the previous question is important to me because……….
- Keep asking the question until you find it hard to answer.
- So, what do you need to do to bring more of what you want into your life?
- Do you need to do or change something right now? If so, what?
- What did you learn?

MOVE AWAY FROM RESISTANCE
- What would my life be like if I didn't get so stressed about……….?
- What would happen if I let my stress control me?

REFRAME: FLIP FROM NEGATIVE TO POSITIVE
Check your language/self-talk around your stressful situation. Place it in the table and flip it into a positive statement.

Negative self-talk	Positive thinking
There's no way it will work	How can I do it differently?
I can't do it	I can do it

> *"The greatest weapon against stress is the ability to choose one thought over another."*
> **William James**

What did you learn?

TIPS TO HELP YOU MANAGE YOUR STRESS

! **Breathe:** breathing can immediately stop the tension from rising when you need an immediate response. Breathe in for six, hold for three, and breathe out for nine. Then, with a little more time to spare, find somewhere comfortable (maybe just sit in the sun) and continue to consciously breathe in and out. Connect to and really feel the breath in your body; allow it to expand from the top of your head to the tips of your toes.

! **Become aware:** ask the right questions. Identify why you are stressed and take action. Journal it out, engage in problem-solving. Meditate. Develop curiosity, find your why, and celebrate your achievements.
When you have awareness around your stress, it's easier to control or limit the effect stress can have on your mind and body.

PART FIVE

- **Work on managing your time better:** work on the things you have to do and don't like doing first – this is when your energy is highest. Put time limits on different things you need to do. Give yourself mini breaks, as it is hard to have full, clear focus for a prolonged amount in time.

- **Establish healthy boundaries:** for example, tell your friend you aren't going to spend time with her if she makes fun of you. Get to know what you need to create the best you. It's imperative that you nurture yourself and respect who you are, your truth and your authenticity. Learn to say no.

- **Ask for support:** from a friend or a health practitioner/professional.

- **Learn how to delegate:** with respect and honour for the other person's efforts. You don't have to do it all.

- **Walk away:** leave a situation that is causing you stress. Once you know that you have done all that you possibly can to resolve the issues that are creating the stress and that there is no chance of reconciliation, walk away.

- **Create a to-do list:** prioritise it from most important to least important. At the end of each day, pick the top six tasks on your list and work through them one at a time. Cross them off your list as you do them and see how much you have achieved.

- **Create an attitude of gratitude:** it's always good to be thankful for the small things in life. Connect with your feelings that make you feel good around what you are grateful for, and in turn, recognise and connect with who you really are, refer to the Toolbox at the back of the book.

YOUR GUIDE TO ACTION AND EMPOWERMENT

! **Create positive affirmations** for each of your learnings. Repeat the affirmations three times a day. Say them out loud. Write them on a piece of paper and pin them where you can see them easily or fit into your wallet. For more information on affirmations, refer to the Toolbox at the back of the book.

! **Practise good communication:** talk it out. Talk your stress out with friends, as you may get a different perspective. Have fun; don't get too serious. It's just the journey you are on, so get excited! You can do this. And now you have the tools.

! **Create a 'stress less' plan:** once you are aware of what creates your stress, find out what the most effective de-stress activities or strategies that work for you are, schedule them into your daily routine, weekly, monthly or yearly plan of action. It could be as simple as making a time to journal it out each night before you go to sleep or do the breathing exercise in the car/train on the way to and from work. Book a regular massage.

! **Create your 'stress less' plan.** Write a list of things you could do on the spur of the moment when you feel stress creeping into your day; these include activities that last five, 10 or 20 minutes. Each week. Each month. Each year.

Everyone is different; what works for you may not work for someone else. Think about what you do before the day starts to what you can do to de-stress at the end of the day/week, from breathing and meditation to taking time out to do something you love and *enjoy*.

PART FIVE

IDEAS THAT YOU CAN ADD TO YOUR 'STRESS LESS' PLAN

Exercise	Play with a pet	Play a game with your kids
Go for a walk	Read a book	Go to a show or a movie
Draw	Write in a journal	Think of something funny
Meditate	Use aromatherapy	Watch a YouTube comedy
Pray	Engage in a hobby	Picture your happy place
Colour	Get creative art/craft	Give yourself a pep talk
Garden	Use a relaxation app	Declutter your room/draw
Smile	Go out for a meal	Listen to music
Drink tea	Plan your next holiday	Bush walk
Take a bath	Do what makes you feel good	Put on lotion that smells good
Ask for help	List the things you are grateful for	Reframe the way you are thinking
Cook a meal	Spend time in nature	Join a choir
Sing in the shower	Play a board game with some friends	Use the "Stop, Think and Flick the Switch" strategy

PLEASE NOTE! Avoid avoidance strategies!

Avoidance strategies are not always a positive way to deal with our stress. For example, never resolving your issues can lead to a major roadblock, more stress, anxiety and depression, and so the cycle repeats itself.

Avoidance strategies include
- Overusing alcohol and drugs: substances may numb your pain but they won't solve your issues.
- Overeating: you can develop an unhealthy relationship with food and weight issues.
- Sleeping too much: it's a temporary escape; the issues will still be there when you wake up.

YOUR GUIDE TO ACTION AND EMPOWERMENT

- Continually venting to others: can keep you stuck repeating the problem over and over again. Venting to get support and a different perspective is positive.
- Overspending: retail therapy and spending more than you can afford will backfire and create more stress.

WHAT DID YOU LEARN?

TAKE ACTION!
- Create your stress less plan.
- What do you feel you can do better to help manage your stress levels?
- What action are you going to do today to release some stress from your body?
- What action are you going to do today to move toward building your resilience against stress?

> I AM BLESSED TO LIVE THE LIFE I HAVE CREATED.
> I AM RELAXED, CALM AND ENJOY
> EVERY MOMENT OF MY DAY.

DEPRESSED

Depression is a mood disorder, which causes a persistent deep feeling of sadness. It affects how you feel, think and behave. It can also lead to a variety of emotional and physical problems.

"Depression is feeling like you've lost something but having no clue when or where you last had it. Then one day you realise what you lost is yourself."
Anonymous

The challenge here is to recognise the symptoms of depression, discover your triggers and move away from feeling depressed before it takes over. This whole book is about preventing roadblocks, building resilience and developing a positive growth mindset around how you can live your best life.

Recognising your true authentic self and living a life aligned to your values and beliefs can be a challenge especially when depression rears its ugly head. Research suggests that ongoing difficulties such as long-term unemployment, living in an abusive or uncaring relationship, long-term isolation or loneliness and prolonged stress are more likely to cause depression than recent life stresses. However, recent events (such as losing your job) or a combination of events can trigger depression if you're already at risk because of previous bad experiences or personal factors.

THERE ARE FIVE MAIN CAUSES OF DEPRESSION

1. Family history: if other members of your family have experienced depression you may be more susceptible to developing the disease.

2. Chronic illness and other health issues: physical injuries can also impact mental health (the loss of a limb, head injury, MS, etc).

3. Medication, drugs and alcohol abuse: predominantly side effects of long-term use.

4. Personality: for example, are you a constant worrier or live with chronic stress?

5. Life events: can trigger the symptoms of depression.
    - The loss of a job.
    - Stress at work/ home.
    - Dysfunctional relationships, loss of self-identity.
    - Isolation.
    - Breakups/divorce.
    - Being diagnosed with long-term illness.
    - Unemployed for a long period of time.
    - Grieving for the loss of a loved one.
    - Natural disasters: fire, floods, war.

YOUR GUIDE TO ACTION AND EMPOWERMENT

- Negative environment: work, family, educational, cultural.
- Unreal expectations: motherhood/fatherhood (internal, external expectations), job/work.

Remember everyone is different, depression generally rears its ugly head when we are at a low ebb and unable to cope with what life has thrown at us, generally when one's personal needs are not being met, when the life you are living is not congruent with your unique values and beliefs.

It's often a combination of contributing factors that can lead us down the road to depression, (it can be a combination of mental and chemical imbalance). The key here is to recognise and become aware of what is going on so you can deal with the situation in a positive way.

> *"You say you're depressed – all I see is resilience. You are allowed to feel messed up and inside out. It doesn't mean you're defective – it just means you're human."*
> **David Mitchell, Cloud Atlas**

RECOGNISING THE SYMPTOMS OF DEPRESSION

Are you feeling sad, losing interest in everything around you, having difficulty in dealing with day-to-day activities? You may be experiencing the symptoms of depression. It is so important for you to recognise the symptoms or listen to significant others when they notice a change in your behaviour because, left unattended, it can create bigger problems and your roadblocks can become more frequent, the doom and gloom button will be switched on and the need for medication to control your depression may be inevitable.

On the left side of the table to follow, I have broken up the symptoms into four areas: thoughts, feelings, behaviours, and physical ailments. On the right side of the table, I have noted the want/need (the flip side, what needs to happen) that aligns with the symptom.

PART FIVE

Tick the YES column if you are aware of the symptom in your life.

THOUGHTS/ COGNITION	Yes	WANT/NEEDS	Yes
'I'm a failure'		'I am successful'	
'It's my fault'		'I am responsible for the choices I make'	
'Nothing good ever happens to me'		'I am focused in what I want in my life'	
'I'm worthless'		'I am valuable'	
'Life's not worth living'		'I am loved and appreciated'	
'People would be better off without me'		'I love my life, my life is a journey and has meaning'	
'I can't cope'		'I am capable'	
Lack of concentration		'I am focused'	
Difficulty making decisions		'I am decisive'	
Thoughts of suicide and self-harm		'I love my life'	

FEELINGS / EMOTIONS	Yes	WANTS/NEEDS	Yes
Unhappy		Happy	
Miserable		Comfortable happy	
Frustrated		Satisfied	
Irritable		Good humoured, easy going	
Numb		Sensitive, responsive	
Sad		Happy	
Indecisive		Decision maker	
Lacking in confidence		Confident	
Guilty		Innocent	

YOUR GUIDE TO ACTION AND EMPOWERMENT

BEHAVIOUR	Yes	WANTS/NEEDS	Yes
Not going out anymore		To go out and enjoy life	
Not getting things done at work/school		Enjoying completing work/school projects achievement	
Withdrawing from close family and friends		Being a productive family member	
Not doing usually enjoyable activities		Making time to do the things you love	
Lacking motivation		Motivated	
Crying a lot		Laughing	
Feeling fragile		Strong	
Relying on alcohol and sedatives		Live a healthy balance lifestyle	

PHYSICAL	Yes	WANTS/NEEDS	Yes
Tired all the time		Energetic	
Headaches and muscle pains		Healthy	
Churning gut		Worry-free	
Sleep problems		Enough	
Loss or change of appetite		Hungry, healthy diet	
Significant weight loss or gain		Healthy, consistent body weight	
Sick and run down		Healthy	

Make a list of your YES answers.

What did you learn?
Please note if you experience 2-5 symptoms above on a daily basis for two weeks or more, it is imperative you seek help from a medical professional NOW, today.

It's important to remember that we all experience some of these symptoms from time to time; the key here is to deal with each one before they accumulate and turn into the doom and gloom of depression. It's

PART FIVE

when the symptoms start to interfere with your personal and work life on a daily basis and last longer than two weeks or more that we need to take note and talk to someone or even consult a health professional.

This is my story: rather than dealing with issues, I used to put up with them until it all got too much. In living an isolated childhood, I never developed resilience to life's ups and downs. My self-worth was non-existent. My mother was insecure, and nothing was ever good enough. There was a lot of negative self-talk and as an adult, I turned into a people-pleaser, listened to what other people said and believed them.

I lost my identity through motherhood and when I returned to the workforce, I didn't know how to be assertive and stand up for myself, let alone communicate what I needed in a work situation or live to my full potential. I was miserable, and I just wanted to be happy. Through the depression, I had lost my identity. I just needed to find myself again.

I made the decision to do something about it. There had to be more to life than what I was feeling and living. Generally, a doctor diagnoses depression and that's a good thing because then you can work out how to cope with it as part of your life. But the doctor never told me how to cope; instead, I just got prescribed antidepressants.

I needed to be on them at the time, and I am very proud to say I eventually weaned myself off them and started to live my best life. I rediscovered my strengths, and that enabled me to deal with life's challenges in a much more positive way. I guess that's why I am writing this book; because I believe you can. You can change your life and make it the best it can be. Once you take that first step, you can't go back, and I find this really exciting.

I just wanted to be happy. I made the decision to find out what makes me happy, and then I took action. It takes courage to do the things you need to do, to stand up for who you are and be the person you want to be, it's never too late. My biggest motivator was that I didn't want to stay where I was in the depression spiral. Through personal development and education, I found my way.

Depression and anxiety are common conditions, and the good news is that there is major support out there with treatment options that work. It's important to seek help early; the sooner you become aware and talk to someone, the sooner you'll be on the road to recovery.

AWARENESS: Identify your depression as a roadblock

Depression can be one of the Major roadblocks on your journey through life. Recognising the symptoms and triggers early and working through them one by one, getting to the root cause of why you feel the way you do, can clear the fog and will make your journey through depression much easier. When you get a diagnosis of depression you know that your symptoms have gone on for too long unattended.

Generally speaking, when you are feeling like you are in a depressed state, at some level you are what I would call emotionally stuck, and it's hard to think clearly. The question you have may be, 'Where do I start?' Depression can be a complex state to be in and at times I found it difficult to answer the questions, but more importantly I didn't give up and asked for help when I needed it.

The most important thing to point out is that you need to be aware of what you specifically want? I was lucky I knew I wanted to be happy, so why wasn't I happy? That was my starting point and I was able to make the decision to do something about my depression and I started the process.

Answer the following questions and follow the process, there is a light at the end of the tunnel, so let your light shine.

ENGAGE YOUR SELF-AWARENESS

Breathe
1. Find a quiet place, breathe in for six, hold for three, and breathe out for nine. Repeat until you feel a sense of calm come over you.

2. Allow the answers to the following questions to bubble up and make a list.

PART FIVE

- If you were to know, what do you specifically want?
  I want to be............
  Why do you want to be..........?
  I want to be..........because............
  Why are you not..........now?
- Is it a work situation?
- Is it a relationship situation?
- Is it a traumatic event?
- Is it a negative experience?
- Do you live/work in an environment that does not support you?
  For each symptom from your list, answer the following questions. Breathe and allow your thoughts to bubble up.
    - What specifically is the challenge around............?
    - Why is it a challenge?
    - If you were to know, what triggered the symptom?

Response: How did you react?
- What specifically was your reaction?
- Was it a thought, a feeling, an emotion or a behaviour?

Outcome: What is the result of having this symptom?
- Is it internal or external? A limiting decision, a negative emotion, a habit, an avoidance strategy, etc.
- Was it a physical reaction ie, a headache, an ache, pain or did you just remove yourself from the situation?
- Has this symptom become a roadblock?
- If you were to know, what is stopping you from doing what you want?

TAKE OWNERSHIP
- What resistance/excuse is coming up for you around each symptom on your list right now?
- Are you blaming others?
- Are you taking responsibility for your choices, your thoughts and your reactions that have created this symptom?

YOUR GUIDE TO ACTION AND EMPOWERMENT

- If not, why not?
- What is it you have to do to take ownership?

WHAT HAVE YOU LEARNT?
- What have you learnt from this exercise so far?
- How do you feel about your symptoms now?

MOVE AWAY FROM RESISTANCE
- Is everything you do getting you closer to your desired outcome, a life you will love living?
- How would your life be if you **DIDN'T** get your depression under control?
- What would happen if you **DID** get your depression under control?
- Is there something you need to change so that you can deal with your depression in a positive way?
- What is it you need to change?
- What else do you need to learn?

JOURNAL IT OUT

You may feel you need to dive in a little deeper to get to the root cause, at the beginning of this Handbook I have listed the most common roadblocks covered in this book. You can go to the relevant section any time and complete the process. Remember one step at a time. If you feel you are getting a little overwhelmed, focus on mastering the four keys first. Refer to the journal contents at the beginning of this chapter. Have fun!

Do you feel you can dive in a little deeper to discover the root cause? If NOT ask for help!

TIPS TO SUPPORT YOU THROUGH DEPRESSION AND BEYOND

! **Breathe:** if you are feeling triggered, just breathe. Find a quiet space; breathe in for six, hold for three, out for nine. Repeat at least five times until you feel a wave of calm come over you. Then you can think clearly.

PART FIVE

- **Develop an attitude of gratitude** (refer to the Toolbox at the back of the book). Most important of all, it is one of the first things you should do, as it positively changes your energy and you start to think in a positive way.

- **Surround yourself with positive, like-minded people** who respect, support, know and love you.

- **Develop a positive/growth mindset** (refer to the Journey Handbook). Be empowered to live your best life.

- **Create positive affirmations** to remind you of how strong you really are (refer to the Toolbox at the back of the book).

- **Do what you love and what makes you happy.** Create a list of at least 20 things you love to do and keep it for a time you may need to refer to it.

- **Align your life with your values.** Do the values elicitation exercise (refer to the Bonus Content).

- **Eliminate** the things in your life that do NOT serve you.

- **Create a strong foundation:** live a healthy, balanced lifestyle. Fuel your body, exercise, and challenge your mind, body and thoughts.

- **Create a positive daily routine** if you don't already have one; make sure it is aligned with who you are. Plan one out and start following it one step at a time. Do not make too many changes all at once, as it can be overwhelming and you could be setting yourself up for failure. (Refer to the Habit Tracker, number eight in the Toolbox.)

YOUR GUIDE TO ACTION AND EMPOWERMENT

- **Use the tools** that have been laid out for you in this book to support you on your journey.

- **Eliminate your negative emotions and limiting decisions** (Refer to Limiting beliefs/decisions in part five.)

- **Journal it out.** If something is bothering you, get it out of your head. If you have a mental block and don't know where to start, do the breathing exercise: find a quiet space; breathe in for six, hold for three, and breathe out for nine. Repeat at least five times until you feel a wave of calm come over you. Then, put pen to paper and let the words flow out onto the paper. If this does not work, use the journal prompts in the Toolbox.

- **Take time out:** go away and treat yourself, connect to your power day (the date of your birthday in each month).

- **Ask for help if you need it.** Consult a mentor, a coach or a health practitioner, as they have more resources that can help you along the way.

What did you learn?

TAKE ACTION!

- What can you do today to commence your journey away from depression?

> ALL IS WELL IN MY WORLD. I AM CALM,
> HAPPY AND CONTENT. I LOVE AND APPROVE
> OF MYSELF.

PART FIVE

 ANXIOUS

Anxiety is a feeling of worry, nervousness or unease about something with an uncertain outcome. It is an emotion characterised by feelings of tension, worried thoughts, and physical changes like increased blood pressure etc, that is triggered either consciously or unconsciously.

The challenge here is to understand where your anxiety comes from and what triggers it, so you can take control of your feelings, feel relaxed and start to enjoy your life. Have you ever felt like something bad is about to happen, even though everything seems fine and you have no actual reason to worry, or felt pressure on your chest that makes it hard to breathe and you can't get rid of it? You may be suffering from symptoms of anxiety.

According to epidemiological surveys, one-third of the population can be affected by anxiety during their lifetime. Of course, feeling some anxiety surrounding certain stressful life events is absolutely normal. The important thing here is that when you become more aware of yourself, your body and your reactions, you know that the feelings have been triggered by something and you are able to work through the anxious feeling, discover the root cause and let the anxious feelings go.

It's when the symptoms of anxiety are experienced more frequently or are persistent and not always connected to an obvious challenge, that your anxiety can become a cause for concern. An anxiety condition can affect people's quality of life on a daily basis and anxiety can show up as a major roadblock.

THERE ARE THREE DIFFERENT TYPES OF ANXIETY: find out which one relates to you. These descriptions are not designed to provide a diagnosis (for that, you'll need to see a doctor), but they can be used as a guide:

1. **Physical**: panic attacks; hot and cold flushes; racing heart; tightening of the chest; quick breathing, trembling; restlessness;

feeling tense, wound up and edgy; sweating, insomnia, upset tummy, or crying uncontrollably.

2. **Psychological**: excessive fear and worry; catastrophising; obsessive thinking; feeling nervous, trouble concentrating and focusing, getting irritated easily and feeling tense.

3. **Behavioural**: avoidance of situations that make you feel anxious which can impact your study, work or social life. For example: stressful situations, activities you once enjoyed, crowded places, friends and family.

> *"You don't have to control your thoughts. You just have to stop letting them control you."*
> *Dan Millman*

Normal anxiety tends to be limited in time and connected with a stressful situation or event.

A sign of an anxiety condition is when anxious feelings don't go away or happen without any prior warning for no particular reason on a regular basis.

For example, I was doing some banking for my father the other day and out of nowhere I felt a tightening in the chest; I felt tense, wound up and edgy. The feeling completely took me by surprise. I asked myself the right questions and discovered what had triggered those physical reactions. It felt good because I worked through it using the tools I have collected from my prior learnings and I gained control. How good is that!

 AWARENESS: Identify anxiety symptoms as a roadblock
Do you have any of the symptoms of anxiety explained on the previous page?
- How does anxiety show up in your body?
- Do you have feelings of tension in your body (your neck, your shoulders, your back, etc)? If so, where?

PART FIVE

- Do you find you have worried thoughts that just won't go away? If so, what are they?
- Do you feel your heart racing or your blood pressure rising when confronted with a specific situation? If so, what is the situation?
- Do you ever feel irritable on a regular basis? If so, do you know why?
- Do you ever feel restless on a regular basis? If so, do you know why?
- Make a list of your symptoms.

Event: What's happening/not happening?

If you were to know, what situations in your everyday life trigger your symptoms of anxiety?

- Is the situation work related?
- Is the situation relationship related?
- Is the situation related to family?
- Is the situation related to another environment you spend time in?

Outcome: What is the result of the way you reacted to the event?

- What DON'T you do when you have any of these symptoms? Make a list.
- What specifically is the challenge around how your body reacts creating each specific symptom on your list?
- Why is it /are they a challenge?
- Was it a thought, an emotion or a behaviour or a physical reaction?
- Is it internal or external? A limiting decision, a negative emotion, a habit, an avoidance strategy, etc.
- Has the outcome of your reaction become a roadblock?

> *"Life is ten percent what you experience and ninety percent how you respond to it."*
> **Dorothy M Niedermeyer**

YOUR GUIDE TO ACTION AND EMPOWERMENT

TAKE OWNERSHIP
- Are you blaming others?
- Are you taking responsibility for your choices, your thoughts and your reactions?
- If not, why not?
- What is it you have to do to take ownership?

What did you learn from the answers to the questions above?

JOURNAL IT OUT: Let's dive in a little deeper
- What are you feeling about your anxious feelings now?
- Do you feel you need help to move away from anxiety? If you do, ask for help NOW.

If you are feeling okay, continue on answering the following questions. Deal with one situation at a time.
- Choose a specific situation that you are anxious about right now.

Breathe
1. Close your eyes. Breathe in for six, hold for three, and breathe out for nine, repeat until you feel a sense of calm come over you.
2. Allow the answers to your questions to bubble up.

Ask the right questions
- Then ask: Is my symptom/roadblock/setback at this point a feeling, an emotion, a thought or a behaviour?
- If you were to know, what specifically triggered your reaction?
- Why are you allowing what triggered you to bother you?
- What was the first thing you did? Was it a thought, an emotion, a behaviour or a physical reaction?
- Write down the answer: *I am allowing (the trigger)..........to bother me because..........*
- Ask the question again and again relating to the previous answer. Keep asking the question until you find it hard to answer.

PART FIVE

DISCOVER THE ROOT CAUSE: Find the solution

When you get deep enough you will notice if your answer is a limiting decision, a negative emotion, overwhelm or whatever, then proceed to the appropriate section listed in the contents page of this Handbook and continue the process.

MOVE AWAY FROM RESISTANCE

Three-point reality check. To dive in a little deeper there are three points of observation:

1. **You as in experiencing the situation**
2. **You as an observer of what's happening**
3. **You as the adviser of a solution**

1. **You as in the situation**
   - Close your eyes and visualise yourself in the situation looking through your own eyes and experiencing your feelings and your behaviour.
   The situation that is triggering my anxiety is..........
   - Describe exactly what is happening.
   - Is it just you or are there others involved?
   - What are you feeling?
   - Complete the following statements:
   I am feeling..........because..........
   I am allowing myself to feel..........because..........
   The reality of the situation is..........

What did you learn?

2. **You as an observer of what's happening**
   - Close your eyes and use your active imagination to stand outside the situation and observe what's happening with you in the situation.
   - What is the reality of the situation?

- What is happening as an observer?
  What can you see?
  What can you hear?
- What can you see is triggering your reactions of anxiety in the situation?
- Write a list.

NOTE! Are they the same things you reacted to when you were in the situation?

What did you learn?

3. **You as the adviser of a solution**
   - Close your eyes and use your active imagination to stand outside the situation and observe what's happening, this time you are going to advise the 'you' in the situation, what to do for each trigger/reaction on the list you created from step two.
   - For each trigger/reaction what advice would you give to the answers of the following questions?
     1. What was your reaction to the situation?
     2. What specifically triggered your reaction in the situation?
     3. Is your reaction in the situation in reality a symptom of anxiety?
     4. Is your reaction in the situation, at this point a thought, a feeling, an emotion, or a behaviour? (Negative emotion, limiting belief, an excuse or avoidance behaviour or a bad habit, etc).
     5. How would your life be if you DIDN'T get anxious/react to this trigger in this situation?
     6. What would happen if you hung onto your anxious symptoms and allowed yourself to be triggered in this situation?
     7. Do you still need to feel anxious about this situation now?
     8. What positive advice would you give 'you' in this situation?
     9. If you were to know, what do you need to change?
     10. If you were to know, what do you need to do next?

PART FIVE

What did you learn?

REFRAME: FLIP FROM NEGATIVE TO POSITIVE

Be aware of your self-talk around your anxiety.

Negative self-talk	Positive thinking
I don't want to..........	If I did..........what is the worst thing that would happen?
I can't do it	I can do it. How can I do it differently?
I am worried about..........	Can I change the outcome? If not, then I don't need to worry about it. If I can change the outcome, what actions do I need to take to release the anxiety?

Do the above exercise with your negative self-talk around the situation.

TIPS TO TAKE CONTROL AND SUPPORT YOU THROUGH YOUR JOURNEY AWAY FROM ANXIETY

! **Breathe:** when you are feeling anxious, breathe in for six, hold for three and breathe out for nine. Repeat at least five times or until you feel calm and relaxed.

! **Ask questions:** when you start to feel your anxiety rear its ugly head, straight away answer the following four important questions:
1. What situation is triggering my anxiety?
2. Why am I feeling worried?
3. Why am I feeling nervous and uneasy?
4. What is the reality of the situation?

- **Take action:** journal it out and focus on the positive. Create a habit of journalling out your feelings on a regular basis. Journal at least once a day if you can, preferably in the evening before you go to sleep so you can reflect on the day. Proactively manage your anxiety. It's hard to stop worrying entirely, so set aside some time to indulge your worries. Get your thoughts out of your head.

    > *"Nothing diminishes anxiety faster than action."*
    > **Walter Anderson**

- **Create an attitude of gratitude.** (Refer to number two in the Toolbox at the back of the book.)

- **Challenge your negative self-talk:** how you think affects how you feel and behave. Anxiety can make you overestimate the danger in a situation and underestimate your ability to handle it. Look at the facts for and against your thoughts.

- **Be kind to yourself:** remember that you are not your anxiety. You are not weak. You are not inferior. Talking with others who also experience anxiety or are going through something similar can help you feel less alone.

- **Practise relaxing activities:** meditation and mindfulness. Listen to soothing music. Anxiety can make your thoughts live in a terrible future that hasn't happened and probably won't. The past is gone, the future has not happened yet. Bring yourself back to where you are right now and stay in the present moment.

- **Spend time with your pet:** it's something that can make you happy and you don't have to worry. Just indulge in the unconditional love and acceptance of who you are.

PART FIVE

- **Exercise:** keep active, eat well, go out into nature, spend time with family and friends, reduce stress, and do activities you enjoy. Physical exercise can relieve mental stress, raise your endorphins and give you space to think clearly.

- **Laugh:** find humour in everyday life, spend time with funny friends, watch a comedy show, read a book of jokes, and have a 'joke of the day'. Laughing helps you relax.

- **Learn to say no:** try not to take on more than you can manage.

- **Become aware,** prioritise what needs to be done and do it. Avoid procrastination.

- **Lower your caffeine intake:** high doses can increase anxiety.

- **Spend time with those who love and support you:** your social network gives you a sense of belonging and self-worth. Who can you spend time with who supports you and accepts you for who you are?

- **Ask for help:** if your anxious feelings or behaviours don't go away, ask for help! Your priority here is to live to your fullest potential and enjoy your life. DON'T let your anxiety get out of control.

- **Create new habits:** commit to practising daily what will help you feel less anxious. This might be affirmations, an attitude of gratitude, practising a positive mindset, taking time out, and painting, relaxing, doing yoga or going for a walk.

Be aware of other things you may need to change at a deeper level.
- Is it your language, negative self-talk, a limiting belief, a negative emotion or a combination of two or more of the above?

YOUR GUIDE TO ACTION AND EMPOWERMENT

- Make a list and deal with each one, one at a time.
- What did you learn about yourself from this exercise?
- What action do you need to take today to start your journey away from anxiety?

> I AM SAFE AND IN CONTROL. I BREATHE IN RELAXATION, AND I BREATHE OUT TENSION.
> I AM HAPPY AND RELAXED.

Behaviour

PROCRASTINATION

Procrastination is the action of delaying or postponing something; it can eat away at your momentum and stop you from making real progress. Some people spend so much time procrastinating that they are unable to complete important daily tasks.

Your challenge is to understand why you procrastinate, believe in yourself and your capabilities and make sure your motivation/why is strong enough to override any reason/excuses you may have to avoid taking action, so that you can keep moving forward easily and effortlessly.

SIGNS AND SYMPTOMS OF PROCRASTINATION

- Last minute deadline.
- Continually putting tasks off for another day.
- Getting stuck in neutral, unable to move forward or complete anything.
- Needlessly delaying or not finishing tasks.

"Your Life Is Happening Right Now: Don't let procrastination take over your life. Be brave and take risks. Your life is happening right now."

Roy T Bennett

PART FIVE

- Postponing doing things you don't like to do.
- Always making excuses for not doing things.
- Putting off making decisions.
- Constantly putting off improving your work habits.
- Perfectionism.

Can you relate to any of the above symptoms? If so, make a list.

THE MAIN CAUSES OF PROCRASTINATION

- **Excessive perfectionism.** One of the common reasons for people to procrastinate is the feeling of extreme perfectionism. When you are a self-confessed perfectionist, you will not want to start the work unless you are totally sure about it and you will not complete the task unless it is picture perfect. Perfectionism tricks the mind that you are not ready for the work, you will indefinitely put off the task until you think you can do it correctly. Which could be never.

- **Abstract goals.** Unreasonable undefined goals, vague goals that are not specific enough and not aligned with who you are. Your why/motivation is not strong enough.

- **Indecisiveness.** When people are unable to make decisions in a timely and organised manner. With so many decisions to make one might struggle to decide the right course of action.

- **Fear of failure.** When you are afraid of failing at the tasks at hand you avoid or delay the task, feel you are not good enough and maybe expect perfection.

- **Task aversion.** Often one may delay the task because they really don't want to do it, it could be tedious or boring. Delaying the work to the last minute when you are unable to do your best work. Interesting, yes?

- **Lack of perseverance.** One can lack the will to persevere, overcome obstacles and finish the task and in doing so lose focus and motivation, keeping it aside and procrastinating on it indefinitely.

Do any of the above points resonate with you? If so, make a list.

AWARENESS: Procrastination as a roadblock

The effects of procrastination can lead to low self-esteem, stress and anxiety. You may lack focus, have low energy levels and waste time. You may become a dreamer, a perfectionist, an overdoer. It's important to think about what you want to achieve and why you want to achieve it. Is it for someone else, or is it for you? Is your why big enough?

As long as laziness and task aversion outweigh your motivation and productivity you will always procrastinate your tasks. Here you have a choice to make: to live with your procrastination or move through it and live to your fullest potential.

> *"I never put off till tomorrow what I can possibly do the day after."*
> **Oscar Wilde**

Identify your procrastination

Procrastinators are good at making excuses and finding a reason not to do a said task.

If I asked you why you procrastinate, what reason/excuse would you justify your procrastination with?

- **Not knowing what needs to be done.** Why don't you know what to do? How can you find out what needs to be done? Is what needs to be done important? If so, why?
- **Not knowing how to do something.** Why don't you know how to do it? Is there a way you could find out how to do it? If so, what do you need to do?

PART FIVE

- **Not wanting to do something.** Why don't you want to do it?
- **Not caring if it gets done or not.** Why don't you care when it gets done?
- **Not feeling in the mood to do it.** Why are you not feeling in the mood? Is the task important to you? If not, why not?
- **Believing that you work better under pressure.** Why do you think you can work better under pressure?
- **Thinking that finishing it at the last minute is okay.** Why do you think it is okay to finish it at the last minute?
- **Lacking the initiative to get started.** Why are you lacking initiative to start? What needs to change so you can become motivated?
- **Forgetting.** What specifically are you forgetting? Why are you forgetting these things? What would you gain if you remembered those things?
- **Blaming lack of action on sickness or poor health.**
- **Waiting for the right moment.** When will the right moment be?
- **Needing time to think about the task.** Why do you need more time to think about the task? What is more time going to change?
- **Delaying one task in favour of working on another.** Why have you delayed one task over another? Is the other task more important? If so, why?
- **Avoiding people with whom you are upset.** Why are you specifically avoiding the person who has upset you? What specifically did they do to upset you?
- **Not talking to people when you are angry at them.** Why is it difficult for you to talk to people when you are angry at them? What specifically did they do to make you angry?
- **Putting off doing things as a way to punish others.** What is the point of putting things off to punish others? What will you gain by putting those specific things off?
- **Using sarcasm to avoid engaging in meaningful conversations.**

Make a list of the reasons that resonate with you, and answer the questions that follow each one you chose.

WHAT HAVE YOU LEARNT?

In reference to your procrastination, if I were to ask you what excuses do you make on a regular basis, which ones do you choose?
- *I just don't know where to begin.* Why don't you know where to begin? Can you find out where to begin? If not, why not?
- *I don't have time.* Why don't you have time? Is it important to make time to do the task? If not, why not?
- *It's just too difficult.* Is it too difficult? What is it that makes it too difficult? Can you do things differently?
- *It just isn't the right time.* Why is it not the right time? When would it be the right time?
- *I don't have enough time to discover what I like.* Why not?
- *I've already dedicated myself to a different path.* Why did you give up on this one?
- *I'm not motivated enough.* Why not? Is the task important enough? What would make you motivated? Why have you lost interest?
- *I'm too easily distracted by other things.* Why do you allow other things to easily distract you?
- *I will start tomorrow.* Why not start today? What is stopping you from starting today?

Make a list of excuses you make on a regular basis. Now answer the questions that follow each excuse you chose as above. Are there any other excuses you make on a regular basis? Add them to your list and ask yourself why you are making this excuse.

WHAT DID YOU LEARN?
- What are you feeling about procrastination now?
- Let's dive in a little deeper.

PART FIVE

IF YOU NEED TO; let's dive in a little deeper and find out what's happening and what's not happening.
- Close your eyes. Breathe in for six, hold for three, and breathe out for nine, repeat until you feel a sense of calm come over you.
- Allow the answers to your questions to bubble up.
- In which area of your Life Circle do you procrastinate the most?
- When do you procrastinate?
- What do you specifically procrastinate about?
- Do you know why you procrastinate? If so, why?
- Do you know what triggers your procrastination? If so, what is it?

Response: How did you react?
- What specifically is your reaction?
- Is it a thought, an emotion or a behaviour?

Outcome: What is the result of the way you reacted to the procrastination?
- Is it internal or external? A limiting decision, a negative emotion, a habit, an avoidance strategy, etc.
- Was it a physical reaction ie, a headache, an ache, pain or did you just remove yourself from the situation?
- Are there any other symptoms at a deeper level that may have come up for you during this process? If so, what are they?

You could be procrastinating because you have a limiting belief, or you may feel guilty. You could be stressed, overwhelmed or afraid. If so, go to the relevant section and get to the root cause?
- Has the outcome of your procrastination/excuse become a roadblock?
- If you were to know, what is it stopping you from doing……….?

TAKE OWNERSHIP
- Are you blaming others?

- Are you taking responsibility for your choices, your thoughts and your reactions? If not, why not?
- Are you living at cause? If not, why not?
- Do you have clarity around what you want out of life?
- Are you living your life to your fullest potential?

MOVE AWAY FROM RESISTANCE

- Is everything you do getting you closer to your desired outcome, a life you will love living?
- How would your life be if you DIDN'T let go of procrastination?
- What would happen if you DID let go of your procrastination, find clarity around what you want and love the life you live?

WHAT HAVE YOU LEARNT ABOUT YOUR PROCRASTINATION SO FAR?

Fill in the spaces in the following statement

The main causes of my procrastination are..........

The reasons why I procrastinate..........

The excuses I make around my procrastination on a regular basis are..........

I need to work on..........to get to the root cause of my procrastination.

TIPS TO ELIMINATE PROCRASTINATION

! **Create a to-do list** with specific deadlines: when you have a to-do list, you become accountable.

! **Break it down:** breaking down tough jobs into easy chunks is the quickest way to make sure that they actually get done.

! **Do one thing at a time:** sticking to one job at a time until it is finished is rewarding, and you can see what you have achieved at any one point in time.

PART FIVE

! **Set aside the right time:** and space for work when you are able to focus without distraction. Depending on the task at hand, identify the energy you need for that task, make a plan. If a task is difficult or challenging, do it when you have more energy. When you have less energy, do the easier tasks. You may work better in the morning or in the afternoon – it's all about finding out what works best for you.

! **Try the two-minute rule:** if it's a task that you just want to run away from, the idea of facing it head-on for only two minutes can relieve a ton of pressure.

! **Reward yourself with breaks:** especially when you feel your energy is fading. Take a break, get some fresh air, and revive and restore your energy.

! **Let go of perfectionism:** perfectionism is what keeps us from moving forward. Focus on getting the job done and then review it. We have a hard time letting things go when they aren't exactly as we pictured them.

! **Make yourself accountable:** we tend to feel more motivated when we're held accountable to something outside ourselves. Identify what needs to be done for the week, month, and year. Ticking off the tasks as you move through your to-do list can be rewarding.

! **Remove distractions:** identify the possible distractions depending on the task at hand.

! **Become aware:** of the little voice in your head and the language you speak, flip from excuse to action.

YOUR GUIDE TO ACTION AND EMPOWERMENT

FLIP FROM EXCUSE TO ACTION

Negative excuse	Positive action
It's just too difficult	How can I find an easier way to do it? Who can help me?
I don't have enough time	What can I do to make time?

- **Get to know your triggers** and move away from procrastination.

- **Think about the big picture.** What do you specifically want? Focus on the end result, what you want and can achieve. Make sure your why is strong enough to keep you motivated and inspired.

- **Don't beat yourself up.** Be nice to yourself and celebrate your achievements.

- **Create a get out of procrastination strategy/plan** for when you feel your procrastination creeping in.

- **Use the Stop, Think and Flick the Switch strategy** (explained in the Toolbox).

- **Get it sorted** before the doom and gloom button is switched on and ask for help if you need it.

It all comes back to the fact that you have a choice. Once you become aware of and really connected with who you are, life begins to flow and you become more confident and ready to take on the world.

To live with procrastination can be a challenge. So, make a decision now and release it, let it go and make a plan using the tools and tips you have learnt from this exercise.

PART FIVE

MY GET-OUT-OF-PROCRASTINATION STRATEGY IS:
a)
b)
c)
d)
e)
f)

WHAT DID YOU LEARN?
- What do you need to change or do differently to move from procrastination to anticipation and action?
- What can you do today to start your journey away from procrastination?

> I MAKE THE MOST OUT OF EVERY DAY – I TAKE ACTION AND GET THINGS DONE.

PERFECTIONISM

Perfectionism is a personal standard, attitude, or philosophy that demands perfection and rejects anything less from self and others. It is just an excuse for self-criticism and is often defined as the need to be or appear to be perfect.

"Let go of who you think you're supposed to be and embrace who you are."
Brené Brown

The challenge here is to understand why we feel the need to be perfect and why it is so important to us. Left unattended, it can become a difficult way to live. Trying to improve something until it has no mistakes or flaws can become a roadblock. In reality, perfectionism can become associated with depression and anxiety. It can lead to a

YOUR GUIDE TO ACTION AND EMPOWERMENT

lack of self-worth, and you may have a negative belief that you are not good enough.

SYMPTOMS OF PERFECTIONISM
You may be experiencing perfectionism in one of the following ways:
- You expect perfection from everyone.
- You struggle to complete tasks in a timely manner.
- You view mistakes as proof you are inadequate.
- You invest a lot of energy in masking your flaws.
- You avoid doing things that may cause you to fail.
- You find it hard to celebrate success.
- Your self-worth depends on your achievements.
- You are never satisfied with life.
- You feel like you fail at everything you try.
- You procrastinate regularly, you might resist starting a task because you're afraid that you'll be unable to complete it perfectly.
- You struggle to relax and share your thoughts and feelings and lack self-confidence.
- You become very controlling in your personal and professional relationships.
- You become obsessed with rules, lists and work, or conversely become extremely apathetic.

Can you identify with any of the above symptoms? If so, make a list.

A FEW CAUSES OF PERFECTIONISM
- Rigid, high parental expectations.
- Highly critical, shaming or abusive parents.
- Low self-esteem and feeling inadequate.
- Believing your self-worth is determined by your achievements.
- Black and white thinking. An effort to feel in control.
- Cultural expectations.
- Specifically, a fear of judgement or disapproval from others.

PART FIVE

Can you relate to any of the above causes of your perfectionism? If so, what are they? Make a list.

 AWARENESS: Recognise perfectionism as a roadblock
- Are you a perfectionist?
- Specifically in which area of your Life Circle are you a perfectionist?

Choose a symptom from your list and answer the following questions.
The symptom I am working on is..........
The symptom appears in the..........of my Life Circle.
- If you were to know, what is this symptom stopping you from doing?

Breathe
- Close your eyes. Breathe in for six, hold for three, and breathe out for nine, repeat until you feel a sense of calm come over you.
- Allow the answers to the following questions bubble up.
- What are you feeling about your symptom now?

Event: What's happening/not happening?
- What specifically is the challenge around this symptom?
- Why is it a challenge?
- What part of the challenge triggered a reaction?

Response: How did you react?
- What specifically was your reaction?
- Was it a thought, an emotion or a behaviour?

Outcome: What is the result of the way you reacted to the event?
- Is it internal or external? A limiting decision, a negative emotion, a habit, an avoidance strategy, etc.
- Was it a physical reaction ie, a headache, an ache, pain or did you just remove yourself from the situation?

YOUR GUIDE TO ACTION AND EMPOWERMENT

If your perfectionism is linked to a limiting belief, a negative emotion or behaviour/state, you may be feeling guilty, stressed, overwhelmed or afraid. If so, go to the relevant section and get to the root cause. (Refer to the contents page of this Handbook.)

"Done is better than perfect."
Sheryl Sandberg

TAKE OWNERSHIP
- Are you blaming others?
- Are you taking responsibility for your choices, your thoughts and your reactions? If not, why not?

MOVE AWAY FROM RESISTANCE
- Is everything I do getting me closer to my desired outcome, a life I will love living?
- How would my life be if I DIDN'T challenge my symptoms of perfectionism?
- What would happen if I were able to let go of this symptom of perfectionism?

WHAT DID YOU LEARN?

TIPS TO SUPPORT YOU IN MOVING AWAY FROM PERFECTIONISM

! **Set realistic, attainable goals and lower your expectations:**
- Do you have realistic goals and expectations that truly align with your values in the area of your life? (Refer back to your core values if you have not already done so.)
- Break up overwhelming tasks into small steps.
- Focus on one activity or task at a time.
- Acknowledge that everyone makes mistakes.
- Confront fears of failure by remaining realistic about possible outcomes.

PART FIVE

! **Recognise that most mistakes present learning opportunities:** realise that there is more than one perfect outcome: Yes, from time to time, things don't work out how we hoped; but we need to recognise that every mistake we make is a learning opportunity. Be graceful in letting go of the things that don't serve you. Your best is good enough.

! **Don't take life too seriously:** learn to dust yourself off, have a good laugh, learn from the experience and do it all again. Remember that time off is not time wasted.
  • Do you give yourself time off?
  • Do you have fun in your life? If not, why not?

! **Care less about what others think of you, as what they think is not your business:** what others say to you has absolutely no meaning, unless YOU attach a meaning to it. So, get clear on the requirements. With any negativity that you come across from others at home or at work that isn't constructive criticism, just drop it and move on as it does not serve you.

! **Create a positive mindset supported by positive affirmations.** (Refer to the article on Affirmations in the Toolbox at the back of the book.)

! **Release self-judgement and stop comparing yourself to others:** you never know success unless you reach your outcome. Be kind to yourself, as you can only do the best that you can at any one point in time. Remember to celebrate each step along the way.

! **Accept compliments and positive feedback from others:** acknowledge your skills, what you can do and what you love to do.

YOUR GUIDE TO ACTION AND EMPOWERMENT

! **Forgive yourself and others:** most importantly, know how to forgive yourself and look for enrichment and experience. Prioritise self-care, invest in yourself, and trust that it will all get done in time.

! **Challenge your inner critic and dispute negative thoughts**: flick the switch from negative to positive on limiting beliefs and negative emotions. Get to the root cause of your negativity and keep moving forward.

! **Reframe the language** you use around your symptom from negative to positive.

Negative self-talk	Positive thinking
It's NOT good enough	It's the best I can do at this point in time
There's no way it will work	How can I do it differently so it will work?
I can't do it	I can do it
They can do it better than me	I always do my best at any one point in time And that's okay

! **Live a life of grace and creativity:** embracing your own authenticity and letting go of the need to be accepted by others. Your best is good enough – it does not have to be perfect.

WHAT DID YOU LEARN?
- How do you feel about perfectionism now?

PART FIVE

TAKE ACTION!
- What do you need to do/change to move away from your perfectionism in the future?
- What action can you do TODAY to move towards releasing your perfectionism?

> I AM CONFIDENT, I AM CAPABLE, I AM POISED, AND I AM STRONG. I CAN ONLY DO MY BEST AT ANY ONE POINT IN TIME.

HABITS

A habit is a usual way of behaving; something that a person does often in a regular repeated way that has become automatic or habitual. Habits are triggered by cues, which are the signals that tell us to act in a certain way.

The challenge here is recognising whether or not the habit serves you. Is it a good habit or a bad one? A good habit is a behaviour that is beneficial to one's physical or mental health and often linked to a high level of discipline and self-control. A bad habit is usually a negative behavioural pattern that you deem to have a negative impact on a part of your life. Some common examples include procrastination, overspending, and nail biting.

We can separate our habits into two areas: CONSCIOUS, and ADDICTIVE behaviour. Any conscious behaviour is one that you do as part of your daily routine (cleaning your teeth, locking the door before you leave home). Addictive behaviour is a behaviour you do to an excessive degree and one you feel unable to stop or control.

When a habit has become a roadblock to achieving your goals and living your best life, you need to change something. You don't eliminate a bad habit, you replace it with a good one, for example if you smoke when you are stressed to relax, what is a good habit you could encourage that gets that same feeling of relaxation or stress release? In other words, bad habits address certain needs in your life. And for that reason, it's better to replace your bad habit with a healthier behaviour that addresses the same need, get to the root cause of why you do what you do, and strive to develop new habits that will support you on your journey.

Keep in mind that breaking a habit can be difficult, especially when it's deeply entrenched.

> *"Watch your thoughts, they become your words; watch your words, they become your actions; watch your actions, they become your habits; watch your habits, they become your character; watch your character, it becomes your destiny."*
> **Lao Tzu**

THE FOLLOWING FACTORS CAN DETERMINE HOW EASY OR HARD THE HABIT WILL BE TO QUIT

- **Time:** a habit you've had for five years is going to be more entrenched and harder to break than a habit you've had for five months.

- **Desire:** breaking a habit takes a lot of willpower and motivation. Is your why strong enough? Make sure the desire to break the habit is linked to something you really, really want to do!

- **Personality:** you may have a harder time quitting the behaviour if you have an obsessive or addictive personality type.

- **Biology:** habits that involve a chemical dependency are often harder to break. Withdrawal symptoms can be the biggest barrier to quitting an unhealthy habit (smoking, drug addiction, alcohol).

- **Emotional triggers:** eating, drinking, exercising and similar habits can be linked to avoidance or coping strategies, limiting beliefs and negative emotions (from nail-biting to negative self-talk to building resistance).

Can you relate to any of the above factors? If so, which ones?

 AWARENESS: Identify if your habit is a roadblock
Answer the following questions.
- At this point in time do you recognise you have some bad habits?
- Write a list of your habits that don't serve you at work.
- Write a list of your habits that don't serve you at home.
- Write a list of your habits that don't serve you around your personal relationships.
- Write a list of your habits that are detrimental to your health and wellbeing.
- Which of your habits from the lists you have created are triggered at work, at home, or around a personal relationship?
- Which of your habits from the lists you have created have turned into a roadblock?
- If you were to know, what are your bad habits stopping you from doing?

Event: What's happening/not happening?
Choose a habit from your list you would like to work through that you believe is a roadblock. Then answer the following questions.
- What is the specific habit you are going to work on?
- In what way is this habit a roadblock?
- How long have you had this habit for?
- Do you know when you created this habit and why?
- Is breaking this habit something you really want to do?
- Why do you want to change this habit?

JOURNAL IT OUT: Let's dive in a little deeper

Breathe
- Close your eyes. Breathe in for six, hold for three, and breathe out for nine, repeat until you feel a sense of calm come over you.
- Allow the answers to the following questions to bubble up.
    - What specifically is the challenge around this habit?
    - Why is it a challenge?
    - If you were to know, what is this habit stopping you from doing?
    - How is this habit stopping you from doing..........?
    - Is the habit linked to a thought, an emotion or a behaviour?
    - Is it internal or external? A limiting decision, a negative emotion, an avoidance strategy, etc.
    - Is it a physical reaction ie, a headache, an ache, pain or did you just remove yourself from the situation?

If your habit is linked to a limiting belief, a negative emotion or behaviour/state, you may be feeling guilty, stressed, overwhelmed or afraid. If so, go to the relevant section and get to the root cause? (Refer to the contents page of this Handbook.)

TAKE OWNERSHIP
- Are you making any excuses around why this habit exists? If so, what are they?
- Are you taking responsibility for your choices, your thoughts and your reactions around this habit? If not, why not?
- If you were to know, why are you allowing this habit to become a roadblock?

{ WHAT HAVE YOU LEARNT ABOUT THIS HABIT SO FAR?
What are you going to do next?

PART FIVE

MOVE AWAY FROM RESISTANCE
- Is maintaining this bad habit getting you closer to your desired outcome, a life you will love living?
- How would your life be if you created a new habit (to replace the bad one) that would support you and allow you to live a life you can love?
- What would happen if you did NOT change anything?
- Do you believe it would be a good idea to replace this habit?
- What would be a good habit that you could create that would support you and replace the bad one.
- Write a list of your good habits.

THE FOLLOWING TIPS MAY HELP YOU BREAK A HABIT

Never give up; remember it can take up to 90 days to set a new habit in concrete.

! **Become aware and manage the emotions** that feed into the habit: habits are often coping mechanisms for anxiety, sadness or boredom. What emotions are feeding or triggering this habit? Addressing these triggers can prevent the need for unhealthy responses. For example, if you gamble to relieve stress, then learning relaxation techniques may decrease your urge to gamble.

! **Replace the bad habit with a healthier one:** it is often easier to redirect one's energy and emotions towards creating a new good habit with the idea of replacing a bad habit.

! **Seek out emotional support:** friends and family can offer encouragement and sympathy during the process of breaking a habit. They can also keep you accountable to the changes you need and want to make.

! **Baby steps:** break it up into baby steps and then build on it. One of the biggest mistakes we make with new habits is that

YOUR GUIDE TO ACTION AND EMPOWERMENT

we go too grand, get discouraged and give up. Piggyback off of an existing habit: for example, drink a glass of water before you have your morning coffee – simple but effective.

! **Make a plan:** baby steps, one step at a time. Without a plan, we're destined to fail. So, write out what you are going to do at each step until you are mindfully entrenched in the new habit before you even get started.

! **Prepare your physical environment to support you:** create a path of least resistance. For example:
   ! Hide junk food.
   ! Place your journal and pen on your bed side table.
   ! Smaller plates support us to eat less.
   ! Set an alarm to remind you of your new habit actions.
   ! Set up automatic transfers to make saving painless.

! **Track your progress and celebrate each step along the way:** track what you're doing, whether through a habit tracker, diary or accountability partner. Access the Monthly Habit Tracker in the Toolbox at the back of the book.

> THE POWER OF CHANGE
> COMES FROM WITHIN.

PLEASE NOTE! NEVER, NEVER, EVER GIVE UP.

Be patient and consistent and commit for at least 4 months. Once you have established that new habit over 21 days/three weeks then continue to do it/track it for another 90 days; it should become a permanent lifestyle change habit.

PART FIVE

IF YOU ARE NOT SURE WHERE TO START, START HERE: Incorporate one of the well proven habits below into your daily routine now.

- **Daily exercise:** when you exercise, you move, you get more energy to take on your day, you sleep better, improve your memory and brain function and exercise benefits your general health.

- **Replace one unhealthy meal a day with a healthy one:** giving your body the right fuel will help you feel better.

- **Meditate:** meditation has the power to calm the mind and it can lower levels of stress, anxiety and depression while improving focus and memory function. Don't give up on meditation – find the way that suits you. It can just be a simple breathing exercise or a guided meditation.

- **Establish successful routines:** daily routines help keep us organised so we can focus on what we want to achieve and make it 10 times easier to achieve and stick to our new habits.

- **Follow the 80/20 rule:** the 80/20 principle is the secret to achieving more with less. When one identifies the 20% input (what you need to do) that will essentially create the 80% of (a productive) outcome. It's how you do it and what you focus on to create a successful outcome.

- **Get a good night's sleep:** sleep impacts almost all your daily choices and will give you more energy to get you through the day.

- **Read, read, read:** reading books is a great way to gain knowledge and stimulate creativity. Reading also improves focus and has a calming effect similar to meditation. Moreover, reading before bedtime can help you sleep better and take your mind of any stressors you may have had during the day.

YOUR GUIDE TO ACTION AND EMPOWERMENT

- **Learn to single-task:** make a list of things you need to accomplish in a day. Start with what's most important and make your way down the list, completing one task at a time.

- **Develop an attitude of gratitude:** (refer to the Toolbox) practising gratitude is a great way to create positivity, reduce stress and improve your physical health.

- **Develop good communication skills:** (refer to the Communication Tools in the Toolbox) pay attention to what others have to say. It'll not only make others feel valued but will also help you understand them better and gain a fresh perspective.

- **Go for a social media detox:** take time to cut back on social media to reduce stress and mental clutter. Switch off your phone and laptop for a few hours every day to improve your mood and reconnect with the world around you.

- **Invest in self-care:** taking some time off to unwind can do wonders for your mood, mental health and self-esteem. Do at least one thing every day that makes you feel good. Listen to music, learn a new skill, take a long bubble bath, or prepare a nice meal – whatever floats your boat! It's your private time, value it.

TAKE ACTION: FOUR STEPS TO CREATING A NEW HABIT

STEP 1: Setting yourself up for a new habit
What specifically do you want?
- What new habit would you like to create?
- How will this new habit benefit you?
- Is it aligned with who you are and what you want?
- Is it aligned with your values in the area you are working in?

PART FIVE

- When are you going to start work on creating this new habit?
- What will you see, hear and feel when your new habit is established? (Refer to the Visualisation Exercise in the Toolbox.)

STEP 2: Set the intention
Complete this statement and set the intention.

The new habit I am going to create is……….
When I am fully entrenched in this habit I will feel……….
I will see……….I will hear……….
I am committed to do this, as I want to live my life to my fullest potential.
Sign………. Date……….

STEP 3: Make a plan
It's almost like setting up a mini goal.
- What specific things do you need to change to help you create your new habit? Make a list.
- Create a timeline. Break your plan up into baby steps and write them down.
- Add each step to your daily routine one at a time (please note if it fits, aim for one step a week if you find it challenging).
- How are you going to celebrate each step as you complete it?

Mindset
- Do you have any negative self-talk, limiting beliefs, negative emotions? If so, get to the root cause as soon as you can.
  Go to the relevant section (refer to the contents page of this Handbook).

Environment
- What can you do in your physical environment to make it easier to follow through with the creation of your new habit?

Support
- Make a list of who you can get to support you to make the changes you need to.
- What other habit could you piggyback off to distract you and support you in changing this bad habit?

Accountability
- Make a list of who can assist you to be accountable for achieving the steps you have created.
- Create a tracking card: use this as a visual reminder of what you have achieved as well as tracking your progress. (Refer to the Monthly Habit Tracker in the Toolbox at the back of the book.)

STEP 4: Visualise
- Breathe: breathe in for six, hold for three, breathe out for nine. Repeat at least five times until you feel a wave of calm come over you.
- Close your eyes and focus on your new habit. Looking through your own eyes, see yourself entrenched in your new habit and the outcome it will achieve.
- Now connect with what you are seeing, feeling, hearing by actively imagining stepping into your body and feel the feelings of success.
- How does that feel?

> **WHAT DID YOU LEARN?**
> What did you learn about yourself?
> How do you feel about your habits now?
> What actions are you going to do today to help you create new habits?
> What actions are you going to do in the future to support you in maintaining your new habits?

PART FIVE

> THE QUALITY OF MY LIFE IS DETERMINED BY
> THE QUALITY OF MY HABITS.

VICTIM MINDSET

"It's always easy to blame others. You can spend your entire life blaming the world, but your successes or failures are entirely your own."
Paulo Coelho

Victim mentality is an acquired personality trait in which a person tends to recognise or consider themselves a victim of the negative actions of others, "It's not my fault." They have often suffered through trauma or hard times, and haven't developed a healthier way to cope.
The challenge here is twofold:

- **Firstly,** take responsibility for your actions/thoughts, etc, to recognise the difference between the things you can change and accepting what you can't change. While understanding that what other people think, say or do is not your business.
- **Secondly,** take back control and get back into the driver's seat. You are the only one who can control your thoughts/behaviour. You might not be able to control others, but you can control how you react to them.

We all have our ups and downs in life, bad things happen to you or people you know on a daily basis. People with victim mentality develop a negative view on life where they don't believe they have any control over what happens to them. Because they don't think anything is their fault, they have little or no sense of responsibility for their own lives. It just happens to them.

Left unattended this mindset can be a huge roadblock. Whatever you can do to shift yourself out of victim mentality, will be the first step towards becoming that person who can live to their fullest potential and live a life they can love.

> *"When you complain you make yourself a victim. Leave the situation, change the situation or accept it, all else is madness."*
> **Eckhart Tolle**

SIGNS AND SYMPTOMS OF A VICTIM MINDSET
Lack of accountability
- Does your victim behaviour/feeling bad for yourself, give you relief or pleasure, because it's never your fault?
- Are you constantly blaming other people or situations for feeling miserable? If so, why? How does it make you feel?
- Do you continually make excuses for not achieving your desired outcome and give up? If so, why?
- Do you see your problems as catastrophes and blow them out of proportion? If so, why do you catastrophise? How does it make you feel?
- Even when things go right, do you find something to complain about? If so, why?
- Do you believe you're not responsible for what happens in your life, and others are? If so, why do you believe that you are not responsible for what happens in your life?
- Is it difficult for you to examine yourself honestly, take responsibility for your actions/choices and make changes? If so, why?

Make a list of the above reasons that you can relate to and answer the questions that follow each one.

What did you learn?

PART FIVE

Negative self-talk, self-sabotage statements
- *Everything bad happens to me.* If so, why do you believe this?
- *I have a negative attitude to life's challenges.* If so, why?
- *The world is a scary, mostly bad place.* If so, why do you believe this?
- *I can't change my life or do anything about it so why try?* If so, why do you believe you can't change anything?
- *I constantly put myself down.* If so, why? How does it make you feel?
- *I enjoy feeling sorry for myself.* If so, why?
- *I deserve the bad things that happen to me.* If so, why?
- *No one cares about me.* If so, why do you believe this? What evidence do you have to prove this statement true?
- *I am the only one being targeted for mistreatment.* If so, why? What evidence do you have to prove this statement true?
- *I refuse to consider other perspectives when talking about my problems.* If so, why?
- *I enjoy sharing my tragic stories with other people.* If so, why? How does it make you feel?

Make a list of the above negative statements that you can relate to and answer the questions that follow each one.

What did you learn?

Frustration anger and resentment
- Do you tend to 'one-up' people when it comes to sharing traumatic experiences? What do you feel when you one-up people when it comes to sharing traumatic experiences?
- Do you keep reliving past painful memories that made you feel like a victim? Why do you relive past painful memories? How does doing this make you feel?
- Do you feel stuck, unable to maintain motivation and complete tasks? If you were to know, why do you feel stuck?

- Do you feel powerless to change your circumstances? If so, why? How does it make you feel?
- Are you cynical or pessimistic? If so, why?
- Do you feel hurt when you believe loved ones don't care about you? If so, why? How do you know your loved ones don't care about you?
- Do you think others are purposely trying to hurt you? How do you know they are trying to hurt you? What specifically are they doing?
- Do you expect to gain sympathy from others, and when you don't get it, you feel upset? If so, why?
- Do you feel resentful of people who seem happy and successful? If so, why?
- Do you feel attacked when you're given constructive criticism or offered helpful feedback? If so, why?
- Do you believe that everyone is 'better off' than you? If so, why?
- Do you find it difficult to say 'no' to doing something you don't want to do, because in letting them down you would feel guilty? If you were to know, why do you feel guilty if you say no?
- Do you attract people like you (who complain, blame, and feel victimised by life)? How does that make you feel?

Make a list of the above negative statements that you can relate to and answer the questions that follow each one.

What did you learn?

> *"Be thankful for what you have, and you'll end up having more. If you concentrate on what you don't have you will never ever have enough."*
> **Oprah Winfrey**

AWARENESS: Recognise victim mindset as a roadblock
From your signs and symptoms list of victim thinking you have created, which ones do you think are presenting themselves as a roadblock? Make a list.

If you were to know, what is your victim mindset stopping you from doing? Choose a symptom one at a time and work through the following sections.

There are four main points that you need consider when you want to flick the switch on victim mindset.
- You need to be responsible for your thoughts, actions and the choices you make. Start replacing 'you' with 'I'.
- You need to commit to the process, discover the root cause and believe in the possibility of change by understanding why you do what you do.
- You need to focus on flicking the switch from negative to positive.
- Ask for help if you need it.

I believe in you and I know you can do this. Are you ready? Let's go.

Event: What's happening/not happening?
- *The symptom I am working on is..........*
- What specifically is happening?
- What do you believe about this symptom?
- Is your belief true? If so, how do you know it's true?
- When you think about this belief what do you feel?
- Do you need to feel the way you do? If so, why?
- Can you take responsibility for your thoughts around this symptom?
- What are you feeling about your symptom now?
- Can you create a positive statement around this symptom? If not, why not?

JOURNAL IT OUT: Let's dive in a little deeper

Breathe
- Close your eyes. Breathe in for six, hold for three, and breathe out for nine. Repeat until you feel a sense of calm come over you.

YOUR GUIDE TO ACTION AND EMPOWERMENT

- Allow the answers to your questions to bubble up.
- What specifically is the challenge around this symptom?
- Why is it a challenge?
- Is it a thought, an emotion or a behaviour?
- Is it internal or external? A limiting decision, a negative emotion, a habit, an avoidance strategy, etc.
- Was it a physical reaction ie, a headache, an ache, pain or did you just remove yourself from the situation?
- Has the outcome of living with this symptom become a roadblock?
- If you were to know, what is it stopping you from doing..........?
- Do you know what triggers your negative behaviour/emotions around this symptom?
- If yes, what are the triggers?
- If there are any negative emotions, negative self-talk, limiting beliefs that need more work to discover the root cause, please go to the appropriate section (refer to the contents page of this Handbook) to dive in a little deeper.

WHAT DID YOU LEARN?

TAKE OWNERSHIP
- Are you living at cause or effect?
- What is it you have to do to take ownership?

MOVE AWAY FROM RESISTANCE
- Is everything I do getting me closer to my desired outcome, a life I will love living?
- How would my life be if I DID NOT change anything around my victim mindset?
- What would happen if I developed a positive mindset and learnt to love and believe in myself?

FLICK THE SWITCH FROM NEGATIVE TO POSITIVE
- Do you need to allow this belief/symptom to control your thoughts?

PART FIVE

- Can you change your thoughts around this belief/symptom?
- If so, what can you change your thoughts to?
- What is your new positive statement?

Symptom/belief	Positive statement/affirmation
I believe that everyone is 'better off' than me	I am grateful for who I am and what I have; I do not need to compare myself to others
I feel stuck, unable to complete tasks	I am resourceful and I can find a way to complete the task

Please note: ask for help.
If you're struggling to get past the victim role or any of
the above questions, practise self-care by asking for help.

TAKE ACTION!

- From the list below, what can you do to move away from the victim mindset?
- Make a list of the things you need to think, believe or do to change your mindset from negative to positive around this symptom.

TIPS THAT CAN SUPPORT YOU ON YOUR JOURNEY AWAY FROM A VICTIM MINDSET

! Journal it out. Go within to find the answers.

! Become aware of your reactions/triggers and your negative self-talk.

! Stop, Think and Flick the Switch (refer to the Toolbox).

! Replace self-loathing with self-compassion. Remember you can only do your best at any one point in time.

YOUR GUIDE TO ACTION AND EMPOWERMENT

- See yourself as a survivor; develop a positive mindset.

- Create an attitude of gratitude. Focus on the positive (refer to the Toolbox).

- Create some positive affirmations and implement them into your daily routine (refer to the Toolbox).

- Implement mindful meditation into your daily routine. Alternatively find a way to quieten the mind, do the things you love to do that make you feel good.

- Practise self-care and self-love; be gentle and kind to yourself.

- Prioritise yourself, take care of your energy and start saying no to some things you don't want to do.

- Change your environment, who you socialise with, work with and spend quality time with like-minded positive people. You may need to change your work, family or social life.

- Live at cause. Take responsibility for your life, your thoughts, choices, and your behaviour and you will be empowered and take control of how you live your life.

VICTIM OR VICTOR, THE CHOICE IS YOURS.

WHAT DID YOU LEARN?
What did you learn about yourself?
How do you feel about your victim mindset now?
What actions are you going to do today to support you to move away from a victim mindset?
What actions are you going to do in the future to support you in maintaining a positive mindset?

PART FIVE

> I AM RESPONSIBLE FOR MY THOUGHTS, MY ACTIONS AND THE CHOICES I MAKE. I AM EMPOWERED TO CREATE CHANGE. I ACCEPT MYSELF FOR WHO I AM; THE GOOD AND THE BAD. I AM RESPONSIBLE FOR MY LIFE.

DISTRACTIONS

A distraction is something that prevents someone from concentrating on something they need to be focusing on.

"Starve your distractions, feed your focus."
Daniel Goleman

The challenge here is to recognise when we are distracted, or using a distraction as a coping or avoidance strategy. Avoidance is a passive coping tool that helps us temporarily block out feelings like anxiety and fear as a way to avoid getting to the root of an issue or potentially even discovering a solution. A distraction, however, is active, time-limited and intentional and is employed to divert attention away from a stressor and towards other thoughts or behaviours that are unrelated to the stressor and can either be conscious or unconscious.

A distraction is caused by the lack of ability to pay attention, caused by a lack of interest in the object of attention or the novelty or attractiveness of something other than the object of attention.

THERE ARE THREE MAIN TYPES OF DISTRACTION

1. **Visual**: something you see, such as taking your eyes off the road.

2. **Manual**: something you do, such as taking your hands off the wheel.

3. **Cognitive**: something you think about, such as taking your mind off driving.

Distractions come from both external and internal sources. Internal distractions are your own thoughts and emotions. These can include thoughts about pressing responsibilities or pleasant things you would rather be doing, or emotions related to life circumstances, fears and worries.

External distractions result from something outside of yourself, including factors such as visual triggers, social interactions, music, text messages, phone calls, loud noises, other people speaking, smells and temperature. Today, devices, emails and social media all demand your attention at any given moment. The costs of these distractions to your personal and professional lives are well documented.

AWARENESS: Recognise your distraction as a roadblock
- Do you find that you are easily distracted?
- In which area of your Life Circle do you usually get distracted?
- When specifically, do you get distracted?

Event: What's happening/not happening?
- Is it related to your work, family or personal environment?
- What specifically is the situation that triggers your distraction?
- What do you do?
- What is the purpose of the distraction?
- Is your distraction an avoidance strategy?
- If so, what are you avoiding?
- Is your distraction a bad habit?
- If so, what is your bad habit?
- What is your distraction delaying you from doing?
- If you were to know, why do you allow yourself to get distracted around this situation?
- What part of the event/challenge specifically triggered your distraction?
- Was it a thought, an emotion or a behaviour?

- Is it internal or external? A limiting decision, a negative emotion, a habit, an avoidance strategy, etc.
- Was it a physical reaction ie, a headache, an ache, pain or did you just remove yourself from the situation?
- In what way has your distraction become a roadblock?
- If you feel you need to go a little deeper to establish the root cause of why you are easily distracted, especially if there are any negative emotions, limiting decisions or bad habits hanging around, go to the appropriate section (refer to the contents page of this Handbook) to dive in a little deeper.

TAKE OWNERSHIP

- Are you blaming others? If so, why?
- Are you taking responsibility for your choices, your thoughts and your reactions around this distraction? If not, why not?

MOVE AWAY FROM RESISTANCE

- Is everything you do getting you closer to your desired outcome, a life you will love living?
- How would your life be if you DIDN'T get rid of your distractions and didn't reach your desired destination/outcome?
- What would happen if you DID get rid of distractions and take the appropriate action?

TIPS THAT CAN HELP YOU ELIMINATE DISTRACTIONS

! Become aware of when a distraction is actually a distraction, and why.

! Evaluate if the distraction is productive (providing you with relief, helping you cope and acting as an outlet) or negative (detaching you from reality and becoming a bad habit or an avoidance strategy).

YOUR GUIDE TO ACTION AND EMPOWERMENT

! Check out your environment. Are you living/working in a supportive environment?

! Eliminate or minimise negative people in your life. These are people who play the victim, are stuck in unhealthy habits or generally make you feel drained or bad about yourself. Surround yourself with those who are positive, focused, productive and ambitious. Remember late iconic speaker Jim Rohn's rule: "You are the average of the five people you spend the most time with."

! Build positive distraction habits. Try something different and new. Take that positive break that you need so that you can get back on track. Take a walk, do a DIY project, have a short nap, call a friend, meditate, laugh, increase quality time with those who you love, whatever is comfortable and natural for you to do (no stress).

! Be mindful of your physical health. Exercise, eat well, get plenty of sleep, and be mindful of all those things you can do to promote good mental health and focus.

! Create a balanced daily routine. Carve out blocks of time for work:
a) Knock out the most dreaded duties first thing in the morning, when your energy levels are higher.
b) Give yourself frequent breaks. Your mind and body aren't designed or meant to work 24/7.
c) Include time out for exercise, the people you care about taking into account your own personal needs.

! Turn off smartphone notifications. Remove the temptation to constantly keep an eye on these pests.

PART FIVE

! Communicate, communicate, communicate (refer to the Communication Tools in the Toolbox at the back of the book).

! Have clear boundaries.

! Set U C A N B S M A R T goals if you need to stay focused, inspired and motivated (refer to part three, Your Road Map).

WHAT DID YOU LEARN?

TAKE ACTION!
- What do you need to do differently?
- What actions are you going to take in the future to move away from your distractions? Refer to the tips above if you are having difficulty.
- What action can you take today to start you off on your journey away from distractions?

> EVERY MOMENT OF EVERY DAY I AM MORE AND MORE FOCUSED.

EXCUSES
Is it an Excuse or a Reason?

An excuse is when you give up ownership of a problem or solution: the explanation/excuse offered is to justify and release one from an obligation or promise.

On the other hand the main function of reasoning is to explain. It is when you take ownership of something, a problem or a solution and justify your actions, whether positive or negative.

The challenge here is to know the difference.

YOUR GUIDE TO ACTION AND EMPOWERMENT

Realise that when you make excuses you are not taking responsibility for your thoughts, actions and behaviours.
Imagine what life would be like if it was excuseless.

There are several points to consider when you are evaluating your excuses:

- **Spotting the danger zone:** knowing when you are making an excuse will help.

- **Difficulty:** is it something you don't want to do because it could be difficult?

> *"Excuses will always be there for you, opportunity won't."*
> **Anonymous**

- **Perspective:** are you feeling stuck and not sure why?

- **Fear:** what are you afraid of?
    a) Fear of the unfamiliar: stepping out of your comfort zone
    b) Fear of failure: what mistakes are you afraid of making?
    c) Fear of uncertainty: lack of knowledge.

- **Avoidance:** what is it you don't want to do?

- **Protection:** what are you protecting yourself from?

- **Motivation:** why are you unmotivated?

- **Lack of resources:** what is it you don't have?

- **Self-belief:** are you set in your ways? What is that little voice in your head telling you?

- **Take responsibility and live at cause:** are you taking responsibility for your thoughts and your behaviour?

PART FIVE

Can you relate to any of the above points? If so, make a list.

AWARENESS: Identify excuses as a roadblock
You may have reasons for why you have not done or achieved something but don't justify it with an excuse.

Here are just a few common excuses, you might like to add some more.

It's too hard	I don't know what to do
I am stuck	I don't care what happens
I don't want to do it	It does not interest me
I give up	I don't have enough time
I keep making mistakes	I don't have enough money
I am scared	I don't have any friends
I don't like it	
I don't know	

Pick out an excuse you have made recently and answer the following questions.
The excuse I am working on is..........

Breathe
- Close your eyes. Breathe in for six, hold for three, and breathe out for nine, repeat until you feel a sense of calm come over you.
- Allow the answers to your questions to bubble up.
- If you were to know, why did you make this excuse?
- Are you feeling stuck and not sure why?
- Are you feeling unmotivated? If so, why?
- Is it an age-old excuse you are repeating over and over again?
- When did you decide to make this excuse?
- Are you set in your ways and telling yourself you are unable to change?

- When you think about it, is it that you can't change or that you don't want to change?
- Is it something you don't want to do because it could be difficult?
- What is it you don't want to do?
- What are you protecting yourself from?
- What are you afraid of?
- What mistakes are you afraid of making?
- What is it you don't know?
- Who are you comparing yourself to and why?

Event: What's happening/not happening?
- What specifically is the challenge around the event that triggered your excuse?
- Why is it a challenge?
- What specifically was your reaction?
- What was the first thing you did?
- Was it a thought, an emotion or a behaviour?
- Is it internal or external? A limiting decision, a negative emotion, a habit, an avoidance strategy, etc.
- What is the result of the excuse, the way you reacted to the event?
- Has the outcome become a roadblock?
- If you were to know, what is it stopping you from doing?

If your excuse is linked to a limiting belief, a negative emotion or behaviour/state, you may be feeling guilty, stressed, overwhelmed or afraid. If so, go to the relevant section and get to the root cause. (Refer to the contents page of this Handbook.)

TAKE OWNERSHIP
- Are you taking responsibility for your choices, your thoughts and your reactions? If not, why not?

"Be stronger than your excuses."
Eric Thomas

PART FIVE

MOVE AWAY FROM RESISTANCE
- Is everything you do getting you closer to your desired outcome, a life you will love living?
- How would your life be if you kept making excuses and didn't reach your destination/outcome?
- What would happen if you DIDN'T make excuses anymore?

WHAT DID YOU LEARN?
- What are you feeling now?
- What have you learnt about yourself?

TIPS TO SUPPORT YOU TO STOP MAKING EXCUSES

! **Commit:** making changes takes effort and commitment, and it can be very difficult. It's your choice – you either do it or don't do it, as long as you realise the consequences of your excuse and are willing to live with the choices you make. Then it's okay, you are in control.

! **Reevaluate:** take responsibility as you alone control your destiny. Live at cause and be empowered to live your best life. For example, you are running late for an appointment and you make the excuse that the traffic was bad. If the appointment is important to you then perhaps you could take the responsible choice and have left a little earlier to compensate for the traffic.

! **Shift your perspective:** problems/challenges are opportunities not obstacles, life is happening for you not to you. Find the lesson, look closely at your mistakes and determine what went wrong and apply the learnings to future decisions.

! **Take baby steps:** instead of giving into the fear, take baby steps. Get excited and embrace the idea that you may fail and make mistakes, get the learnings and keep moving forward.

YOUR GUIDE TO ACTION AND EMPOWERMENT

- **Celebrate:** create a milestone map and celebrate each baby step when achieved.

- **Uncover limiting beliefs** and find clarity about what you really want.

- **Define your vision,** set U CAN B SMART goals and you will always have a pathway to follow.

- **Move from negative to positive mindset.** See failure as an opportunity, get your learnings and keep moving forward.

- **Stop overthinking:** let go of the past and take massive action or nothing will change.

- **Check your WHY is strong enough:** the light at the end of the tunnel is your destination, where you want to be.

- **Stepping back** from the excuse and aligning yourself with your values and what you want will help you make aligned choices.

- **A positive affirmation:** put your challenge into perspective, and change your thoughts and beliefs around it. A positive affirmation can support the change in perspective (refer to the Toolbox).

- **Be prepared:** think of every possible obstacle, do some research; find out what you don't know. This will give you the confidence to deal with the situation and keep moving forward.

- **Focus on your strengths:** what are your strengths in the area in question? Do not compare yourself to others.

PART FIVE

! **Develop an attitude of gratitude:** be grateful for the opportunities that are available to you to help you grow.

TAKE ACTION!
From the tips above, what can you do to move away from making excuses? Make a list.

What action are you going to do TODAY to start your journey away from making excuses?

> I LET GO OF ALL EXCUSES, EVERYTHING I NEED IS WITHIN ME, I AM EMBRACING THE LIFE I AM MEANT TO BE LIVING.

Feelings

UNHAPPY

Understanding what happiness is, is a necessary element to realising when you are unhappy. No matter what it is that you want more of in your life, finding happiness is all about taking an honest look within and being willing to make the changes necessary that allow you to realise and do what gives you those feelings of pleasure, contentment, and puts a smile on your face.

> *"When it rains, look for rainbows. When it's dark, look for stars."*
> **Anonymous**

AWARENESS: What makes you happy
The challenge around Unhappy is to find out what makes you happy so that you can make the choice to be happy and do what you need to do to move from unhappy.
What does happiness look like in your life?

Breathe

1. Close your eyes. Breathe in for six, hold for three, and breathe out for nine, repeat until you feel a sense of calm come over you.

2. Allow the answers to your questions to bubble up.

3. Can you remember a time when you were really happy, imagine you were there right now: what do you see, hear and feel?

4. Connect back to that time, what specifically were you doing?

5. What specifically were you feeling? Make a list.

6. Now think of some other times when you were happy. Make a list of at least 5 events/activities (more if you can think of them).

7. What specifically is happiness for you? What does it look, feel and sound like? Make a list.

8. What are you NOT doing now that would bring more happiness into your life?

For happiness to exist in anyone's life, I believe there are three major understandings that need to take place: **firstly**, understanding the theory of basic human needs, as I outlined earlier with Maslow's hierarchy of basic human needs (refer to Understanding Life Balance in your Journey Handbook).

Secondly, understanding who you are, your thoughts, your values and why you do what you do. It is imperative to understanding what makes you happy/fulfilled.

And **thirdly**, understanding that happiness is a choice.

PART FIVE

1. MASLOW'S THEORY OF BASIC HUMAN NEEDS

Are your basic needs in your life being met? Please answer the following questions and make a list.

Physiological: Do you have:
a. Access to air, water, food, exercise, rest and shelter?
b. A balanced life

Safety needs: Do you have:
a. Personal security?
b. Employment?
c. Good health?
d. Clear boundaries?

Love and belonging: Do you have:
a. Good friends that you know you can trust and depend on when needed?
b. A good personal relationship and intimacy?
c. A supportive family that loves and accepts you for who you are?
d. A sense of connection with self and others?

Esteem needs: Are you:
a. Respected and acknowledged for who you are?
b. Strong in the area of your self-identity?
c. Free to be yourself?

Self-actualisation: Do you:
a. Have the desire to live to your full potential?
b. Fill your life up with things you love to do?
c. Know your life's purpose?
d. Allow yourself to dream?
e. Set U CAN B SMART goals?

What did you learn?
Is there anything you need to consider and implement in your life from this list?

2. UNDERSTANDING WHO YOU ARE: Your thoughts, your values and why you act the way you do

Becoming aware: answer the following questions and make a list.
Self-actualisation: achieving one's full potential. Do you feel you are living your best life, to your fullest potential, in all areas of your life?

Now let's apply his theory into the different areas of your Life Circle.

Relationships: personal, friendships and family
- Do you have good friends that you know you can trust and depend on when needed? If not, why not?
- Do you have a loving family that accepts, loves and supports you for who you are?
- Do you have a loving, intimate personal relationship in your life right now? If not, why not?
- Do you live in a positive supportive home environment? If not, why not?

Emotionally
- Do you feel you are living your best life?
- Do you have an understanding of what makes you happy? If not, why not?
- Do you have self-confidence/positive self-worth?
- Do you have a sense of accomplishment?
- Are you allowing yourself to grow?
- Do you have an understanding of who you are, who you want to be and how to achieve this?
- Do you have control over your emotions? If not, why not?

PART FIVE

Finances
- Do you feel you are managing your finances well?
    a. Are you earning enough to do the things you want to do?
    b. Are you paying your bills on time? If not, why not?

Living a spiritually fulfilled life
- Do you feel you are living your best life now to your fullest potential? If not, why not?
- Do you fill your life up with things you love to do, things that make you happy?
- Do you make time to have fun and connect with self and others?
- Do you know your life's purpose?
- Do you allow yourself to dream?
- Do you set U C A N B S M A R T goals to keep you motivated?
- Do you meditate or just take time out to smell the roses?

Health and wellbeing
- Do you feel you are making your health and wellbeing a priority? If not, why not?
- Do you live a balanced lifestyle, eat nutritious food, exercise regularly, rest and sleep well?

Fun/social life
- Do you have fun?
- Do you create time to have a social life? To live, laugh and love, whether it be having coffee with friends, partying or just doing things with like-minded people that know, love and accept you for who you are.
- Do you make time to just be and do the things you really enjoy in life? Those things that make you feel alive? Like playing sports or enjoying your hobbies, walking, swimming, etc.

Business and career
- Do you have a successful business that you love? If not, why not?
- Do you feel you have a career doing the work you love? If not, why not?
- Do you work in a positive supportive work environment? If not, why not?

I hope you found this exercise interesting and you may have a better understanding of the cause of why you are unhappy.

What did you learn about yourself?

AWARENESS: Identify if unhappiness is a roadblock

Down in the dumps? We get it because we've had our fair share of bad days too. Maybe you woke up on the wrong side of the bed, maybe you recently had a heated argument with a family member and it's still got you in a funk, or maybe you're just plain grumpy. Are you unhappy?

If yes, connect with yourself and go within to discover why you are unhappy.
- Choose a specific event where you are unhappy.
- Is it personal, family or work related?

> *"Nurturing yourself is not selfish – it is essential to your survival and your well-being."*
> **Renee Peterson Trudeau**

Event: What's happening/not happening?
- What specifically is the challenge around being unhappy?
- How is this unhappiness showing up in your body? (This could be behaviours, emotions and/or limiting decisions.)
- Is how it shows up for you a challenge? If so, why?

PART FIVE

Response: How did you react?
- If you were to know, what creates or triggers your unhappiness?
- How does being unhappy make you feel?
- What specifically is your reaction?

Outcome: What is the result of the way you reacted to the event?
- Is it internal or external? A limiting decision, a negative emotion, a habit, an avoidance strategy, etc.
- Was it a physical reaction ie, a headache, an ache, pain or did you just remove yourself from the situation?
- Has the outcome become a roadblock?
- If you were to know, what is stopping you from being happy?

TAKE OWNERSHIP
- Are you blaming others?
- Are you taking responsibility for your choices, your thoughts and your reactions? If not, why not?
- Are you living at cause? If not, why not?
- What is it you have to do to take ownership?

JOURNAL IT OUT: Let's dive in a little deeper

- What are you feeling about the situation now?

Breathe
1. Close your eyes. Breathe in for six, hold for three, and breathe out for nine, repeat until you feel a sense of calm come over you.
2. Allow the answers to your questions to bubble up.

Ask the right questions
- Then ask, Why are you feeling unhappy about..........? How does the feeling of unhappy about..........make you feel?
  Feeling unhappy makes me feel..........
- What specifically triggered these feelings?

YOUR GUIDE TO ACTION AND EMPOWERMENT

- What is the first thing you do when you realise you are unhappy? How did you react?
- Was it a limiting decision, a negative emotion, a habit, an avoidance strategy, etc?
- Go to the relevant section around your previous answer to dive in a little deeper, or continue below.

DISCOVER THE ROOT CAUSE: Find the solution
- What are you feeling now? *(I am feeling..........)*
- Is this feeling important to you? If so, why?
  The answer to the previous question is important to me because..........
- Keep asking the question of the previous answer until you find it hard to answer.
- So, what do you need to do to bring more happiness into your life?
- Do you need to do or change something right now? If so, what?

WHAT DID YOU LEARN?

MOVE AWAY FROM RESISTANCE
- Is everything I do getting me closer to experiencing more happiness in a life I will love living?
- How would my life be if I remained unhappy; what would NOT happen?
- What WOULD happen if I did more things that created more happiness in my life?

REFRAME: FLIP FROM NEGATIVE TO POSITIVE
When we become aware of our Negative self-talk, it's generally a sign for us to change the way we think and take action.

Do you have any negative self-talk around allowing yourself to be happy?

PART FIVE

Negative self-talk	Positive thinking
I am lonely	What do I need to do so I don't feel lonely?
There's no way it will work	How can I do it differently?
I can't do it	I can do it if I have the right tools. Who can I talk to, to find out how to do it?

WHAT DID YOU LEARN?
- If you were to know, what specifically is stopping you from being happy right now?

3. CHOICE

To make progress with any personal development, you need to become aware of your thoughts, and your feelings, as they are the key to what you think and how you behave at any one point in time; negative and positive. Connect with who you are, what makes you happy/sad and what creates the real, authentic you. Realise your thoughts create your emotions, your feelings are a reaction to your emotions and how you behave is governed by choice. Once you understand this, how empowering can it be to know that you and you alone are in control? As long as we know what we want and where we are going, the choices we make along the way are not so difficult to make. Understanding your why (why you do the things you do and the way you think) can be the key to making the right choices for the right reasons and living a happy and content life.

We make choices every day, when to get up, what to wear, who to go out with, etc. So why is it so hard to realise that happiness is a choice? I guess things just get in the way and it all becomes too hard.

Everything that is happening in your life right now is a result of the choices you made in the past.

YOUR GUIDE TO ACTION AND EMPOWERMENT

> No hidden secrets; just wise choices:
> diet, exercise, clean water,
> and balancing the mind,
> body and spirit.

Our thoughts can create positive and negative emotions, reactions and behaviours that do or don't serve us on our journey.

Please NOTE! here that we need to have and acknowledge the negative so that we can appreciate and understand the positive.

TIPS TO THINK ABOUT AND GET YOU BACK ON THE ROAD TO HAPPINESS

- ! Choose to be happy.

- ! Be mindful; become aware of the choices you make every day.

- ! Take responsibility/own your thoughts and your behaviour.

- ! Manage your stress levels. Breathe, meditate, and bring a sense of calm into your life.

- ! Boost your self-esteem.

- ! Live a healthy lifestyle.

- ! Reconnect with others and yourself.

- ! Build your resilience.

- ! Have fun, and do the things that make you happy.

- ! Smile a lot.

> *"Everything that is happening at this moment is a result of the choices you've made in the past."*
> **Deepak Chopra**

PART FIVE

! Develop an attitude of gratitude.

! Lend a hand when needed.

! Be kind to yourself and others.

! Check that your environment is supporting you.

! Ask for help if you need it.

WHAT HAVE YOU LEARNT ABOUT YOURSELF?

TAKE ACTION!
- What do you need to do next to bring more happiness into your life?
- What action are you going to do TODAY to get closer to having more happiness into your life?

> I HAVE THE POWER TO SHAPE MY OWN REALITY. HAPPINESS IS A CHOICE AND TODAY I CHOOSE TO BE HAPPY.

SCARED

Being scared is being fearful, frightened, nervous and maybe a little panicked.

The challenge around being scared/fearful is to realise if it is a roadblock, (an excuse, or an avoidance strategy) does the feeling or belief stop you from enjoying your life and doing what you want? Does it originate from an unpleasant experience, or is it just a worry of something that has not happened yet? Either way it's okay as long as it does not develop into a more serious state if left unattended (stress, anxiety or depression etc).

YOUR GUIDE TO ACTION AND EMPOWERMENT

It may not seem like it, but fear can actually be a good thing. Being scared is usually what makes us act in ways to protect ourselves, for example if you were afraid of catching COVID-19, you would probably follow the rules of washing your hands for 20 seconds or wearing a mask. You might not enjoy feeling this way, but it can serve as an important purpose, keeping you safe right now.

AWARENESS: Scared as a roadblock

When scared/fear appears as a roadblock you need to delve in a little deeper. Especially when you can't stop thinking about what scares you, or if it's interrupting your daily activities by sending you into full-on panic mode and triggering off any limiting beliefs that may be hovering in the background.

Your response can be physical (a universal biochemical response) or psychological (a high individual emotional response) or a combination of both. Understanding your scared state can help you move through the roadblock.

> *"Fears are educated into us, and can, if we wish, be educated out."*
> **Karl Augustus Menninger**

Event: What's happening/not happening?

Choose a situation that puts you in a scared state.
- Is it personal, family or work related?
- Let's determine specifically where you are at by asking the following questions:
    - What are you specifically scared of?
    - Why does it scare you?
    - What is the purpose of being scared of this?
    - What specifically is the challenge around being scared of this?
    - Why is it a challenge?
    - How does being scared of this make you feel?

PART FIVE

Response: How did you react?
- What specifically is your reaction in this situation?
- Is it physical or emotional?

Outcome: What is the result of the way you reacted to the event?
- Is it internal or external? A limiting decision, a negative emotion, a habit, an avoidance strategy, etc. If so, what?
- Was it a physical reaction ie, a headache, an ache, pain or did you just remove yourself from the situation? If so, what did you do?
- What is being scared stopping you from doing..........?
- If you were to know, does being scared originate from an unpleasant experience from the past?
- Is it a worry of something that has not happened yet?
- What evidence do you have to prove that it is going to happen?
- How does the information/evidence present itself to you?

TAKE OWNERSHIP
- Are you blaming others?
- Are you taking responsibility for your choices, your thoughts and your reactions around the event?
- Has scared become a roadblock?

WHAT DID YOU LEARN?
- *I learnt that my scared/fear originates from..........*
- With the understanding you have now, do you still need to feel scared around this event?

MOVE AWAY FROM RESISTANCE
- How would your life be if you continued to feel scared around this event?
- What would happen if you let go of your fear around this event?

COMPLETE THE FOLLOWING SENTENCE:
- *The reality of the situation is that..........*

YOUR GUIDE TO ACTION AND EMPOWERMENT

If you feel you need to go a little deeper to establish the root cause of why you are feeling scared/fearful and find a solution, go to the questions in the FEAR section (refer to page 312).

> *"It's okay to be scared. Being scared means you're about to do something really, really brave."*
> **Mandy Hale**

TIPS TO RELEASE SCARED FEELINGS

! **Take time out:** it is impossible to think clearly when you are experiencing the emotion of scared/fear.

! **Breathe:** find a quiet space. Breathe in for six, hold for three, and breathe out for nine. Repeat at least five times until you feel a wave of calm come over you.

! **Go within:** ask the right questions. Look at the evidence, is it real? Do I need to feel scared of this? What can I do differently to release the feeling of scared around this situation?

! **Be flexible:** deal with each life challenge one step at a time.

! **Choose to be happy:** do the things that make you feel good, worthwhile and amazing.

! **Maintain:** a healthy balanced lifestyle.

! **Celebrate:** and recognise each step along the way to achieving your desired outcome.

! **Ask for help:** talk about it (friends, colleagues, a coach or a mental health specialist). A challenge shared is a challenge solved.

PART FIVE

TAKE ACTION!
What action do you need to take today to start moving away from feeling scared?

> I AM CONFIDENT AND DETERMINED. MY STRUGGLES ARE OPPORTUNITIES TO GROW.

CONFUSED

Confusion is a state of uncertainty about what is happening, intended or required; it is a state of being unclear in one's mind.

Your challenge here is to realise that you are in a state of confusion and that you need to do something about it, move from confusion to clarity, get clear in whatever situation you are in (what is happening, intended or required).

A lack of clarity creates chaos and misunderstandings. You can feel so alone. When you are unfocused and distracted it's easy to start doubting yourself and talk yourself out of things, and you can become frustrated. That little voice in your head goes into overtime and your limiting decisions, etc start to creep back into your life. Confusion can so easily become an excuse and if left unattended it can create a roadblock.

The key to moving from confusion to clarity is to just Stop, Think and Flick the Switch.

AWARENESS: Identify your confusion
- What specifically are you confused about?
- Is it work, family or a relationship situation?
- What really matters to you in the area that you are confused about?
- What specifically is the challenge around being confused in this situation?

YOUR GUIDE TO ACTION AND EMPOWERMENT

- Why is it a challenge?
- Did part of the challenge trigger a reaction?

Response: How did you react?
- What specifically was your reaction?
- Was it a thought, a feeling, an emotion or a behaviour?

> *"Someday everything will make perfect sense. So, for now, laugh at confusion, smile through the tears and keep reminding yourself that everything happens for a reason."*
> *John Mayer*

Outcome: What is the result of the way you reacted to the event?
- Is it internal or external? A limiting decision, a negative emotion, a habit, an avoidance strategy, etc?
- Was it a physical reaction ie, a headache, an ache, pain or did you just remove yourself from the situation?
- Has the result of how you reacted become a roadblock?
- If you were to know, what is it stopping you from finding clarity in this situation?

TAKE OWNERSHIP
- Are you blaming others? If so, why?
- Are you taking responsibility for your choices, your thoughts and your reactions? If not, why not?

JOURNAL IT OUT: Let's dive in a little deeper

Breathe
- Close your eyes. Breathe in for six, hold for three, and breathe out for nine. Repeat until you feel a sense of calm come over you.
- Allow the answers to your questions to bubble up.
- What specifically is the result of the way you reacted to the

PART FIVE

confusion? (At this point a thought, a feeling, an emotion, or a behaviour?)
- What are you feeling about the event now?
- Are there any negative emotions, limiting beliefs or specific behaviour patterns attached to this confusion? If so, what are they?
- You may need to go to the section relevant to the negativity that is showing up for you to find the root cause.
- Is it low self-esteem, negative self-talk, a limiting belief or a negative emotion?

MOVE AWAY FROM RESISTANCE

- What would your reaction be if you did have CLARITY in this situation?
- What would happen if you did NOT have clarity around this situation?

TIPS TO SUPPORT YOU IN ELIMINATING CONFUSION IN YOUR LIFE

! **Communicate, Communicate, Communicate:** maybe you need to learn how to communicate better. Realise the importance of good communication. You are not a mind-reader and neither is the other person involved. Learn what you need to say and how to say it. How you communicate can make all the difference. Check your blinker! Refer to page 372 and the communications tools in the Toolbox at the back of the book.

! **Develop an inquiring mind:** educate yourself on the topic. Do a course, listen to a webinar, read a book – anything that will give you more clarity on your topic of confusion.

! **Take time out** and release the emotion attached to the confusion.

- **Talk to a friend:** just voicing your confusion to someone who knows you well can give you a different perspective.

- **Ask for advice:** ask someone who knows more or is an expert in the field of your confusion.

- **Talk it out:** with those involved with the situation creating the confusion. Have a discussion if the confusion is around an experience with another person involved. You may not know all the facts relevant to the situation; ask them questions to clarify. Sometimes, we can assume or place judgement on another, and these assumptions can confuse our thinking. Then, emotions arise that can cloud our thinking, creating even more confusion. Get the facts or the knowledge that's missing and find clarity.

- **Declutter:** your mind must process everything that crosses your field of vision. If your home or work environment is cluttered and messy, the mess and clutter can result in brain fog. Clear the clutter at least once a week.

- **Remove distractions:** decide what is important. Get clear on what matters by getting rid of everything that doesn't serve you and focus on what you want.

WHAT DID YOU LEARN ABOUT YOURSELF FROM THIS EXERCISE?
- What action can you do today to start your journey from confusion to clarity?

> I MAINTAIN STRENGTH, CLARITY, AND PEACE OF MIND. ALL THINGS FALL INTO PLACE WITH EASE AND GRACE.

PART FIVE

OVERWHELMED

Overwhelm most commonly means to be overcome with emotion as a result of the amount of something that is just too much to handle. When you feel overwhelmed by emotion, it can be positive or negative. You can be ecstatically happy because someone has surprised you and given you an amazing gift or surprise, or you can hit a roadblock where you are temporarily unable to think clearly as

> *"The secret of getting ahead is getting started. The secret to getting started is breaking your overwhelming tasks into small manageable tasks, and then starting on the first one."*
> **Mark Twain**

the negative emotions and limiting beliefs become overbearing. If left unattended your overwhelm can lead to stress, depression, anxiety and sooner or later, create dis-ease in your body.

Your challenge with feeling overwhelmed is to release any negative emotions, etc, start to think clearly so that you can move through being in overwhelm and choose to be in control.

AWARENESS: Identify your overwhelm as a roadblock

Feeling overwhelmed comes from thinking too much, and you drown beneath a huge mass of something and never finish anything.

Do you have any of the following symptoms?
- Are you experiencing mental slowness and find it hard to focus?
- Are you forgetting to do the things you need to do on a regular basis?
- What types of things are you forgetting to do?
- Do you feel Confused? With a lot on your mind you are not sure which task to do first.
- What are you feeling Confused about?
- Do you feel physically fatigued, tense or over emotional and don't know why?
- How is the overwhelm showing up in your body?

YOUR GUIDE TO ACTION AND EMPOWERMENT

- Are you having trouble focusing on or even completing even the smallest of tasks?
- What tasks are you having trouble focusing on or completing?
- Are you finding yourself withdrawing from friends and family?
- If yes, if you were to know, why are you withdrawing from friends and family?
- Do you find yourself overreacting to the smallest of issues?
- If yes, do you know why you are overreacting?

If you said yes, to any of the above questions, you just may be overwhelmed.

Make a list of your YES answers.

Event: What's happening/not happening?
- Are you feeling overwhelmed right now?
- How do you feel when you are overwhelmed?
- Is your overwhelm relationship, family or work related?
- If you were to know, what created your overwhelm?
- Are your feelings of overwhelm caused by things you find challenging? If so, what are they?
- Are your feelings of overwhelm caused by things you don't want to do but have to do? If so, why?
- What specifically is the challenge around feeling overwhelmed in this situation?
- Why is it a challenge?
- When you become overwhelmed what specifically DO you do?
- When you become overwhelmed what specifically DON'T you do?

Response: How did you react?
- What specifically happens next?
- Is it a thought, an emotion or a behaviour?
- Is it positive or negative?
- Is it internal or external? A limiting decision, a negative emotion, a habit, an avoidance strategy, etc. Be specific!

- Was it a physical reaction ie, a headache, an ache, pain or did you just remove yourself from the situation? Be specific!

Outcome: What is the result of the way you reacted to the event?
You may need to go to the section relevant to the negativity that may be showing up for you to find the root cause.
- Is it low self-esteem, negative self-talk, a limiting belief or a negative emotion, etc?
- Has the outcome become a roadblock?
- If you were to know, what is your overwhelm stopping you from doing..........?

TAKE OWNERSHIP
- Are you blaming others?
- Why specifically are you allowing yourself to feel the way you do?
- Are you taking responsibility for your choices, your thoughts and your reactions? If not, why not?

MOVE AWAY FROM RESISTANCE
- Is everything I do getting me closer to my desired outcome, a life I will love living?
- How would your life be if you DIDN'T get overwhelmed and you were able to think clearly and get things done?
- What would happen if you allowed yourself to go into overwhelm every time you faced a similar situation?

WHAT DID YOU LEARN ABOUT YOUR OVERWHELM?
Here is an array of tips and strategies that can support you to move away from overwhelm.

TIPS FOR ON THE SPOT

! **Breathe:** breathe in for six, hold for three and breathe out for nine. Repeat at least five times, or until you feel calm and relaxed.

- **Take time out:** go for a walk, have a cuppa, stretch, breathe or talk to a friend. Give yourself space to calm down, get a new perspective, regain your motivation and become refreshed, so that you can think clearly, especially when working on a monster project or a difficult situation.

- **Journal it out:** find clarity on the issue that is causing you to feel overwhelmed. Discover what specifically is creating the feelings of overwhelm?

- **COMMUNICATE:** communicate, communicate!

- **Stay well:** keep hydrated and nourish yourself. Drink water and eat a balanced diet. The bus won't go unless you put in the right fuel.

- **Don't be too hard on yourself.** Remember everything you do is the best you can do at any one point in time.

Sometimes the feelings of overwhelm can be caused by things you find challenging or things you don't want to do but have to do.

TIPS FOR PRODUCTIVITY

- Write a list of things you need to do. You may need 2-3 lists; personal, work or family related.

- Prioritise each list in order of most important to least important.

- Working from the top of your lists, create a daily to-do list of 6 tasks or less.

- Be aware, you may need to break down each task into baby steps that can be spread out over the day or week.

PART FIVE

- Do one task at a time. Do not move on to the next task until you have completed the previous one.

- Do your best and don't get disappointed if you don't complete all six tasks in the day. Just reassess at the end of the day and prepare your list for the next day including those tasks you were unable to complete.

- Delegate. You don't have to do it all yourself.

- Alternatively, get it done in one swoop – often, the longer you leave something, the harder it is to get on with it and get it done.

- Schedule personal time and work time into your day. Work out your most productive time of day and do the more challenging tasks when you have more energy. Including time to work on your to-do lists.

- Stick to your original to-do list. Keep your original to-do list so that you can map your progress. Cross each task off when completed.

- Celebrate the successful completion of what you have achieved at the end of each day, week, month and year.

TIPS FROM AWARENESS

- Be mindful. Be fully present and aware of where you are and what you are doing.

- Declutter. Clean up your desk, your room or your car. Clearing your living and working spaces has a profound calming effect.

- ! Learn to say no. You don't have to do everything. Put your life into perspective. Make sure you are doing everything for the right reasons and take control.

- ! Talk it out. Talk it over with a friend, partner or coach. You will gain a different perspective and find some clarity and maybe some inspiration.

- ! Develop an attitude of gratitude (refer to the Toolbox). Be thankful for the small things at the end of the day. Let your light shine. It feels good, doesn't it?

Create your own get-out-of-overwhelm strategy

Your strategy can be for work, personal or family, taking into account the following steps.

Step 1. Determine in which area of your Life Circle you are going to work in: finance, emotional, health, relationships, personal, work or family related issues.

Step 2. Be mindful. Are there any roadblocks in the section you want to work in?

Step 3. Journal it out and find clarity on the issue that is causing you to feel overwhelmed. What specifically is creating the feelings of overwhelm?

Step 4. Be clear about what you want to achieve.

Step 5. Write lists of things you need to do in the area you have chosen.

Step 6. Prioritise each list in order of most important to least important.

PART FIVE

Step 7. Break down each task into baby steps that can be spread out over the day or week.

Step 8. Do one task at a time.

Step 9. Delegate some tasks if you need to and decide to whom.

Step 10. Map your progress and cross each task off when completed.

Step 12. Celebrate the successful completion of what you have achieved at the end of each day, week, month and year.

Important points to remember when creating your strategy:
- Schedule personal time and work time into your day. (Take into consideration your most productive time of day.)
- Stay hydrated and nourish yourself to keep your energy up.
- Communicate well to maintain clarity around your challenge in overwhelm.
- Take time out when you need it.
- Be mindful. If you say 'yes' to something, is it going to get you closer to the end, desired result?
- Learn to say no. Make sure you are doing everything for the right reasons and take control.
- Develop an attitude of gratitude.

OVERWHELM STRATEGY FOR WORK

When I am starting to feel overwhelmed at work from.........I will follow the process I have created:

1.
2.
3.
4.
5.
6.

YOUR GUIDE TO ACTION AND EMPOWERMENT

OVERWHELM STRATEGY FOR FAMILY
When I am starting to feel overwhelmed around..........(family issues) I will follow the process I have created:
1.
2.
3.
4.
5.
6.

OVERWHELM STRATEGY FOR PERSONAL
When I am starting to feel overwhelmed around..........(a personal issue) I will follow the process I have created:
1.
2.
3.
4.
5.
6.

REMEMBER, take one step at a time
What did you learn about yourself?
- Do you need to work on any other areas of negative self-talk or limiting beliefs, etc?
- What are the main things you need to change to move away from overwhelm?
- What action can you do today to start you on your journey away from, and eliminate your feelings of, overwhelm?

> I AM IN HARMONY AND BALANCE WITH LIFE.
> ONE DAY AT A TIME, ONE STEP AT A TIME.

PART FIVE

Negative emotions

Negative emotions can be described as any feeling that causes you to be miserable and sad. These emotions make you dislike yourself and others and take away your confidence. When we allow these negative emotions to become firmly entrenched it is more likely they will turn into a roadblock.

The challenge here is to become aware and understand why you are experiencing a particular negative emotion, what triggers it and your reaction to the experience (why you feel the way you do).

Once we begin the process of discovery we realise that our emotions can stop us from thinking and behaving rationally and seeing situations from their true perspective thus the emotion is generally seen as a call to action.

Once you realise you have been triggered you need to 'Stop, Think and Flick the Switch.' (Refer to 'Stop, Think and Flick the Switch' in the Toolbox.)

There are three important things you need to consider;
1. What specifically is happening? (the event) What specifically has triggered your reaction?
2. What is the thought process attached to the trigger? (Resulting in your mental, physical and emotional responses.)
3. What is the root cause that has been locked away and created the trigger?

You can attend to these reactions without judgement through observation of the negative emotion you experienced and how specifically you responded.

Your physiological reactions – your heart rate, respiration and perspiration.

Your behaviour. What did you do?

Your feelings that are influenced by your interpretations of our world (beliefs, values, experiences, internal and external etc).

The five major negative emotions we experience are 1. Anger, 2. Sadness, 3. Fear, 4. Hurt and 5. Guilt.

Do you feel you experience any of the 5 major negative emotions on a regular basis? If so, which ones?

> *"Negative emotions are like unwelcome guests. Just because they show up on our doorstep doesn't mean they have a right to stay."*
> **Deepak Chopra**

HOW I LEARNT THE IMPORTANCE OF GOING WITHIN TO FIND THE ANSWERS WHEN I WAS EXPERIENCING A NEGATIVE EMOTION

I am not an angry person, although every now and then I get frustrated. My anger flares, but once the emotional outburst is over, the moment is gone. Conflict can often cause frustration and lead to some sort of emotional reaction.

From personal experience, one example of frustration is when I had conflicting emotions around my eldest son. I was angry and frustrated with him, and I couldn't do anything about it. One possible reason could be that I had a conflict of values and beliefs that came from within. I had a choice: I could keep going the way I was going, getting emotional and crying, or I could go within and find the answer.

During my son's formative teenage years, someone told me that when a child hits double figures, the aliens come and take their brains away, and when they get into their twenties, they bring them back. I like that generalisation – the logic seems to make sense and is a bit of fun. In actual fact, it is during this time when their brains develop their identity, what their place is in the world and how they fit in. Once I understood this, it made things a little easier in my mind, but it did not stop me from getting emotional. From my studies, I learnt that it was my issue and my conflict that was creating my emotion.

PART FIVE

LET ME EXPLAIN

There was a time when I could not communicate with him. He did not and would not listen to anything I had to say. He would hold up his hand in front of my face, saying, "Speak to the hand." Not very nice, right? I knew he was unhappy and stuck. With all the wisdom of a mother, I recognised this.

The situation was getting out of control. My reaction was to cry and get frustrated and annoyed, and it was getting worse. I knew and recognised his reality but couldn't do anything about it. I realised I had a conflict. I needed to go within because I could not keep going like this, and my emotional reactions were getting worse even to the point where I would avoid having a normal conversation with him as it was proving too difficult.

I asked the right questions and made two lists: one was headed, *Motherly Nurturing*. All I wanted for my son was for him to be happy. I wanted to fix it, make him safe and give him a big hug, but he wouldn't even allow me to do that. The second list was headed, *Independence*. I needed him to leave home, grow up, communicate better and consolidate his learnings.

With each column, I asked the question: *Why was the previous answer important to me?* I wrote down the answers and repeated the question again and again till I could find no more answers. Then, I switched between the columns to see if there was something else I could think of and so on, until I had no more answers.

By the time I had completed the process, I found that the conflict had the same actual outcome, and the next time I spoke to my son, I was able to do it without the emotion. Even more interestingly, he spoke to me also.

I had created the situation without even knowing it. **Perception is projection.** In my mind, I did not want to get involved with the situation because it caused me grief and in the process of this thinking,

> "The emotions you once thought of as negative are merely a call to action. In fact, instead of calling them negative emotions…let's call them action signals."
>
> **Tony Robbins**

YOUR GUIDE TO ACTION AND EMPOWERMENT

I was anticipating his behaviour before it happened. Thus, he would react to my perception as I projected it. If we can release our perceptions based on our beliefs and values, we may find it easier to move on.

I actually went through this process while at a training. I had not spoken to my son for three weeks. I had just completed this exercise when five minutes later, I received a text saying, *Love you, Mum*. No more, no less. Out of the blue. How cool was that, it brought happy tears to my eyes. It does not have to be difficult – I believe our emotions are an indication that we need to take some positive action. One emotional reaction could be triggered by a conflict of values and beliefs that comes from within. We just need to become aware of how to do it and what action to take.

Let's have a look at the 5 major negative emotions and then dive in a little deeper by following THE PROCESS THROUGH YOUR NEGATIVE EMOTIONS on page 321

1. ANGER

Anger is when your body is reacting to things not going your way. To be angry is to be furious, mad or enraged. It can give you a sense of control and power in the face of vulnerability, through feeling or showing strong annoyance, displeasure or hostility. You may see red; your blood begins to boil, and you may even throw something, get annoyed or walk away and stew.

The challenge here is to understand your triggers, release your anger and take responsibility for your thoughts and actions. Remember when we are in an emotional state, clarity disappears and it's wise to take some time out before you review your actions/words and get to the root cause.

SYMPTOMS OF ANGER

Anger feels different for everyone; you may be experiencing some of the symptoms from the list below.
- A churning feeling in your stomach
- Tightness in your chest

PART FIVE

- An increased and rapid heartbeat
- Legs go weak
- Tense muscles
- Feeling hot, flushed
- Sweating profusely or sweaty palms
- A pounding head
- Shaking and trembling
- Dizziness
- Your voice gets louder
- Feeling tense, nervous, and unable to relax
- Feeling guilty
- Feeling resentful towards others
- Easily irritated

The two main points to consider when we are reviewing our reactions around anger:

1. Feelings of anger can arise from how we interpret and react to certain situations. Everyone has their own triggers for what makes them angry. Several of the most common triggers are:
    - Feeling threatened or attacked.
    - Feeling powerless and frustrated.
    - Feeling like we are being treated unfairly, being rejected and not listened to.
    - People are not respecting our feelings or our possessions.

2. How you interpret and react to a situation can depend on different life experiences stemming from:
    - Your childhood and upbringing.
    - Past negative life experiences.
    - Current circumstances.

We need to understand where our anger is coming from so that we don't put our body through unnecessary trauma and tension. You can learn how to manage it by changing your perspective and thinking in a different way.

> "Anger is an acid that can do more harm to the vessel in which it is stored than to anything on which it is poured."
> **Mark Twain**

To dive in a little deeper and discover the root cause of your anger, follow THE PROCESS as written for Negative Emotions on page 321.

TIPS TO MANAGE THE ANGER IN YOUR LIFE

! **Breathe:** as soon as you feel anger taking over your body, close your eyes. Breathe in for six, hold for three, and breathe out for nine, repeat until you feel a sense of calm come over you.

! **Communicate communicate communicate:** if you don't have good communication skills with self and others, misunderstandings can create our symptoms of anger. (Refer to the Communication Tools in the Toolbox at the back of the book.)

! **Think before you speak:** in the heat of the moment, it's easy to say something you'll later regret. Take a few moments and count to 10 slowly to collect your thoughts before saying anything and allow the others involved in the situation to do the same.

! **Express what is creating your anger when you are calm:** as soon as you're thinking clearly, express your frustration in an assertive but non-confrontational way. It is important to say what you need to say in a positive way. State your concerns and needs clearly and directly, without hurting others or trying to control them.

- **Stick with 'I' statements:** avoid criticising or placing blame, as it can only increase tension. For example, instead of saying "you never do any house work", you could say "I'm upset that you left the table without offering to help with the dishes".

- **Identify possible solutions:** instead of focusing on what made you mad, work on resolving the issue at hand. Does your child's messy room drive you crazy? Close the door. Is your partner late for dinner every night? Schedule meals later in the evening, or agree to eat on your own a few times a week. Remind yourself that anger won't fix anything and might only make it worse.

- **Use humour to release tension:** lightening up can help diffuse tension. Avoid sarcasm, though, it can hurt feelings and make things worse.

- **Take a timeout:** timeouts aren't just for kids. Give yourself short breaks during times of the day that tend to be stressful. A few moments of quiet time might help you feel better prepared to handle what's ahead without getting irritated or angry. Please note that it's important to deal with anger in a positive way. If you're feeling angry, you should blow off steam or count to 10 to calm down instead of doing something you'll regret.

- **Get some exercise:** physical activity can help reduce stress that can cause you to become angry. If you feel your anger escalating, go for a brisk walk or run or spend some time doing other enjoyable physical activities.

- **Don't hold a grudge:** if you allow anger and other negative feelings to crowd out positive feelings, you might find yourself swallowed up by your own bitterness or sense of injustice.

Forgiveness is a powerful tool. To gain more clarity, take a look at the Relationship Triangle, number six in the Toolbox at the back of the book.

! **Practise relaxation skills:** practise deep-breathing exercises, listen to relaxing music, practise some yoga, and then journal it out when you can, to get it out of your head. Do whatever suits you that encourages relaxation, the calming of the mind.

! **Know when to ask for help:** if your anger seems out of control, seek help.

! **Journal it out.** (Refer to the Toolbox at the back of the book.)

WHAT DID YOU LEARN?

TAKE ACTION!

What actions are you going to do to release your negative emotion of anger? Make a list.

What action are you going to do TODAY to start your journey towards managing your anger in a positive way?

> I AM IN CONTROL OF MY LIFE AND EMOTIONS.

2. SADNESS

Sadness is feeling sorrow and unhappiness, ranging from mild to extreme, and is usually aroused by the loss of something highly valued.

The challenge here is not to dwell on your sadness, as it can become a roadblock and take over your life and may develop into a depressive

PART FIVE

episode. You need to realise how sadness naturally fits into your life. Sadness can also piggyback onto other emotions:

Anger: (eg, the loss of a loved one or someone who has abandoned you)

Fear: (that we will not be able to move on in life without them)

Joy: (pleasure from the comfort of others when reminiscing about a time spent with a loved one)

SYMPTOMS OF SADNESS

- A persistent low mood
- A loss of pleasure in everyday activities
- Feeling irritable
- Feelings of despair, guilt, worthlessness
- Low self-esteem
- Tearfulness
- Feeling stressed or anxious
- Depressed
- Reduced sex drive
- Less sociable
- Difficulty concentrating

> *"It will never rain roses: when we want to have more roses, we must plant more roses."*
> **George Eliot**

COMMON TRIGGERS OF SADNESS

- Sickness and death of a loved one.
- A loss of identity when life circumstances are changed.
- Being disappointed by an unexpected outcome.
- Endings and goodbyes.
- Rejection by a lover or a friend.

AWARENESS: Identify your sadness as a roadblock

The key here is to check there are no other roadblocks piggy-backing on your sadness.

- What is the main trigger of the sadness you are feeling right now?
- What symptoms of sadness are showing up for you? Make a list.

Breathe
1. Close your eyes. Breathe in for six, hold for three, and breathe out for nine. Repeat until you feel a sense of calm come over you.
2. Allow the answers to the following questions to bubble up.

Event: What's happening/not happening?
If you were to know, why are you experiencing this symptom..........?
Ask the above question again and again using the previous answer from each time you asked the question. Keep asking the question until you find it hard to answer.
Your final answer is, *I am experiencing* (the last answer you gave).......... *because*..........

Response: How did you react?
- Are there any other emotions underlying the emotion of sadness (fear, anxiety, worry, sadness, loss, disappointment, discouragement, hurt, guilt)?
- If so, make a list and go to the appropriate section and keep working on it.
- Are there any other limiting beliefs or decisions showing up for you right now?
- Was it a thought, a feeling or a behaviour?
- Is it internal or external? A limiting decision, an excuse, a habit, an avoidance strategy, etc. If so, make a list.

What did you learn?

Outcome: What is the result of the way you reacted to the event?
For each item on your list answer the following questions:
- How does reacting this way make you feel?
- Was it a physical reaction ie, a headache, an ache, pain or an action you may regret? Or did you just remove yourself from the situation and hold onto the negative emotion internally?
- What is the outcome of feeling this way?

PART FIVE

- Has the outcome become a roadblock?
- If you were to know, what is it stopping you from doing..........?

WHAT DID YOU LEARN?

MOVE AWAY FROM RESISTANCE

- How would your life be if you DIDN'T let go or manage this negative emotion, sadness.
- What would happen if you DID let go or manage this negative emotion?
- Is everything I do getting me closer to my desired outcome, a life I will love living?

Feelings of sadness can be a normal part of life. How you manage these feelings is the key to keep moving forward and living your life.

TIPS TO HELP YOU TO MANAGE SADNESS IN YOUR LIFE

! **Ask the questions** and work out why you are feeling sad. Has your sadness become a roadblock?

! **Stop any negative self-talk** that may be bubbling up. Become aware and work through each one.

! **Journal it out:** not sure where to start? (Refer to the Journal Prompts in the Toolbox at the back of the book.)

! **Do some of the things you love to do:** make a list of go-to activities for when you are feeling a little sad. Listen to music, meditate, exercise, go for a walk, read a book, play with your pet, go for coffee with friends or go see a movie.

! **Take time out to nurture yourself, re-energise and reconnect:** eat well, get your hair done or get a beauty treatment, massage or acupuncture, etc.

- **Accept what is:** if you can't change the situation that has created your sadness, accept it as is, get your learnings. Keep moving forward and change the things you can. One step at a time.

- **Ask for help:** get some help from a counsellor. You may need to just talk it out.

- **Reframe:** flick the switch from negative to positive to see your way through.

- **Check in with your environment:** surround yourself with those who love and support you.

- **Communicate, communicate, and communicate!** Remember the blinker story and communication triangle.

- **Develop an attitude of gratitude.**

- **Create some positive affirmations that will support you.**

TAKE ACTION!

What actions are you going to take to manage your sadness in a positive way? Make a list.

What action are you going to do TODAY to support the changes you need to make?

> MY LIFE IS NOT DEPENDENT UPON CIRCUMSTANCES. I AM STRONG AND I CAN OVERCOME ALL THE CHALLENGES LIFE THROWS AT ME AND SMILE.

 3. FEAR

Fear is an unpleasant emotion caused by the threat of danger, pain or harm.

The challenge here is to understand that fear has its good and bad points and to realise the difference. When you move through fear, a whole new world opens up and you can smile.

The universal trigger for fear is the threat of harm, either real or imagined. This threat can be to our physical, emotional or psychological wellbeing. While there are certain things that trigger fear in most of us, we can learn to become afraid of nearly anything. Embracing the emotion of fear and exploring why it arises can help you prepare yourself proactively and create the tools to tackle challenges instead of being afraid of them.

When I think of fear, I think of this acronym and it becomes a check in point for me when I feel fear creeping into my life:

> **F** – False. Is what you are feeling true?
>
> **E** – Evidence. What evidence do you have to prove that what you are feeling is going to happen?
>
> **A** – Appearing. How does the information/evidence present itself to you?
>
> **R** – Real. Is the evidence/reality of the situation real?

SYMPTOMS OF FEAR

- Increased heart rate
- Faster breathing or shortness of breath
- Dry mouth
- Butterflies or upset stomach
- Sweating and chills
- Trembling muscles
- Limiting beliefs
- Negative emotions

"Underneath your fears lie great opportunities."
Lydia Sweatt

CAUSES OF FEAR

Fear can result from:
- Experiences of trauma
- Negative experiences from the past (either conscious or unconscious)
- Loss of control
- Certain specific objects (spiders, heights, snakes, flying)
- Real environmental dangers
- The unknown

When fear is left unattended/not dealt with it can turn into different types of anxiety/phobias and create major roadblocks.

 AWARENESS: Identify fear as a roadblock
- What symptoms of fear are showing up for you right now? Make a list.
- If you were to know, what is the main trigger of the fear you are feeling right now?

NOW go to page 321, follow THE PROCESS as written for Negative Emotions to dive in a little deeper and discover the root cause of your FEAR.

Once completed, name the fear you have been working on and fill in the following statement.

The fear I have been working on is..........
If the feelings I am feeling around (this fear..........) were true, the worst case scenario is that..........
If (the worst case scenario..........) were to eventuate from my fear, I would feel..........and it would stop me from doing..........
If I released the fear and kept moving through the roadblock (do it anyway) I would be able to..........

And that would make me feel..........
The benefits of releasing this fear would enable me to..........

WHAT DID YOU LEARN?

TIPS TO SUPPORT YOU TO MOVE THROUGH YOUR FEARS
When you feel any symptoms of fear creeping into your body:

! **Take time out** so you can physically calm down because you can't think clearly when in a negative emotional state. Go for a walk, make a cup of tea, have a bath, and breathe.

! **Breathe:** when you feel your heart beating faster, slow it down. Feel the fear and focus on your breath, until you feel a sense of calm come over you.

! **Visualise a happy place:** close your eyes and connect to the feelings that happy place creates for you. Let the positive feelings soothe you until you feel more relaxed.

! **Face your fears and do it anyway:** avoiding your fears can make them scarier the next time you are in a similar situation.

When you can think more clearly
- **Journal it out:** get to the root cause and find clarity around your fear. When you know what you are dealing with, it's easier to let it go or find a strategy to help you move through it.

- **Look at the evidence:** challenge your fearful thoughts. What evidence do you have to prove your fear to be true? Is it real or is it a figment of your imagination? What is the purpose of holding on to this fear?

- **Realise stepping out of your comfort zone is part of your journey:** accept your challenges and keep moving forward.

YOUR GUIDE TO ACTION AND EMPOWERMENT

- **Check in with your supportive environment:** talk about your fears. It always helps to talk as it can dissipate the intensity of the fear and you may find a solution by sharing your concerns.

- **Ask for help:** if your fears don't go away, ask for help before it gets out of hand. Your GP can refer you to the right practitioner to support your needs.

- **Go back to basics and nurture yourself:** sleep well, eat well and exercise.

- **Create positive affirmations to support you.** (Refer to the Toolbox.)

- **Develop an attitude of gratitude** and focus on the positive aspects of your life. (Refer to the Toolbox.)

- **Celebrate every step you make away from fear:** do the things you love.

- **Use your active imagination to visualise a positive outcome.** (Refer to number three, the Active Imagination Exercise in the Toolbox at the back of the book.) What will happen if you are not fearful of your fear anymore?

> "Nothing in life is to be feared, it is only to be understood. Now is the time to understand more, so that we may fear less."
> *Marie Curie*

TAKE ACTION!
Connect to what you will see, hear and feel when you are no longer afraid of said fearful experience.

PART FIVE

- How do you feel about the fear now? Maybe it still exists, or maybe it's gone – well done!

- What action are you going to take next?

- Schedule these tasks in your calendar right now.

- What is the first step you are going to take TODAY to manage your fear?

> I WILL FOLLOW MY HEART TODAY
> AND ENJOY MY LIFE.

4. HURT

Hurt is unhappiness or sadness caused by someone's words or actions.

The challenge here is to know that you are capable of putting this feeling into perspective and understand that feeling hurt is a representation of what you believe to be true.

In every moment, you have a choice – to continue to feel bad or to *start feeling good*. You need to *take responsibility* for your own thoughts and reactions and not put power into the hands of another person. Why would you let a person who hurt you have such power?

If the feelings and emotions connected to the hurt are left unattended, the psychological pain can become intense and significantly affect different areas of your life and become a major roadblock.

SYMPTOMS OF HURT LEFT UNATTENDED
- Deep sorrow
- Panic
- Sadness

YOUR GUIDE TO ACTION AND EMPOWERMENT

- Rage
- Depression
- Shame
- Intense distress
- Worthlessness
- Loneliness and isolation
- Other Limiting beliefs
- Other negative emotions

"Nobody can hurt me without my permission."
Mahatma Gandhi

Are you feeling any symptoms of hurt right now? If so, make a list.

Feeling hurt isn't necessarily a bad thing; it can be a kind of 'wake-up call'. Only YOU know the reasons you are feeling hurt; it's your interpretation of what has happened that makes you feel this way. Feelings of hurt can make us feel miserable and worthless. The best solution is finding out why you are allowing yourself to feel hurt and what is behind the feeling/emotion, dealing with it and being empowered to move on.

Every hurt you experience gives you an opportunity to learn more about yourself. As you learn, you grow, and as you grow, you will make better choices and decisions in the future based on your values, rules, boundaries and personal expectations.

Now go to page 321 and complete the Awareness process through your negative emotions. And journal it out.

TIPS TO RELEASE AND UNDERSTAND YOUR HURT

! **Breathe:** close your eyes. Breathe in for six, hold for three, and breathe out for nine, repeat until you feel a sense of calm come over you. Remove yourself from the situation and take time to calm your emotions and settle your mind.

! **Journal it out (follow 'The Process' on page 321):** get very clear about what exactly happened. Understand what the person said or did and how events transpired.

- **Communicate:** the key is to be open to possibilities and be willing to fully understand the other person's point of view and true intentions. (Refer to the Communication Tools in the Toolbox at the end of the book.)

- **Consider your choices:** make a decision – you have the choice to either forgive and move on, or simply let go of the relationship and distance yourself from the person or people involved as they do not serve you. They may not be aligned with who you are, your values and your belief systems. No matter what you choose to do, it's vital that you accept what has happened, commit and allow your feelings of hurt to subside. Check in with your decision and make sure you are making it for the right reason.

- **Create an attitude of gratitude.** (Refer to the Toolbox.)

- **Create an affirmation:** focus on your strengths. Revisit your strengths list, pick three strengths that relate to your hurt. Repeat your affirmation daily.

- **Smile:** it costs you nothing and brings so much joy.

- **Do what you enjoy:** move, exercise, go for a walk, read a book, or cook.

- **Spend time with those who support you, love you and inspire you.**

- **Live at cause.** (Refer to your Journey Handbook.) Always accept responsibility for your thoughts and actions.

- **Don't take things personally:** it's YOUR interpretation of the event; let it go. And what other people think or say is not your business.

YOUR GUIDE TO ACTION AND EMPOWERMENT

What did you learn?

TAKE ACTION!
What actions are you going to do to release your negative emotion of hurt?
Make a list.
What action are you going to do TODAY to support you on your journey of letting go of hurt?

> I HAVE CONTROL OVER MY THOUGHTS AND WHAT I ALLOW MYSELF TO FOCUS ON.

5. GUILT

Guilt is a feeling of worry or unhappiness that you have because you have done something wrong, or you blame yourself for everything that goes wrong.

"Guilt is like a gauge or light on the dashboard. It means that something is wrong."
Wade Powers

The challenge is to pay attention when the emotion arises and seek to make the changes you need to get your learnings and keep moving forward. Remember you can only do your best at any one point in time, whatever you feel, do or think at that point was influenced by what was happening in that particular situation (your growth, your experience and your outside influences/environment at the time).

When you feel guilty it's your moral compass telling you something is awry. You can't go back and change past behaviours. We can feel this complex emotion not only in relation to ourselves and past behaviours that we wish hadn't happened, but also in relation to how our behaviour impacts those around us in the present.

Don't be too hard on yourself. Understand why you are feeling the way you feel and take the following steps to release your guilt.

PART FIVE

NOW follow THE PROCESS as written for Negative Emotions on page 321 to dive in a little deeper and discover the root cause of your Guilt.

What did you learn?

TIPS TO SUPPORT YOU TO MOVE AWAY FROM FEELING GUILTY

! **Identify your feelings of guilt:** and find out why you feel the way you do. Follow the process.

! **Accept what has happened:** get your learnings and recognise that you might approach it differently in the future.

! **Forgive yourself:** we are not perfect and when we come from a place of self-compassion, we realise that we have the ability to fix our mistakes.

! **Change your self-talk:** looking at it from a different perspective is being able to have a more realistic view, as we tend to make something bigger than it actually is. (Refer to number six, Reality Check, in the Toolbox.)

! **Talk to someone and seek objectivity:** chances are you are being too hard on yourself, a coach or a family friend will give you positive support and keep you accountable.

! **Take action:** accept responsibility if you have wronged someone or something, apologise. Flip your negative thoughts/feelings to positive ones, get your learnings and move on.

! **Develop a positive/growth mindset.** (Refer to your Journey Handbook.)

YOUR GUIDE TO ACTION AND EMPOWERMENT

- ! **Consolidate your learnings:** focus on your strengths. Create positive affirmations around your guilt. (Refer to the Affirmations article in the Toolbox.)

- ! **Focus on the positives in life:** turn the guilt into gratitude and get your positive learnings.

- ! **Ask for help:** if your guilt doesn't go away and is interfering with your everyday activities, ask for help before it becomes a roadblock. Your GP can refer you to the right practitioner to support your needs. Accept that it's totally cool to take care of your own needs.

TAKE ACTION!
- What actions are you going to do to release your negative emotions of guilt? Write a list.
- What can you do right now to feel better about yourself?
- What action can you do TODAY to support your journey away from feeling guilty?

> I GIVE MYSELF THE GIFT OF FORGIVENESS.

THE PROCESS FOR WORKING THROUGH YOUR NEGATIVE EMOTIONS

AWARENESS
Recognise your negative emotion.
The negative emotion I am working on is..........
- Choose a recent event where you experienced this negative emotion.
- In which area of your Life Circle is this event situated?

PART FIVE

- Which symptoms of this negative emotion did you experience in this event?

Event: What's happening/not happening?
- What specifically is the event?
- What specifically is the challenge around this event?
- Why is it a challenge?
- Are there any other emotions underlying the emotion of..........(fear, anxiety, worry, sadness, loss, disappointment, discouragement, hurt, guilt)?
- What specifically was your reaction?
- What did you do?
- Was it a thought, or a behaviour?
- Is it internal or external? A limiting decision, an excuse, a habit, an avoidance strategy, etc.
- How does reacting this way make you feel?
- Was it a physical reaction ie, a headache, an ache, pain or an action you may regret?
- Or did you just remove yourself from the situation and hold onto the negative emotion internally?
- Has the outcome become a roadblock?
- If you were to know, what is it stopping you from doing..........?

> *"Nothing is all good or bad, and that includes people. We are human, and that means we make mistakes. Those are actions, not character traits."*
> **Lesli Doares**

TAKE OWNERSHIP
- Are you blaming others?
- Are you taking responsibility for your choices, your thoughts and your reactions around your symptoms?
- If not, why not?
- Are you living at cause? If not, why not?
- What is it you have to do to take ownership?
- What are you feeling about the event now?

Breathe
- Close your eyes. Breathe in for six, hold for three, and breathe out for nine, repeat until you feel a sense of calm come over you.
- Allow the answers to the following questions to bubble up.

THE TRIGGER: Your reaction
- What part of the challenge triggered a reaction/your negative emotion?
- Specifically, what is the trigger?
- Why are you allowing (the specific trigger)..........to trigger your reactions?
- Ask the above question again and again using the previous answer from each time you asked the question. Keep asking the question until you find it hard to answer.
- When you have reached the last reason you came up with, complete the following statement.

Outcome
I am allowing..........to bother me because..........
- Is my reaction to the trigger at this point at a deeper level; a thought, a feeling, an emotion, a behaviour, a limiting belief/decision etc?

You may find you need to go to the appropriate section that relates to your final answer to completely release or control your negative emotions.

What did you learn?

JOURNAL IT OUT: Let's dive in a little deeper to discover the root cause and find the solution

- What are you feeling now about your negative emotion?
- Is this feeling important to you? If so, why? If not, why?
..........*(The answer to the previous question)..........is important to me because..........*

- Ask the above question again and again using the previous answer from each time you asked the question.
- Keep asking the question until you find it hard to answer.

When you have gone as far as you can go, complete the following statement.

..........*(the answer to your last question)*..........*is important to me because*..........

- So what do you need to bring more of into your life right now? Make a list!

MOVE AWAY FROM RESISTANCE

- How would your life be if you DIDN'T let go or manage this negative emotion?
- What would happen if you DID let go or manage this negative emotion?
- Is everything you do getting you closer to your desired outcome, a life you will love living?

TAKE ACTION!

- Do you need to do or change something right now? If so, what? What do you need to do next? Make a list!

WHAT DID YOU LEARN?

> I AM WORTHY OF LOVE, HAPPINESS AND FULFILMENT. EACH DAY IS FILLED WITH INFINITE POTENTIAL AND POSSIBILITY.

"I have the power within me to create the life I desire. Thoughts become things – choose the good ones."
Mike Dooley

YOUR GUIDE TO ACTION AND EMPOWERMENT

Thoughts

LOW SELF-ESTEEM/ LACKING CONFIDENCE

Low self-esteem is characterised by a lack of confidence, and feeling badly about oneself. People with low self-esteem often feel unlovable, awkward or incompetent. They have a fragile sense of self that can easily be wounded by others. When you are not feeling confident, you surround yourself with limiting beliefs and a lot of negative self-talk. Thus, creating yet another roadblock. Interesting, right?

Your challenge here is to build your confidence around your true authentic self and let go of self-doubt. You are worthy, so be empowered to live your best life because it's your life and no one else can live it for you.

"When you start seeing your worth, you'll find it harder to stay around people who don't."

Unknown

AWARENESS: Identify your symptoms

Signs of low self-esteem are predominantly negative and lead to negative self-talk:
- Being critical of self in a negative way
- Focusing on your failures and ignoring your achievements
- Thinking others are better than you
- You find it difficult to accept compliments
- Thinking you don't deserve to have fun
- Being overly upset by disapproval or criticism
- Feeling sad, depressed, anxious, angry or worthless
- Difficulty speaking up
- Saying I am sorry or feeling guilty for everyday actions
- Not rocking the boat, following along with what others are doing is easier than carving your own path
- Difficulty in making your own choices
- Lack of boundaries
- Negative self-talk

PART FIVE

Create a list of any of the above symptoms that you can identify with at this stage.

Some causes of low self-esteem/self-confidence
Life experiences from birth can play an important part in feeling completely unsure of yourself and worthless.

- **Trauma:** the emotional response/trigger from a terrible event like an accident, rape or natural disaster.

- **Parenting style:** the way we were treated as children, constant belittling, high expectations, or no expectations, nothing was ever good enough and finally the parents may have unresolved issues as well.

- **Bullying and harassment:** from school, work, sport or other environments you engage in.

- **Discrimination:** being on the receiving end of discrimination, culture or sexual.

- **Misinformation:** believing something/standards required that may not be true.

- **Living in an unsupportive environment.**

- **Anxiety, depression.**

- **Any long-term chronic illness,** etc.

Understanding where these negative beliefs/triggers come from can give you an insight into the first step of claiming your confidence back. If you were to know, which of the contributing factors above resonate with you the most?

- Write a list.
- For each item on your list explain specifically what happened, why you think it happened and your reaction to what happened (what did you do?). As below:
  I feel that the life experience that influenced my self-doubt was……….
  Specifically,……….happened.
  I think it happened because……….
  And my reaction was……….

PLEASE NOTE! The most important thing here is to remember that you were doing the best that you possibly could with the knowledge and experience you had at that point in time.

Do not be hard on yourself, it is just a past experience that has memories locked away in your unconscious mind that have created triggers in the present time that can create roadblocks.

WHAT HAVE YOU LEARNT FROM THIS EXERCISE SO FAR?
There are two main areas we need to address in this section:
1. Becoming Aware of the root cause of your limiting beliefs/negative self-talk and
2. Rebuilding your self-confidence. Please note that over time low self-esteem leads to a lack of confidence.

AWARENESS: Becoming aware of the root cause
First, we need to identify where you lack confidence and take ownership. Self-confidence is when you believe in yourself and your abilities, showing certainty in everything you do. When you are not feeling confident is when the negative self-talk can rear its ugly head.

- Are there any areas in your life right now where you don't feel confident?
- If so, what are they? Make a list.
- What specifically is it about each area that leads to your lack of confidence?
- Do you have any negative self-talk in this area? If so, what is it?

PART FIVE

You should end up with a statement something like this for each area in your life where you lack confidence:
The area I lack confidence in is..........
I specifically lack confidence around..........
And my negative self-talk specifically in this area is.........

TAKE OWNERSHIP
- Are you blaming others?
- Are you taking responsibility for your choices, your thoughts and your reactions? If not, why not?

NEGATIVE SELF-TALK
Negative self-talk is the main symptom of low self-esteem and has been seen to feed anxiety and depression if left unaddressed. It can cause an increase in stress levels and lead to decreased motivation as well as greater feelings of helplessness.

Below are seven of the most common negative self-talk phrases that can lead to low self-esteem.

1. No one likes me.

2. No one wants me.

3. No one loves me.

4. I don't do anything right.

5. I'll never be able to..........

6. There is no way it will work.

7. No one bothers to communicate with me.

Do you have any other negative self-talk around your low self-esteem? Make a list of your negative self-talk.

YOUR GUIDE TO ACTION AND EMPOWERMENT

LET'S CHALLENGE YOUR NEGATIVE SELF-TALK

If someone says to me, "No one likes me", I will ask the following questions:
- When did you decide that no one likes you?
- Is this statement true?
- How do you know no one likes you?
- What evidence do you have to support the belief that no one likes you?
- How do you feel when you think no one likes you?

REVIEW: What is the positive feeling opposite to the negative feeling expressed in the last question?

Can you remember a time when you last felt that positive feeling? What were you doing/experiencing at the time?

BREATHE: Close your eyes and breathe in for six, hold for three, and breathe out for nine. Repeat at least five times until you feel a wave of calm come over you.
- Visualise yourself in that experience, embody that positive feeling and understand how good it feels.

Open your eyes and write down what you have learnt about yourself.

RESET: Write a list of 20 positive things that you like about yourself (your smile, your great sense of humour, your skill set, your achievements, etc).

ACTION: Coming back to now is there something you need to do or change to let go of the limiting belief that no one likes you?
- Write a list of the things you need to do or change and how you are going to achieve them.
- What is your new positive statement/belief about yourself?
  I believe..........
- What are you feeling now?
- Create a positive affirmation (refer to the Affirmations article in the Toolbox at the back of the book).

If someone says to me, "No one wants or loves me", I will ask the following questions:
- Is this statement true?

PART FIVE

- When did you decide that no one wants or loves you?
- What makes you feel unloved?

The definition of being loved is a strong affection and concern toward another person and being accepted unconditionally for who you are.
- What specifically does being wanted and loved mean to you?
- What evidence do you need to prove that someone wants and loves you?
- Is this evidence a possibility in your current circumstance?
- If not, what do you need to do or change to feel wanted and loved?
- Why is it important to you to be wanted or loved?
- How does it make you feel when you are wanted and loved? **(I recommend you read *The 5 Love Languages* by Gary Chapman.)**
- Why is that feeling important to you?

Make a list of what you are grateful for in your life right now. All the things you love in your life and why (your cat, your parents, etc).

What have you learnt about yourself?
- What is your new positive statement/belief about being wanted and loved?
  I am……….
- What are you feeling now?
  Create a positive affirmation (refer to the Affirmations article in the Toolbox at the back of the book).

If someone says to me, "I don't/can't do anything right", I will ask the following questions:
- Is this statement true?
- When did you decide that you can't do anything right?
- What is it specifically you don't/can't do right?
- Who said you can't do anything right?
- What evidence do you have that you don't/can't do anything right?
- If you were to know, why can't you do them right?

- Can you do some things right?
  Write a list of at least 20 things you can do right.
- When you do something wrong can you learn how to do it right?
- If not, why not?
- What is it you think you need to do/change so that you can do things right?
- Is this possible?
- How are you going to achieve that?
- What is your new positive statement/belief about yourself?
  I can……….
- What did you learn?
- What are you feeling now?
  Create a positive affirmation (refer to the Affirmations article in the Toolbox at the back of the book).

If someone says to me, "I will never be able to……….", I will ask the following questions:

- Is this statement true?
- When did you decide that you will never be able to……….?
- Who said that you will never be able to……….?
- Is it important for you to be able to……….?
- What is it you need to do so you can do……….
- What is stopping you from being able to do……….?
- What is it you think you need to do/change so that you will be able to do……….?
- Is this possible? If not, why not?
- What do you need to do next?
- How are you going to achieve that?
  Write an "I can" statement if it is important for you to be able to do……….
  ie; *Where there is a will there is a way; I can learn to do……….because it is important to me. I can do anything I put my mind to.*
- What is your new statement/belief about yourself?
  I will be able to……….when……….

- What did you learn?
- What are you feeling now?
  Create a positive affirmation (refer to the Affirmations article in the Toolbox at the back of the book).

If someone says to me, "There is no way it will work", I will ask the following questions:
- Is this statement true?
- When did you decide that it will not work?
- How do you know it won't work?
- What evidence do you have to support the belief that it won't work?
- How do you feel when you believe you can't make it work?
- Do you think if you thought about it differently that you could make it work? If not, why not?
- Why do you think you can't make it work?
- What negative self-talk are you experiencing right now?

If you answered 'yes' to being able to think differently, what do you need to do/change?
- Make a list of what you can do and take action one step at a time.
- How do you feel about taking action?
- How does taking action make you feel?
- What is your positive self-talk now around believing that it can work?
  I believe..........can work because I can..........
  Create a positive affirmation (refer to the Affirmations article in the Toolbox at the back of the book).

Do you have any other negative self-talk around your self-esteem that you could add to this list? If so, write them down and answer the following questions for each one and alter them where appropriate.
- Is this statement true?
- When did you decide that this statement is true?
- What evidence do you have to support the belief that this statement is true?

- What is it you think you need to do/change so that this statement is no longer true?
- Is this possible?
- How are you going to achieve the changes you need to make?
- What is the opposite of this statement?
- What is your new statement/belief about yourself?
- Can you let the negative self-talk go now? If not, why not?
- What would the negative self-talk be if you reframed it into a positive self-talk? (What would your truth statement be?)
- If you believed the positive self-talk was possible, how would that make you feel?
- What are you feeling now?
  Create a positive affirmation (refer to the Affirmations article in the Toolbox at the back of the book).

FLICK THE SWITCH FROM YOUR NEGATIVE SELF-TALK TO POSITIVE SELF-TALK

Negative self-talk	Your truth statement
I can't..........	I can..........
There is no way it will work	I will find a way to do it if it is important to me
No one loves me	I am loved I love myself unconditionally

WHAT DID YOU LEARN FROM THIS EXERCISE?

MOVE AWAY FROM RESISTANCE

- Is everything you do getting you closer to your desired outcome, a life you will love living?
- How would your life be if you believed in yourself and became more confident?

PART FIVE

- What would happen if you did NOT change your negative self-talk, believe in yourself or become more confident?

BECOME MORE SELF-CONFIDENT:
Now let's flick the switch and focus on the unique, incredible you

How to become more self-confident
What you focus on is what you get, right? So, let's change your focus. To be truly confident in yourself you need to understand who you are and what motivates you to do what you do.

- Align yourself to your values. Revisit your core values.
- Connect with your body and listen to what it says (breathe and be mindful).
- Get to know yourself; become your own best friend (go within to find the answers).
- Understand and acknowledge what makes you tick and what makes you feel amazing, inspired, and motivated. Honour yourself and let your light shine.
- Love what you do. When you love what you do your motivation to do it is generally aligned with your values, your needs and your goals. You can become passionate and unstoppable.

5 STEPS TO REIGNITE YOUR SELF-CONFIDENCE

STEP 1: Identify your uniqueness
What you love to do.

- Write a list of all the things you love to do.
- When you look at this list how you do feel?
- Why do you feel this way?
- What motivates you to do the things you love?
- How do you feel when you do the things you love?

YOUR GUIDE TO ACTION AND EMPOWERMENT

- Are you doing the things you love in your life right now? If not, why not?
- Is there any negative self-talk around you doing the things you love? If so, what is it?
- Is there something you need to change so that you can do the things you love?
- Write a list.

Write a positive truth statement about each thing you love to do.
I love doing..........because it makes me feel..........

> *"Once you embrace your value, talents and strengths, it neutralises when others think less of you."*
> *Rob Liano*

Write an affirmation around what you feel when doing what you love (refer to the Affirmations article in the Toolbox).
For example: *I am strong, creative and my life is filled with happiness when I do the things I love.*

YOUR ACHIEVEMENTS

- Write a list of all that you have achieved in your life so far (at least fifty).
- When you look at this list how you do feel?
- Why do you feel this way?
- What motivated you to do the things you have achieved in your life? Write a list.
- What have you learnt about life and yourself from each thing you have achieved?
- Make a list of your learnings.
- Is there any negative self-talk around anything you have achieved in your life? If so, what is it?

Now I want you to write a list of what/who you are grateful for around your achievements.
ie; *I am now on the other side of my divorce and I am really grateful*

for my ex-partner as I now realise how strong I really am and what is important to me in my life.

Now I want you to write a positive truth statement around your major achievements and what you are grateful for for each one.
For example: *I achieved my Diploma of Education and Diploma of Visual Arts and I am grateful for the knowledge I have because I became a teacher not only of art; the skills I developed have extended into other areas of my life as well.*

Write an affirmation that acknowledges your achievements and represents where you are now or where you want to be. (Refer to the Affirmations article in the Toolbox at the back of the book).
For example: *I am a teacher and I am passionate about helping others to live a life they can love.*

YOUR SKILL BASE
- Write a list of all the skills you have developed and learnt in your life so far, (aim for 50) dig deep you may be surprised. It would be good if you wrote your skill base for each area of your Life Circle.
- When you look at this list how you do feel?
- What did you learn?
- Is there any negative self-talk around your list of skills in a certain area of your Life Circle? If so, what is it?
- Is there anything you need to learn to support you on your journey to being confident and the best you can possibly be?
- Make a list.

Write a positive truth statement around your skill base.
For example: *I have skills and am willing to learn new skills to support me on my life's journey to live my best life.*

YOUR GUIDE TO ACTION AND EMPOWERMENT

Write a positive affirmation around your skill base.

For example: *Each and every day my skills are improving.*

YOUR MOTIVATIONS AND INSPIRATIONS

Sometimes when we are in the doom and gloom of our emotions we find it difficult to focus on the positives. The aim here is to create some lists, etc to remind you of the good stuff.

- Be clear about what you want to achieve in your life? Make a list.
- Create a bucket list. Things you would love to do in your life.
- Create U C A N B S M A R T goals. The pathway to achieving what you want, the light at the end of the tunnel.
- Create a list of people who inspire you and why?
- Read some motivational autobiographies.
- Make a list of what motivates you. Use the Active Imagination Exercise (refer to the Toolbox at the back of the book).

Use the Active Imagination Exercise in the Toolbox to get in touch with the last time you were highly motivated. What did you see, hear and feel at the time?

STEP 2: Print out your positive truth statements and your affirmations

Pin them where you can see them easily. Read them out loud and repeat three times a day. (For more information on affirmations, refer to the Toolbox.)

STEP 3: Write a letter to yourself

Write a letter to yourself acknowledging and celebrating your unique abilities, what you have achieved, what you love to do and why. What motivates and inspires you and what you hope to achieve in the next 6 months.

Put it in an envelope and address it to yourself and put the date on it six months into the future when you can open it. Place it in a safe place (on the fridge, stapled into your diary on the date you can open it or give it to a friend who can give it to you in 6 months' time, etc).

PART FIVE

STEP 4: Mirror Mirror

Stand in front of a mirror daily and have a positive conversation with yourself.

- Look into your eyes and start by saying I love you three times; it may seem a little awkward at first and that's okay. As your confidence builds you will start to relax.
- Next, while still looking into your eyes, state three things you are grateful for and how each one makes you feel. (Refer to the Attitude of Gratitude article in the Toolbox.)
- And then finish off by saying your affirmations out loud. Enjoy.

What did you learn about yourself from Steps 1, 2, 3 and 4?

STEP 5: Check in

There are times when you might feel a little nervous and a little self-doubt may creep into your mindset, you may be starting a new job, going on a first date, your first time at a networking event/club or interest group, whatever you are feeling at that moment is normal.

This is the time to check in, breathe and take that step into the unknown. Become aware of why you feel the way you do and let go of that negative self-talk/negative belief.

BREATHE

- Find a quiet space, breathe in for six, hold for three, and breathe out for nine. Repeat at least five times until you feel a wave of calm come over you.
- Allow your thoughts to bubble up.
- Determine the event where your lack of confidence has been triggered.
- Ask yourself why you are feeling a lack of confidence around.......... (this new event)?
  I am feeling.........because.........
- Why is..........(the answer to the previous question) important to me?
  It is important to me because..........

- Then continue to ask the question above about the answer to the previous question until you find it hard to answer.
- What is stopping you from feeling confident in this situation now?

Now, Flick the Switch
How would you feel if you were confident in this situation?

Breathe in, close your eyes and imagine yourself in the event. Realise the importance of being confident and successful in the event and how that would feel.

Just be in that moment for a while and indulge in those positive feelings. Embody and really connect to what you are seeing, hearing and feeling.

Open your eyes and ask yourself how good did that feel?
Is there any negative self-talk or have you let it go?
What is your new positive self-talk around this event? Make a list.

PLEASE NOTE! Some other roadblocks may rear their ugly heads. Is there anything else coming up for you right now? For example, negative self-talk, limiting decisions, avoidance strategies etc. Work through it now. Go to the appropriate page and let it go.

TIPS TO SUPPORT YOU IN BECOMING MORE CONFIDENT

! **Check in** on a regular basis and become aware of when your negative self-talk appears and what triggers it. Discover the root cause and ask why you feel the way you do.

  ! **Connect with who you are and be aware:** understand what makes you tick and what makes you feel amazing, inspired, and motivated to be the best you can be. Honour yourself and become your own best friend.

  ! **Surround yourself with positive people:** these are people who are like-minded, support you to be the best version of yourself, make you feel good and who you enjoy being around.

PART FIVE

Be inspired by others and choose role models who have the same values.

! **Communicate:** you need to have the freedom to be able to communicate well with others. You need to say what you need to communicate and understand other's points of view (refer to the Communication Tools in the Toolbox at the back of the book). Avoid demanding and abusive people. Learn to say no and be assertive.

! **Don't compare yourself to others:** there is no one else on this earth that can be you. Celebrate your uniqueness and allow your light to shine. You were born with potential, goodness, trust, ideas and dreams. Learn to love who you are. You are the only one in charge of you. What anybody else says or thinks is not your business.

! **Practise positive affirmations:** when we practise positive, self-orientated affirmations, we sow seeds of positivity into our lives. We are verbalising and visualising the person we know we are or can be.

! **Take care of yourself:** look after yourself, practise mindfulness, breathe, eat and drink well, keep your body hydrated, exercise, and love the life you live; you only get one chance at it. Make it a habit to treat yourself well every day and celebrate all your achievements. Don't forget, as your happiness is your priority.

! **Accept compliments:** breathe in, say thank you, and smile. Allow yourself to feel the feeling you get from the compliment and understand that they would not have said it unless they meant it.

! **Acknowledge that you can change if you need to:** it takes work, and it's worthwhile. Once you have taken that first step,

YOUR GUIDE TO ACTION AND EMPOWERMENT

you can't go back. Commit, believe you can, and nothing can stop you. Get excited.

! **REMEMBER:** one step at a time.

! **Ask for help:** if you are having any trouble at all with these exercises, ask for help. Generally, there is someone else out there who has experienced what you have. Make sure you ask advice from someone who is aligned with your values and you feel comfortable with.

Now I want you to write a positive "I am" statement about who you are. *My name is..........I am..........*

WHAT DID YOU LEARN FROM THIS SECTION?
What actions are you going to do today to start building your self-esteem and confidence?

"You are braver than you believe, stronger than you seem, and smarter than you think."
Christopher Robin

LIMITING BELIEFS/DECISIONS

Limiting beliefs/limiting decisions are always negative. They are something you believe to be true about yourself or the world you live in that limits you in some way. Limiting beliefs are often about ourselves and our self-identity but may also be about other people and the world in general.

The challenge here is to realise that it's a CHOICE to let go of your limiting belief, become aware of what your triggers are, flick the switch

"Everybody is a genius. But if you judge a fish by its ability to climb a tree, it will live its whole life believing that it is stupid."
Albert Einstein

PART FIVE

from negative to positive and develop a positive/growth mindset.

When it comes to building an incredible life, there is no limit to what you can do. The only thing keeping you from reaching your full potential is a lack of self-belief.

Our limiting beliefs/decisions are often fear-driven and can provide us with a safe haven. If left unattended the results of thinking this way can develop into negative behaviours, bad habits, ill-health and eventually major roadblocks.

When someone says, "I can't", I ask what it is they don't want to do, see or believe. You see, it's a choice. When you feel a limiting belief appear, think about what you are saying to yourself.

HERE ARE SOME EXAMPLES OF LIMITING BELIEFS:

A self-judgement limiting belief appears as an "I can't", "I don't", or "I am" statement. Beliefs driven by values, laws and rules appear as, "I mustn't" statements.

I can't	I'm not educated enough
I can't handle failure	I'm not confident enough to do this
I can't swim	I'm not ready yet
I can't dance	I'm not creative enough
I don't	I'm too old to start
I don't have enough experience	I'm not talented enough
I don't believe I can do it	I'm not educated enough
I don't have a choice	I'm not destined to succeed
I don't have enough time	I'm not smart enough
I'm not good with money	I am not good enough

When your beliefs are based on the judgement of others, realise that you are not them and you have not walked in their shoes.
- I believe others are more superior/capable than I am.
- Nobody believes in me.
- I come from a poor background.

Can you relate to any of the above limiting beliefs/decisions? If so, make a list.

- In which area of your Life Circle are each of these limiting beliefs being triggered?
- Put your limiting beliefs in the table below.

Limiting belief/ decision	Life Circle section	Is it an excuse?	What is it stopping you from doing?
I can't handle failure	Career	yes	It is stopping me from achieving the desired outcome Success Promotion
I'm not ready yet	Personal relationships	yes	Being happy in a personal relationship

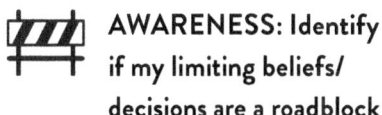 **AWARENESS: Identify if my limiting beliefs/ decisions are a roadblock**

"More than anything else I believe it's our decisions, not the conditions of our lives, that determine our destiny."

Tony Robbins

Event: Identify your roadblock

Choose a limiting belief from your list and ask the following questions.
The limiting belief I am working on is.................

- In which area of your Life Circle is this limiting belief triggered?
- When did you decide that your limiting belief is true?
- What is this limiting belief stopping you from doing?
- If you were to know, what specifically is this limiting belief stopping you from doing?
- Why are you allowing it to stop you from...........? (doing it?)
- What evidence do you have that would prove your limiting belief to be true?

PART FIVE

Outcome: What's happening/not happening?
- What specifically is the challenge in this situation?
- Why is it a challenge?
- What part of the challenge triggered your limiting belief/reaction?
- How specifically did you react?
- Was it a thought, an emotion or a behaviour?
- What specifically did you do?
- Has the outcome of this belief become a roadblock?
- What are you feeling about the situation now?
- How important is it for you to achieve your desired outcome.

TAKE OWNERSHIP
- Why are you allowing this limiting belief to take control of your actions?
- Are you blaming others?
- Are you taking responsibility for your choices, your thoughts and your reactions around this limiting belief? If not, why not?
- What would happen if you took responsibility for your choices, your thoughts and your reactions around this situation?
- What could you do differently?
- What have you learnt so far about your limiting belief?

MOVE AWAY FROM RESISTANCE
- Is everything I do getting me closer to my desired outcome, a life I will love living?
- How would your life be if you DIDN'T let go of your limiting beliefs?
- What would happen if you DID let go of your limiting beliefs?
- Write a list of at least 20 things you could achieve if your limiting belief did not exist.
- Now let's dive in a little deeper: discover the root cause.

JOURNAL IT OUT: Let's dive in a little deeper

Breathe

1. Close your eyes. Breathe in for six, hold for three, and breathe out for nine, repeat until you feel a sense of calm come over you.
2. Allow the answers to your questions to bubble up.
   - If you were to know, what specifically triggered your limiting belief?

     Now close your eyes and go back as far as you can into your past, go to the very first time you ever experienced your limiting decision.
   - What happened?
   - How specifically did you react?
   - What is the first thing you did?
   - What happened next?
   - What did you learn from this experience at that time around your limiting belief?

     Come back now to the present moment.
   - How do you feel about your limiting belief/decision now?
   - Why are you still allowing this trigger to bother you and create this limiting belief/reaction now?
   - Write down the answer: *I am still allowing it to bother me because……….*
   - Ask the question again and again relating to the answer to the previous question. Keep asking the question until you find it hard to answer.
   - What is the last answer you came to when you realised you could not go any further? You may find you end up with a positive and find clarity around what you really, really want. Well done!
     I am allowing it to bother me because……….
   - What are you feeling now?

DISCOVER THE ROOT CAUSE: Find the solution

- Is this feeling important to you? If so, why?
  The answer to the previous question is important to me because……….

PART FIVE

- Ask the question again and again relating to the answer of the previous question.
- Keep asking the question until you find it hard to answer.
- What did you learn?

REFRAME: FLIP FROM NEGATIVE TO POSITIVE

Limiting belief	Positive thinking to solution
I am not good enough	I can achieve anything I put my mind to
I am too old to start	I am never too old to follow my dreams
I can't do it	I can do it

Complete the following statement:
My positive belief around what I need to achieve is………..in the………..area of my Life Circle. And I am going to achieve it by taking the following actions………..

The good thing about limiting beliefs is that you have the power to change them at any time. This doesn't mean that doing so will be an easy process, but commitment and a greater level of self-awareness can make it possible. Don't forget to ask for help if you need it.

TIPS TO SUPPORT YOU IN LETTING GO OF YOUR LIMITING BELIEFS

! **Stop, Think and Flick the Switch.** Become aware of:
   a. What the little voice in your head is saying.
   b. What triggers your reactions?
   c. How you react when your feelings, emotions and behaviours are triggered.

! **Journal it out** and ask the right questions.

! **Create positive affirmations** and repeat them at least three times a day. (Refer to Affirmations in the Toolbox.)

- **Develop an attitude of gratitude**. (Refer to the article in the Toolbox.)

- **Create a positive routine** that supports the changes you want to make.

- **Meditate.** Find a way to relax and become more mindful.

- **Find a positive environment** that supports you, that you know loves and accepts you for who you are.

- **Acknowledge your achievements:** remind yourself of the evidence. Can you remember a time when you were the opposite of your limiting belief? Give yourself examples of when you have been good enough and things were more positive in your life.

WHAT DID YOU LEARN?
- How do you feel about your limiting beliefs now?
- What did you learn about your limiting beliefs?
- What did you learn about yourself?

TAKE ACTION!
- So, what do you need to do to bring more of what you want into your life around your limiting beliefs?
- Do you need to do or change something right now?
- What are you going to do today to help you overcome your limiting belief?
- What are you going to do in the future to help you overcome your limiting belief?

> I AM FEELING POSITIVE,
> HEALTHY AND STRONG TODAY.

> *It does not matter how slowly you go so long as you do not stop.*
> **Confucius**

You close the handbook, close your eyes, breathe in for six, hold for three and breathe out for nine, until a state of calm completely washes over you. You sit for a while with the realisation that you now have a 'go-to book' that will guide you and support you in discovering your true authentic self, a self you can love, honour and accept.

Now you can take the steering wheel of your life and become empowered to live your best life, a life you can love knowing you have the tools to make a difference in the way you think and progress through any challenge that comes your way.

You take a deep breath, open your eyes, get up and stretch and decide to take some time out to just BE.

You smile and decide to go to the beach for a walk. You feel the sand between your toes and smell the fresh salt air, with a gentle sea breeze blowing your hair across your face.

You straighten up, feeling even more confident than you have ever felt before; you feel at peace, but at the same time excited.

You have reached this point and it feels great. You know there will be more challenges to come. That's life, let's face it.

Then a tiny thought pops into your conscious mind: How can I maintain this amazing feeling forever? I just love feeling this way.

You didn't get to read that last chapter did you, what was it called? MAINTENANCE.

That's right, *you smile,* the last chapter can be for another day.

PART SIX

MAINTENANCE: THE JOURNEY CONTINUES

"

Not I, not anyone else can travel that road for you.
You must travel it by yourself. It is not far. It is within reach.
Perhaps you have been on it since you were born, and did
not know. Perhaps it is everywhere – on water and land.

Walt Whitman

"

PART SIX

The purpose of this final chapter is twofold: firstly, to celebrate everything that you have achieved on this journey so far, while looking back with gratitude and understanding for who you were before. Secondly, to realise that you are now in the driver's seat, empowered to live your best life. When a roadblock has been triggered around life's challenges (and they will be), you know that you need to pause and focus on some maintenance.

Maintenance

Maintenance is about preserving a specific state or situation, checking how it is functioning and working to repair any issues so the situation can function at its best. You can do this on your journey. Take a deep breath and realise you now have the tools to draw upon to keep moving forward. There will always be another challenge around the corner; that's life.

We crave growth. The destination matters and the journey makes it all worthwhile. So don't be hard on yourself. You need to maintain the resilience you have achieved and trust you have the tools to navigate any roadblock that comes your way.

Whatever has happened in the past stays in the past; you can't go back. Keep moving forward with this new knowledge of yourself, and what you need to do to maintain your life balance. While change can be confronting, it can also bring new and incredible experiences, insights and opportunities into your life.

You know how to do it and what questions to ask, and the more you practise the strategy, the more trust you will develop in your unconscious mind.

You will find the solutions more quickly and easily, and that's when you'll know you are truly connected to who you are and who you want to be. Allow yourself to be authentically you – be happy and grow your resilience, one step at a time.

My journey continues

My mantra throughout my journey has been:

> "Stop, Think and Flick the Switch!"
> And then I ask myself:
>
> "Who's driving your bus?"

I use these two sentences over and over again with my clients, students and myself, and they always lead me to the answers when I need to get back on track.

My lessons from the pandemic

> *"Character cannot be developed in ease and quiet. Only through experience of trial and suffering can the soul be strengthened, ambition inspired, and success achieved."*
> **Helen Keller**

These words remind us that the journey itself becomes the focal point of our lessons in life; it is the innumerable resources gained along the way, which renders the goal far more rewarding in the end.

And so it was that COVID-19 put me in a place I didn't want to be in 2020. My resistance to it was challenging me in a way I couldn't believe, catching me completely by surprise.

I had done so much work on myself that I thought I was managing quite well – when suddenly, boom! The 'doom and gloom' switch appeared in my life again.

The pandemic presented itself and my life seemed to be super challenged all at once, not just for me but seemingly for everyone in the whole world.

My health, my aged father and the stressors that appeared with no warning at all meant I was having trouble maintaining my energy, my momentum, my positivity and my health at that point. I was shocked to realise my depression was creeping back! It was as if I had gone right back to the time when I had depression, sitting on that couch and feeling miserable.

Back then, I didn't know what to do to help myself so I didn't do anything, at least until I experienced my 'enough is enough' moment and found the courage to look for a better way to enjoy my life and develop the tools to stop taking antidepressants.

I thought I had done enough work that new challenges wouldn't be as hard anymore, but life is an ever-evolving journey. You never know what's around the corner. I knew what I needed to do to maintain my energy and happiness in life, however I wasn't able to because lockdown restrictions kept me away from the things that made me happy and fulfilled.

In 2020, I lost myself as well as my business. I was not well. I needed an operation. I couldn't get out to do the things that make me happy. I was challenged in every aspect; I couldn't create my happy spot that is the source of my good mental health and my best life.

I was lying in bed at 3 am one morning, unable to sleep. I was wrestling with writer's block on how to complete this book. I thought to myself at this point it would be so easy to just let go, give up and not pursue the things I love to do.

I thought hard and long on the outcome that would eventuate from this decision, and again I decided that if I let go of doing the things I love to do, I would not be happy.

After recovery from my operation and more tests, I started to feel better. I started asking myself the right questions and delving in a little deeper and I was back on track. Yay!

Oh no! In 2021 during the editing of this book, more major challenges reared their ugly heads: my dad's health, my breast cancer diagnosis and the need for surgery on my back. The cancer prognosis was good as we caught it early and the back op (which happened in 2022, delayed due to COVID-19) has relieved the constant pain I was having in my lower back and legs. All is going well.

My biggest learnings from all this were that I was not nurturing and loving myself enough through these challenges, I was not listening to my

MAINTENANCE: THE JOURNEY CONTINUES

body, and my self-care had gone into survival mode. You see, I have always been there for others – my family, my dad, my friends, my clients – but I was not there for myself.

What would happen if I *didn't* do the things I needed to do and live a life I could love to my fullest potential?

I had all the tools, and I knew they worked. So, how was I going to get out of this and maintain what I had come to cherish?

I needed to go deeper again. I undertook the very process of this book once again and started on the journey to create a plan around what I needed to live a balanced life, fully understanding the principles of loving, appreciating and accepting myself for who I am, so that I could be the best version of myself.

My plan included a daily routine, a structure that would support me to create the new habits I needed to cement into my life, along with my need to do what makes me happy and fulfilled.

I needed to:
- Reconnect through mindful practices and meditation, get back to my attitude of gratitude and work on my positive affirmation daily practice.
- Make time to plan out my week, including a healthy diet and exercise program.
- Do what makes me happy with my business, my environment (I need like-minded people in my life to support, stimulate and inspire me and accept me for who I am).
- Take time out and have fun.

And so my journey continues.

> *"When you finally uncover those beliefs that keep you shackled to an ineffective pattern you give yourself permission to be Free!!"*
> **Sue Krebs**

No matter what happens in your life (negative experiences, trauma, cancer, viruses, relationship/marriage breakups, job loss or natural disasters), every life challenge requires you to dig deep. While change can be confronting, change can also bring new and incredible experiences, insights and opportunities into your life. The real challenge is to keep moving forward, stay positive and stay connected to who you truly are.

Your journey continues

Often, we need some help to stay in the driver's seat and stay on track and that's okay. Maintenance is the key. We were not made to function alone, after all.

"No man is an island"

I remember at a high school assembly some years ago, the school principal gave a talk about this statement. As human beings, we need the company of others to maintain a normal healthy mental state; no one is truly self-sufficient. We need to be able to communicate, collaborate and have healthy and positive relationships in our lives.

One of my biggest challenges through life was to understand that I could ask for help. I was an only child, coming from a socially isolated farming family. This meant that understanding what real friendship was, how to read a social situation, how to trust others and learning the purpose of a supportive environment was beyond me. I was so naive.

As an only child, I had learnt to be fairly self-sufficient, and when I stepped into the big wide world, a social situation or a confrontation, the easiest way for me to deal with this was to NOT deal with it. I guess that's why my book has so many questions – because when I started asking and answering questions, I did it to truly find out who I was and what made me happy. I learnt to do what I enjoyed doing. I learnt so much about myself. On my journey, one of my biggest challenges was taking responsibility for the choices I made and understanding that I always had a choice.

MAINTENANCE: THE JOURNEY CONTINUES

It was not until I decided that enough was enough that I really started my journey to fulfilment. I am not the person I used to be. Now I can allow myself to enjoy my life and I actively choose to be happy. Admittedly, it's tricky sometimes, so that's when I use the tools. I just go a little deeper, and each time it gets easier. The more I trust my unconscious mind, the quicker the solution comes to me. I trust the tools, and the process leads to clarity, accomplishment and empowerment every time.

It's important to check in regularly with yourself about your destination and if you're on track to getting there.

Sometimes we think that things are okay and we say everything's fine, but then small subtle feelings (like our intuition) make us wonder if our life could in fact be better. We could be suffering physically or emotionally and are just not on track to achieving what we want. Be open to changing your mind, your behaviour and your thoughts and listen to what your body is telling you.

A question I should not need to ask is: How do you know when you need to do some maintenance and repair – what's not working?

You may be presenting some of the following symptoms when you regularly check in with yourself, which would indicate that you may be off track or out of balance. Make a list of the symptoms that you can identify with.

- Frustration
- Unhappiness
- Restlessness
- Discontentment
- Feeling overwhelmed
- Sleepless nights
- Stressed
- Depressed
- Confused
- Exhaustion
- Low mood
- Feeling out of control
- Not feeling fulfilled
- Not getting the same results
- Vagueness
- Angry
- Scared

Remember the purpose of maintenance is to:
A) REPAIR WHAT'S NOT WORKING

It's okay to not be okay. Give yourself permission to give in to your emotions

PART SIX

and know that it's okay to give yourself a break. Trust in your ability to heal and celebrate your failures; they hold the lessons you need to learn.

As the wonderful Oprah Winfrey said, "Think like a queen. A queen is not afraid to fail. Failure is another step to greatness." When terrible things happen, there is a lesson to be learnt. Have faith in the fact that, thanks to the experience, you will be better equipped to deal with whatever life throws at you next.

B) LET GO OF THAT WHICH DOES NOT SERVE YOU

Limiting decisions, negative emotions, environmental situations, people, at each point when something just does not feel right, ask the question, "Is this action or person aligned with my values, my goals and where I want to be?" If the answer is no, let go of that which does not serve you, discover the root cause and keep moving forward.

Once you have identified the symptoms, it's time to move through the four pillars of maintenance to empowerment, and refocus on living your best life to your fullest potential when YOU are in the driver's seat of your life.

The four pillars to empowerment and driving your bus

The four pillars to remember and check in with when you are ready to do some maintenance, and repair what is not working are:

FOUNDATION   MINDSET   FLOW   RECHARGE

Pillar 1: Check in with your foundation

The Rule: Find your balance and create a strong foundation.

Belief: A strong personal foundation helps to guide your choices around everything you do. Live a life true to your authentic self.

Revisit: Check in, review your Life Circle and discover what's working and what is not.

MAINTENANCE: THE JOURNEY CONTINUES

> *"Balance is not something you find, it's something you create."*
> **Jana Kingsford**

Your foundation is the first place to check in with when some maintenance is due.

For the purpose of this book, your personal foundation represents your beliefs around how you want to live your life – your values and the rules you live by. Without a strong inner foundation, it's easy to bend and break under pressure. Taking the time to build a strong foundation and doing the inner work to find out who you truly are will create a structural base to support your choices around everything you do, which indirectly affects your personal outcome of living an exceptional, vibrant, happy and authentic life.

A strong inner foundation takes into account:
- Your relationships and the environment that supports you, that makes you feel secure and supported.
- Your mindset and the quality of your positive thoughts around growth and success in life.
- Your values, what is important to you and the rules you live by.
- Your habits and daily routines that support you and keep you on track.
- Your strengths, doing what you love and are naturally good at; your flow.

Hopefully by now you have stopped making excuses; you are learning to take responsibility and are driving your own bus to success and happiness. With a strong foundation, you are in control, empowered to live a life you can love.

Firstly, if something is not working, you are probably out of balance and your personal foundation is off track.

In practical terms, this means revisiting your Life Circle.

When you first workshopped your Life Circle, it was to identify what was not right in your life and where your strengths and weaknesses appeared. Now as you have worked through the book, the map on your Life Circle will have changed.

PART SIX

 Redo your Life Circle on page 20 or a print out is available in the Bonus Content. Answer the questions and compare this with the first one. You may be surprised at how far you have come in certain areas, which is a cause to celebrate!

After you have checked in with your Life Circle map, get specific and ask the following questions:
- Where are you at this point in time?
- What's working?
- What's not working?
- In which area of your Life Circle is your challenge coming from?
- If you were to know, what has triggered the challenge?
- Is your challenge a potential roadblock?

What did you learn?

Secondly, check in with the principles of the U.C.A.N.B.S.M.A.R.T. goals (Part 3) **then revisit your** U.C.A.N.B.S.M.A.R.T. **goal and answer the following questions:**
- Is your challenge (what's not working) aligned with what you want?
- Is your goal and what you are doing aligned with your values?
- Are you committed and taking action by sticking to the habits/daily routines, etc that support you and keep you on track?
- Is a part of what you are doing aligned with your strengths, what you are naturally good at and what you love to do?
- Do you have a supportive environment and relationships, both with work and home, that make you feel supported and secure? If not, why not?
- Are you giving yourself space and time out to review, research, reset and become self-aware of what is and isn't working and celebrate your achievements? If not, why not?

What did you learn?

Pillar 2: Check in on your mindset

The Rule: Stay positive; become resilient, hopeful, optimistic, courageous and kind.

Belief: The right mindset attracts positive circumstances.

Practice: An attitude of gratitude, positive self-talk, set boundaries, and believe in yourself. Practice visualisation and meditate.

Develop a positive mindset, remain optimistic and see opportunities around every corner. Feeling positive can put you in a state of happiness, excitement and enthusiasm, thus creating the motivation you need to keep taking the actions you require to achieve what you want.

Are you maintaining a positive/growth mindset? If not, why not?
What is your biggest challenge around mindset?

You may ask how you can maintain a positive mindset.

10 TIPS TO SUPPORT YOUR POSITIVE ENVIRONMENT

1. **Check your environment**

When re-evaluating our lives and changing our behaviours, we need support. Check in with your environment to make sure that it is supporting you to do what you need to do, what you love to do and what makes you happy.

We tend to get caught up in our busy lives, and sometimes we forget to actually connect with other people. Organise regular catch-ups with people who are likeminded, people who enjoy the same things you enjoy and people who love, support and inspire you to move forward in your life.

> *"Magic is believing in yourself. If you can make that happen, you can make anything happen."*
> **Johann Wolfgang von Goethe**

Make a list of all the people who are supportive in your life right now.

2. **Believe you can**

Believe in yourself, give yourself a break, and you will get there. Make sure your why is big enough and believe that you can achieve anything you want. My mother used to say, "Where there is a will, there is a way." If you want it bad enough, you will find a way to achieve it. Know you have what it takes to respond, grow and change. Keep an open mind, be flexible and strongly believe that you have the ability to adapt moving forward.

3. **Be Grateful.** Develop an Attitude of Gratitude.

The Rule: Write down 3 to 5 "I am grateful" statements before you go to sleep. It puts you in a positive mindset before you close your eyes.

Develop an attitude of gratitude, raise your energy and start to see your life in a positive light. It's about flicking the switch to what's important and positive in your life, being flexible and being open to endless opportunities.

Feeling lucky is a positive, and feeling positive can put you in a state of happiness, excitement and enthusiasm, thus creating the motivation you need to keep taking the actions you need to, to achieve what you want.

Most importantly, to get even more from your gratitude statement you need to connect to the feelings experienced while in a state of gratitude.

I am grateful for ....
because it makes me feel ....

Example 1: I am grateful for my mum and all she does for me because she makes me feel loved. (And when you feel loved, how do you feel?)

Example 2: I am grateful for the birds that visit our birdbath because I am in awe of the magic of nature, their songs and the colour of their feathers. It makes me feel lucky to be able to enjoy their existence.

When you develop an attitude of gratitude around a positive mindset, you remain optimistic and see opportunities around every corner.

4. **Set a daily intention.** Check in with the Power of Intention in the Toolbox at the back of the book.

The power of intention means deliberately thinking thoughts NOW about what you want in the future. What you focus on is what you get, right.

For example, a wellness intention that supports your physical wellbeing can be, "I intend to move my body today in ways that will bring me joy."

An example of an intention at work could be, "Today I am going to make time to organise and prioritise my weekly tasks so I can be more efficient and achieve my weekly goals."

5. **Set boundaries**

A boundary is a limit between you and another person. The purpose of setting healthy boundaries is, of course, to protect and take good care of yourself. They signify a limit or a point that establishes what you will tolerate or expect, particularly about how you let people treat you. Honouring your personal boundaries is more than an act of self-care – it is a fundamental practice that supports you.

Often, our boundaries are related to our values in a specific area of our life. Here are four steps to setting better boundaries in your personal and work relationships that will allow you to communicate your needs:

- Define – identify the desired boundary.
- Communicate – say what you need to.
- Stay simple – don't over explain.
- Set consequences – say why it's important.

If you are a people pleaser as I was, my boundaries were weak and they created a lot of angst and frustration and I ran myself into the ground. I wasn't fully comprehending what was happening, but then I learnt my lesson. Your boundaries can be different in different areas of your Life Circle, so be aware.

6. **Let go of that which doesn't serve you**

At each point when something just does not feel right, ask the question: "Is this thought, action or person aligned with my values, my goals and where

 PART SIX

I want to be?" If the answer is no, let go of that which does not serve you.

Stop, Think and Flick the Switch; stay positive and keep moving forward.

Surround yourself with positive, like-minded people.

7. Be aware of your self-talk

Become aware of what that little itty bitty shitty committee is saying to you, that voice in your head. Flip from negative self-talk to positive self-talk.

Notice the difference between the intention of your intuition and that negative voice in your head.

8. Take time out

We can get caught up in the busyness of our daily activities. Take time out, have some fun and stay connected to your true authentic self. Meditate, be mindful, find that space and allow yourself to just be.

9. Ask for help

It's okay to ask for help. Remember that whatever comes up is not a problem, it's a challenge. Realise all possible solutions to this challenge. If you don't know how to do it, ask someone who does know how. This might be a friend, a mentor, a coach, or a specialist in the field.

10. Celebrate

Acknowledge and celebrate your strengths and what you have achieved at each step along the way.

> "Belief in oneself and knowing who you are, I mean, that's the foundation of everything great."
> *Jay-Z*

Pillar 3: Flow

The Rule: Rediscover your flow. Make finding your flow a priority as often as possible. Celebrate your achievements and acknowledge your skills. Do the things you love and allow yourself to be completely immersed in a feeling of energised focus, peace and creativity.

As our lives are journeys, we need to allow ourselves to get excited and find our flow. In other words, what floats your boat? In positive psychology, a flow state is known as "being in the zone". It is a mental state in which a person performing an activity is fully immersed in a feeling of energised focus, full involvement and enjoyment in the process. Or it can just be a feeling of being in the right place at the right time, doing the right thing.

Who doesn't love being in the zone?

For some people, it takes effort to recognise this state for what it is and not to dismiss it as 'wasting time'. They feel they should be doing something useful, like washing the dishes instead of gardening. But if the sun is shining, then the priority is to recharge your flow and respond to the call of the garden. That's just one example; people find flow in so many activities, situations and environments. When you allow yourself to be in flow regularly, you become reenergised and grounded, and life can become so much easier. This in turn helps you make decisions that benefit you and keeps you on track with what you need to live a life to your fullest potential – a life you can love.

Doing what you love must be a priority. Find out what puts you in the zone and let it be a part of your everyday existence. Be aware of how it makes you feel. Along with a strong foundation, you can create a cycle of reoccurrence where each area of your life consistently flows into the next.

Have you experienced your flow recently? If not, why not?

Pillar 4: Recharge

Take action/recharge
Rule: Never ever give up.
Practice: The five-step system below.
Evaluate/review

> "The only person you are destined to become is the person you decide to be."
> **Ralph Waldo Emerson**

When you recharge, it's all about getting your mojo back, replenishing your energy and resources, and getting back on track to achieving a balanced life you will love and back into the driver's seat.

 PART SIX

When things are not quite right, Stop, Think and Flick the Switch and follow the six-step system below. By now, you know that when things are not quite right or another roadblock has been triggered, you need to pause and focus on some maintenance. It could be that the engine is playing up, a tyre has gone flat, you've lost the map, or the bus might just need a refuel. The key is to use the tools in your toolbox to get back on track and never ever give up.

THE FIVE STEP SYSTEM TO RECHARGE YOUR LIFE

STEP 1. Awareness

In Chapter 1, I talked about awareness being the knowledge or perception of a situation or fact. Self-awareness and connection with self are one of the major gateways to living your best life. The only way we experience the outside world is through our perceptions, and what we perceive drives what we project out into the world. We are the only ones who know the answers to the questions we ask ourselves; no one has walked in our shoes. We need to go within to find the answers.

I became aware by asking myself the right questions. I knew I couldn't stay where I was. I was not happy, and I needed to rekindle my confidence in myself and my love of helping others. I needed to finish my book and get the message out there! I realigned myself to my goal and discovered that my why was big enough to recreate the motivation I needed to keep moving forward. My why was wanting to be happy and running a successful business.

Awareness Tips

! Go within to find the answers and journal it out.

! Stay focused on the challenge.

! Be honest, it's okay. It's the road to your truth. Be honest and take responsibility for your choices and actions.

! Don't be too hard on yourself – you are a human being and no one is perfect.

MAINTENANCE: THE JOURNEY CONTINUES

! Ask the right questions.
What is working?
What is not working?
Is my why strong enough?
Is the outcome aligned with who I am and what I want?
Why am I allowing the trigger to create a reaction and bother me?

! Be non-judgemental of yourself and others. You are the only one who has experienced your journey. You have NO right to judge others, as you have not lived in their shoes.

! Discover the root cause, and do what you need to do to get back on track. Revisit the appropriate section in the Action to Empowerment Handbook.

! Get your learnings and keep moving forward.

> "God grant me the serenity
> To accept the things I cannot change,
> courage to change the things I can,
> and the wisdom to know the difference.
> Living one day at a time;
> enjoying one moment at a time;
> accepting hardships as the pathway to peace."
>
> **Words from the Serenity Prayer**

STEP 2. Acceptance

Acceptance is all about accepting the things you can't change and changing the things you can. Get on the right bus, stop making excuses, and take responsibility for your success and happiness. If it's not in your control consciously, intentionally coming to terms with the experience for what it is allows you to get your positive learnings (which I know can be heartbreakingly difficult sometimes) and keep moving forward. Every negative experience or

PART SIX

life challenge (e.g. trauma, viruses, relationship/marriage breakups or job loss) requires you to dig deep.

That year in question, I needed to accept where I was and not be too hard on myself. I wasn't finding it easy. Some things I could change, but other things I needed to accept for what they were. I realised I needed to get back into balance and do the things I needed to do to feel better.

The trick is that while it is important to accept yourself for who you are or the situation you find yourself in, you need to also challenge yourself so you can grow and get back on track.

The key here is to LOVE YOURSELF and CARE FOR YOURSELF so that you can be the best you can be along the way.

Acceptance Tips

- ! It's all about accepting the things you can't change and changing the things you can. Get in the driver's seat, stay focused on what you want, look for the light at the end of the tunnel and keep moving forward.

- ! Avoid thinking of situations as good or bad. Simply see them for what they are: experiences.

- ! Develop a positive mindset. Flick the Switch from negative to positive. Find your power, honour it, and develop it.

- ! Feel and be grateful for every negative experience or challenge, as it will always teach you something.

- ! Focus on the good and let go of what does not serve you.

- ! Make time to nurture yourself.

- ! Make time to do the things that are important to you.

! When you make a decision, make sure you make it for the right reason.

STEP 3. Choice

We are fortunate in these modern times to have so much choice in how we live our lives. This doesn't make decisions any easier; sometimes it is harder when other people are affected, but we must stick to the values and aspirations of our true authentic selves.

When I was struggling again, I had to make a choice. I could choose to stay where I was, feeling miserable, unhappy and frustrated with the doom and gloom of depression rearing its ugly head – or I could choose to take on the challenge and get back on track, to live a fulfilled life doing what I love. Enough was enough! I had the tools, and I knew they worked. I had to find my way again – and I did. I still am, as life is a journey that will always have its ups and downs. You never know what's around the corner.

Remember that every challenge is different, and you'll need to take a slightly different approach to resolve the issue at hand. Because of where I was in 2020, the effects of living in a pandemic were threatening to overwhelm me, but I very carefully chose to take baby steps and just concentrate on what could be achieved day by day: my routine, my diet and connecting with others however I could. I knew these small steps were taking positive action to do the best I could in a challenging situation.

> *"Everything that is happening at this moment is a result of the choices you've made in the past."*
> **Deepak Chopra**

Choice Tips

! Be aware of the choices you make every day.

! Be aware if the little voice in your head is creating negative self-talk or being triggered by a limiting belief or negative emotion.

 PART SIX

- ! The choices you make should be good for you, good for others, your community and the greater good of the planet too.

- ! Choose with the end in mind.

- ! Align your choices with who you are and what you want.

- ! Don't worry about what other people say; it's not your business!

- ! Simplify your choices by focusing on one thing at a time.

- ! Stay positive and make sure you are making the right choices for the right reasons.

- ! Choose to discover the root cause if it's not working, deal with it now – don't let it fester and create dis-ease in your life.

- ! Take responsibility for your choices, thoughts and actions, rather than playing the blame game of a victim mindset.

This tip relates to the power of cause and effect. Are you living at cause or effect? (Refer to the Journey Handbook.) When you are in control, you are empowered to live your best life. If you blame others for your actions or circumstances, you are giving your power away.

Good questions create clarity. When we realise that we have a choice, it becomes very empowering. When we become aware of how we think, we have the power to change our thoughts and change the outcome. Stop, Think and Flick the Switch. (Refer to the Toolbox.)

It takes practice, but each time you get better at taking the extra second to remember that you have control. When you have a negative reaction that expands the situation, you can choose to accept, flick the switch, move forward and even change what you need to, to create a positive outcome, even if it wasn't the original one you had in mind. How empowering is that?

MAINTENANCE: THE JOURNEY CONTINUES

STEP 4. Focus

Focus on and be really clear on what you want, because what you focus on is what you get.

Always keep the end goal in mind, but don't forget to focus on the step-by-step process to get there. If you fall short on the process, the quality of the desired result may be disappointing or unacceptable.

Tips to help you stay focused

! Create a daily routine.

! Implement the power of Intention.

! Create a positive affirmation.

! Live in a supportive environment.

! Live at cause.

! Eliminate distractions.

! Reduce multitasking.

! Practise meditation and mindfulness.

! Get more sleep.

! Take time out to reset and recharge.

! Connect with nature.

! Exercise.

! Eat well.

> *"Reality is a projection of your thoughts or the things you habitually think about."*
>
> **Stephen Richards**

PART SIX

! Focus on one thing at a time. Use a timer, and switch tasks when you need to.

STEP 5. TAKE ACTION

To take action typically is to choose or achieve an aim by doing something. You can achieve anything if you want it badly enough, you just need to take action; nothing will change unless you do.

Make a plan: Create a U C A N B S M A R T goal. Become organised.

Check: You are aligned with who you are and what you want, and commit to your outcome.

Practice good communication, be inspired and stay motivated.

No matter how dark the clouds above your head are, there are better days right around the corner. Believe and trust in yourself and the process, give yourself a break, and you will get there. Keep an open mind, be flexible and develop a solution mindset, knowing you have what it takes to respond, grow and change what you need to, to achieve what you want.

Ask the right questions

Six important questions to consider when you are checking-in before you take action and reconnect with your outcome are:

1. *Do you have a clear plan to action? If not, why not?*
2. *Are you committed to the outcome, your success, your dreams? If not, why not?*
3. *Are you a good communicator in all aspects of your work, family and personal relationships? If not, why not?*
4. *Are you inspired, excited or stimulated to follow through on what you need to do? If not, why not?*
5. *Are you motivated; is your why strong enough? If not, why not?*
6. *Do you have a supportive environment to keep you accountable? If not, why not?*

Journal it out answer the above questions and make a list of what you may need to change.

- Prioritise your list.

What did you learn?
What action do you need to take next?

> *"A goal without a plan is just a wish."*
> **Antoine de Saint-Exupéry**

Set a goal. Create a plan.
- Create a U C A N B S M A R T goal. Big or small, it does not matter. It can be anything from paying your bills on time to creating that six-figure business.

Dream first and connect with what you really want *(the goal, the light at the end of the tunnel).*

Create a vision board (refer to the Bonus Content) to keep your dreams alive.

Embody your goal. Use your active imagination to visualise, step into and feel the achievement as if it had already happened. Take into account the personal and financial benefits when you achieve your outcome.

Create the pathway, the road to your destination *(the plan).* Your plan or routine shows you how to get there and keeps you accountable.

Believe you can. As long as your why is strong enough and you focus on the light at the end of the tunnel, your goal will keep you moving in the right direction, motivating you and inspiring you to realise that you can do it.

Break it down into small, achievable steps. Revisit and refresh along the way, checking that your actions are aligned with who you are and what you want.

Prioritise your steps, create a daily routine, create a 90-day plan (refer to the Bonus Content) and find out what works best for you.

 PART SIX

Celebrate!! every step along the way. You deserve it – you have put in the hard work and besides, it makes you feel good, right! And you can get excited for what comes next.

Stay committed

To commit to anything, whether it be a life goal or a mini goal, knowing specifically what you want is the key. To be successful and make commitment easier for yourself you need to:

- Be a good communicator.
- Stay inspired/motivated.
- Stay connected along the way, review, research, renew, get your learnings and keep moving towards the goal, the light at the end of the tunnel.

> "There are dreamers and there are planners; the planners make their dreams come true."
> **Edwin Louis Cole**

Commitment helps you stick to your goals during the good times and the bad, especially when roadblocks appear and get in the way. Two factors that contribute to commitment are importance and ability. One needs to see that whatever one is striving for is important to them, and they need to believe they can achieve it and carry out all the behaviours and tasks that are necessary to achieve it.

Communicate well

Communicate, communicate, communicate! We communicate for a variety of reasons: we use communication to share information, to comment, ask questions, express wants and needs, set personal boundaries, to learn, to understand, to acknowledge and to be acknowledged so that we can build, nurture and maintain better personal and work relationships. Communication is imperative to living a successful and fulfilled life.

When driving a car, you communicate with your blinker. This shows the other drivers in front and behind you what you are doing, and you are also aware of what you are doing too. You have communicated appropriately for the situation you are in.

To be a good communicator, you need to learn to listen, pay attention to body language, observe how others communicate in different contexts, ask questions, speak with confidence and find common ground. Refer to the communication tools in the Toolbox.

5 tips to support good communication

! Listen carefully – observe body language.

! Define – be clear, identify the desired outcome/boundary.

! Communicate – say what you need as you deserve to be heard, be positive and think before you speak.

! Keep it simple – don't over-explain.

! Set consequences – say why it's important, be brief and be specific.

Stay inspired

When you need to change something in your life, being inspired, excited or stimulated to move can be a challenge on its own. If you want to see real changes in life, you can only see them if you take the necessary actions consistently. Typically, if you don't take action, nothing will change.

There are four perspectives to take into account when you don't know where to start and you are lacking inspiration.

Review, research, reconnect to your authentic self and consolidate your learnings

- **Review and check in.** Be specific and clear, and make sure your why is strong enough. Know what you want, when you want it and why you want it.
- **Research.** Research what you don't know, find a mentor, ask for help, talk it out or find an accountability partner, and exist in a supportive environment.

PART SIX

- **Reconnect to authentic self.** Go within to find the answers. Take time out to relax and rejuvenate. Get out of your comfort zone and have fun.
- **Consolidate your learnings.** Be flexible and stay open to positive opportunities that come your way. Believe in yourself and practise the 'I can' attitude. If you want something badly enough, know that after reading this book you have the tools to achieve anything you want.

Stay motivated

Motivation is the driving force for why a person does something. Three words that define motivation are intensity, direction and persistence.

Staying on task is not easy; it can become overwhelming. If you are struggling a little, check if there is any negative self-talk, limiting decisions or negative emotions blocking the way and take action to get to the root cause.

The key here is to stay focused on what you want.

Firstly, use the visualisation exercise (refer to the Active Imagination Visualisation exercise in the Toolbox), and reconnect with what specifically motivates you. Think about the last time you were really motivated and ask yourself: *How did it feel? What was I doing that lead me to feel that way? Can I feel this way again? What do I need to do to feel this way again?*

Secondly, if you feel you are still getting distracted, feeling unmotivated, lost and not achieving the desired outcome, ask yourself the following questions:

- Have you lost motivation or the inspiration to keep going?
- If so, why?
- If you were to know, why are you feeling this way?
- Why are you allowing this feeling to bother you?
- Is the outcome important to you?
- Is your why strong enough?
- Is what you are focusing on now getting you any closer to where you want to be?

- If not, why not?
- What is it you need to do to get back on track?

What did you learn?

STOP, THINK and FLICK the SWITCH!

DISCOVER YOUR FLOW, RECHARGE AND BE EMPOWERED TO LIVE YOUR BEST LIFE, A LIFE YOU CAN LOVE BECAUSE YOU CAN. TAKE ONE STEP AT A TIME AND COMMIT TO LIVING A LIFE TO YOUR ULTIMATE POTENTIAL.

The exciting news is that while you might have thought that your journey was difficult on this part of the road, as long as you are going in the right direction, aligned with your values and connected to your body, a problem is only a challenge, and life soon becomes an adventure. How good is that? When you get through it, you can smile, knowing that you have done your best at any point in time.

The destination of our journey is not a static thing. Hopes and dreams can change as we age, and it's good to always have a goal up ahead to keep us striving and motivated physically and mentally. This allows us to grow in personal development, even as our bodies grow older. There will always be another skin to peel off the onion or a challenge that hides just around the corner. Know that you must never, ever give up. Embrace your learnings, embody who you really are and keep moving forward.

For me, my sea change away from depression to living a life I can love has been a really fulfilling experience and I wouldn't have it any other way. I now get excited when a new challenge rears its ugly head. I look at things differently, and I have a greater understanding of who I am and what I want, and I choose to be happy. I now have the tools to get me through any challenge life throws at me and so do you, and if I really get stuck I ask for help, so can you.

REMEMBER: you can be the person you want to be if you want it badly enough! Believe in yourself. Trust your process. Enjoy your life and its ups and downs, stay fit and healthy, and don't forget to celebrate every step along the way.

The bus jolts to a stop. It's been a long day; the driver's training is now complete. You step off the bus and realise that you are now in the driver's seat of your life.

You close your eyes and focus on your breath. You become aware of all the sounds that surround you. The birds singing, etc, and you can feel the warmth of the sun upon your cheeks.

You take a deep breath, check in, and release any tension that may be residing in your body. You take a moment now before you open your eyes. You breathe easy and smile. You feel good, you feel comfortable, and you feel at peace with yourself. You know that after working through this book, everything you do, think and feel is in your control.

It's not about what happens to you. It's about how you deal with it.

You slowly open your eyes, stretch, and there on the other side of the road is a sign showing you that you have arrived. You can't miss it. It is huge and meaningful; it is a destination you will embrace forever.

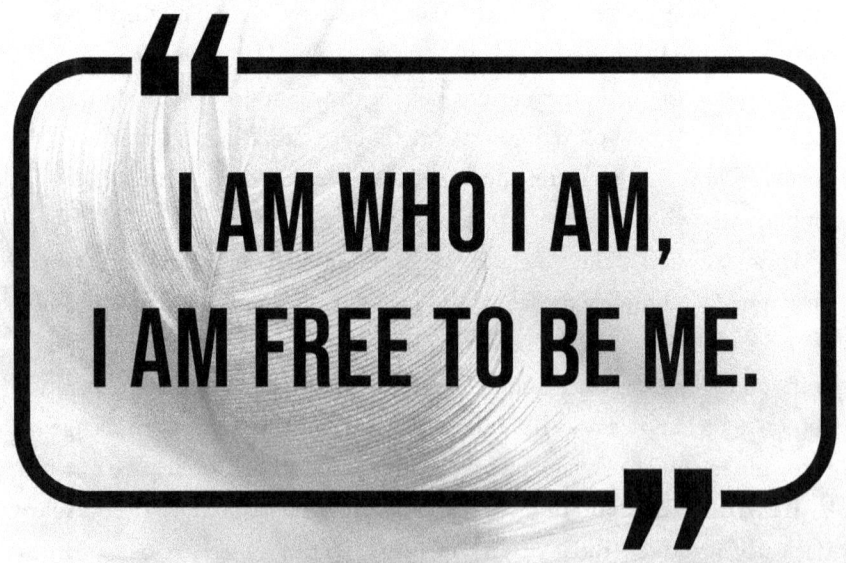

> **I AM WHO I AM, I AM FREE TO BE ME.**

BECAUSE YOU CAN

Because you can
Dare to dream
Reach for the stars
Acknowledge your achievements
and let your light shine

Because you can
Believe in yourself
Be inspired
Reach out
Embark on an adventure
Be honest and seek your truth
Let your light shine as it shows you the way
The way to your truth and understandings

Because you can
Close your eyes and breathe
Choose happiness over turmoil
Trust yourself
Allow the answers to come
Create peace within yourself that only you can understand

Because you can
Recognise inner beauty in self and others
Allow yourself to just be
Draw on your inner strength and
Be empowered to live your best life
Because you can

By Gillian Gorrie, September 2022

The symbol of a feather holds meaning in many different religious practices. For me, I choose to believe that the feather teaches us faith and hope in ourselves and the universe. It can also symbolise trust, honour, strength, wisdom, power and freedom.

What does a feather symbolise for you?

Gillian Gorrie

THE TOOLBOX

The Toolbox is here to support you to take action on your journey. The tools are to help you find clarity and realign your focus away from any roadblock that may appear.

"

*Don't dwell on what went wrong.
Instead, focus on what to do next.
Spend your energies on moving forward
toward finding the answer.*
Denis Waitley

"

Contents

1. Affirmations 381
2. Attitude of gratitude 384
3. Active imagination visualisation exercise 387
4. The power of observation: A different perspective ... 392
5. Breathe 394
6. Communication reality check/relationship triangle ... 396
7. Communication sandwich: A handy tool for communication ... 397
8. Monthly habit tracker 398
9. Journal it out 399
10. Stop, Think and Flick the Switch 403
11. The power of intention 407
12. Asking the right questions 408
13. Lists (A - E) 413
    A. Feelings list 413
    B. Negative emotions list 416
    C. Fear list 416
    D. Values list 417
    E. Body sensations list 422

1. Affirmations

What are affirmations?
The word 'affirmation' originates from the Latin word 'affirmare,' which means "to strengthen, to make steady." In this sense, every thought we regularly entertain strengthens certain beliefs. In most cases, we are entirely unaware of this process.

An affirmation is a declaration, which when repeated over and over again, acts directly on our emotions and our feelings. Then, it penetrates to the very depths of our subconscious minds.

It's one of the most powerful ways to create a vibrational match for what you want to attract in your life. They are a key element in the creation and self-transformation; affirmations help us to literally change the neural pathways in our brains if used correctly.

They work by purposely replacing limiting ideas, negative beliefs, and self-talk you have taken on and internalised over the years (that might even cause us to self-sabotage our progress in life) with positive statements that assert who you want to be, and how you want to experience life, the life you desire.

Six steps to creating the best affirmations ever
1. **Start with the words "I am", "I have" or "My"**

These words "I am", "I have" and "My" are the most powerful words in our language. The subconscious takes any sentence that starts with these words and interprets it as a command, a directive to make your wish a command and make it happen.

2. **Use the present tense**

Describe what you want as though you already have it (as though it's already accomplished). Feel what you feel, see what you see, hear what you hear, as if it has already happened.
For example:
Wrong: I am going to get a new red Porsche 911.

THE TOOLBOX

Right: I am enjoying driving my new red Porsche 911. I have a new red Porsche. My new red Porsche is amazing to drive.

3. **State it in the positive**
Affirm what you want, not what you don't want.
State your affirmations in the positive. The unconscious does not hear the words no, or not. This means that the statement "Don't slam the door" is heard as "Slam the door." The unconscious thinks in pictures, and the words "Don't slam the door" evoke a picture of slamming the door.
Wrong: I am no longer afraid of surfing.
Right: I am enjoying the thrill of surfing the waves.

4. **Keep it brief and make it specific**
Think of your affirmation as an advertising jingle. Act as if each word costs $1,000. It needs to be specific, short enough and memorable enough to be easily remembered. Vague affirmations produce vague results.
For example:
Wrong: I am driving my new sports car.
Right: I am happily driving my new red Porsche 911.

5. **Include at least one dynamic emotion or feeling word**
Include the emotional state you would be feeling if you had already achieved the goal. Some commonly used words are: enjoying, joyfully, happily, celebrating, proudly, calmly, peacefully, delighted, enthusiastic, lovingly, secure, serenely, and triumphant.
For example:
Wrong: I am maintaining my perfect body weight of 78 kilos.
Right: I feel fit and agile at 78 kilos!

6. **Make affirmations for yourself, not others**
When you are constructing your affirmations, make them describe your behaviour, not the behaviour of others.
For example:
Wrong: I am watching Johnny clean up his room.

Right: I communicate my needs and desires to Johnny effectively.

Review and repeat your affirmations one to three times a day. Read each affirmation out loud every day for around one to three months. The best times are first thing in the morning, in the middle of the day, and around bedtime. They will soon become an automatic part of your thinking, woven into the very fabric of your being.

You can place a printout of them on the fridge, on a mirror or in your diary so it becomes a part of your daily routine.

EXAMPLES

I am where I am and where I want to be.
I believe in myself, I am confident, I am a winner!
I confront my fears, confidently and courageously to move forward on my life's journey.
I ask for help when I need it.
I have abundance in every area of my life.
I never give up.
I accept, love and appreciate who I am; I am free to be me.
I am open to new ideas shared by positive-thinking people, and implement them with confidence and optimism.
My body is fit and healthy.
I am strong.
I am confident.
I am resilient.
I am an effective communicator.
I am worthy.
I can stand up for myself.
I am flexible.
I am understanding.
I am assertive.
I do the best that I can at any one point in time.
I am compassionate.
I am a nurturer.
I give love.
I appreciate life and living.

THE TOOLBOX

My life is full of magic and serendipity.
My thoughts and feelings are nourishing.
I am present in every moment.
I see beauty in everything.
I slow my breathing, I relax my body, stress flows out of my mind and I am relaxed.
I can overcome any obstacle when I put my mind to it.
I am a beacon of love and compassion.
My relationships are positive and filled with love and compassion.
Each day of my life is filled with joy and love.
I easily accomplish all of my goals.
My environment is calm and supportive.
I love, laugh and live my best life because I can.

Create, emotionally connect, and embody a positive affirmation for each area of your Life Circle.

2. Attitude of gratitude

Matthew Henry, an author, consciously practised living in gratitude. More than 250 years ago, he wrote these words in his diary after he was robbed of all the money he had in the world: "Let me be thankful first because I was never robbed before; second, although they took my purse, they did not take my life; third, because although they took my all, it was not much; and fourth, because it was I who was robbed, not I who robbed."[8]

> "Gratitude is riches. Complaint is poverty."
> **Doris Day**

He had trained himself so well to live thankfully that even when something vile happened to him, he chose to find the reasons he had to be grateful.

I'm not suggesting that we should all keep a diary for other people to read two centuries from now, but I do know that there is tremendous value in keeping a gratitude journal for ourselves. Appreciating what is right in our lives is a habit well worth the effort. Being thankful is a choice.

Yes, we all have stressful and negative things in our lives. We could let them overwhelm us, but everyone has reasons to be thankful too. If we train ourselves to become more aware of the good things, we will start to find our life changing – maybe not on the outside, but on the inside where it really counts.

Deliberately, even in all our busyness, we can focus for at least a few minutes a day on the reasons we have to be grateful. This can take some practice. A lot of the time we feel too tired, too distressed, too sad, too mad, too frustrated, too overwhelmed by our lives and the load is too heavy – but that is exactly when we need an attitude of gratitude the most. The surprising thing about choosing to be grateful is that it changes our focus, and ultimately, our life.

GROW
RELEASE
ACCEPT
THANK
INSPIRE
TREASURE
UNDERSTAND
DELIGHT
EXPERIENCE

> At the end of each week, write down your I am gratefuls/ achievements on a sticky note and place it in a lidded container.
>
> Open that lidded container when ever you need to lift your energy into a positive state of mind.

It is simple to start keeping a gratitude journal. Personally, I enjoy having a beautiful blank book to write in. It makes me feel…well…thankful!

TIPS TO START YOUR GRATITUDE JOURNEY

! A gratitude journal can be a simple exercise book or a beautiful journal. There are so many to choose from these days.

! I recommend you write at least five things you are grateful for in your gratitude journal before bed, so you can go to sleep in a positive frame of mind.

! It is important to connect your gratitude to your feelings, as it takes the positives inside and connects with your inner self, your subconscious mind and your body!

! Be specific!

THE TOOLBOX

See how you go and feel the difference.
Today I am grateful for..
because it makes me feel ....
For example:
Wrong: I am grateful for my husband.
Right: I am grateful for my husband Peter, because when he washes the dishes, he makes me feel loved and supported. It means I have more time to do what I want.

You can be really grateful for just about anything – the birds that sing, the sun that shines, shelter from the rain, tasty food that is freely available, a cosy bed to curl up in, being able to read, a beautiful sunset or sunrise, laughter, a hot drink when you are cold, people in your life, electric lights, indoor plumbing.

It's just a way of saying thank you and feeling it. Perception is projection right!

AN EXAMPLE

It's pouring with rain, so you want to get a car park close to the shop. There is a girl standing in the rain in front of the shop hailing a taxi. A taxi comes from behind you and takes the car park you were lining up for. What do you do and think?

You have a choice. Do you plant your hand on the horn and get physically and emotionally frustrated or angry? Or do you wait patiently for him to pull out with his passenger, feeling grateful that she has a ride and is out of the rain, that the taxi driver has a fare on this miserable day? He probably has a family to feed and rent to pay. You are not feeling stressed at all and when he pulls out, you glide into the car park and get on with your day.

First, you were not out in the rain waiting for a taxi.
Second, you were able to get a car park in front of the shop and not get wet.
Third, you did not have to make a living from driving a taxi.

Can you think of any more positives?

3. Active imagination visualisation exercise

In simple terms, to visualise is to make visible, to see or form an image of something. An active imagination is the process that helps to bridge the gap between the conscious and unconscious mind. In combining what we see and what we feel, we are able to, for the purpose of this exercise, really connect with senses and feelings that we have already experienced or wish to experience in the future.

It involves the use of mental imagery to achieve a desired outcome. In other words, you must imagine yourself doing (or being) the thing that you want to do or be, successfully, at the same time connecting with the feelings and emotions of the experience.

It doesn't come easily to everyone and it might feel a little awkward at first. But with a bit of consistent practice, it'll start to feel more natural.

It is imperative that you are aware of several important aspects of visualisation that you should follow, if you want it to be an effective process.

- **Be specific** – you have to be specific about your goal. State it how you want it to be and include every detail.
- **Listen to your instincts** – you have to be sure to only visualise those goals that are authentic to you.
- **Picture yourself in your vision** – you have to clearly picture yourself in your vision if you want to truly connect with the positive experience.
- **Take advantage of physical sensations** – you need to incorporate sounds, smells, feelings, taste, and sight into your visualisations to make them clear and realistic.
- **Enforce your visualisation** – inject positive emotion and feel it as if it is happening right now.
- **Revisit regularly** – make it a practice to refine the purpose of the visualisation.
- **Be patient** – a tree won't grow in a day, so you have to be patient and learn how to notice the subtle changes as they begin to happen. Take pleasure in these changes. They affirm your faith in the process.

- **Stay positive** – replace all doubts with a picture of what can go well. Be persistent and diligent about this until the old, negative neural pathways waste away from lack of use. It will always be mind over matter since the brain is the one that dominates. Before you can manifest anything into your life, it has to exist in the brain in the first place. Visualisation is a classic example of mind over matter.

The exercise: Focus on what you want
Part 1. To relax.
Part 2. To evoke a positive state.
Part 3. To set goals or prepare oneself for that all important job interview.

PART 1. To relax
Firstly, put yourself into a positive state and quiet the mind.

1. **Get into a comfortable position. Close your eyes.**

2. **Breathe.**
   - Breathe in for six. Hold for three. Breathe out for nine.
   - Repeat: Continue to breathe slowly and peacefully as you allow any tension to leave your body until a feeling of calm washes over you.
   - Having trouble to quiet the mind? See if you can visualise each number as you say it to yourself with each breathe in and out you take.
   - You could even give the numbers a positive colour that you can relate to.

3. **Ask the question.**
When you are ready, ask your unconscious mind.
   - If I were to know, can I remember a time (or the last time) when I felt completely relaxed?

- Now, think of that place where you were completely relaxed. It might be the beach, or the mountains, or a room in which you feel particularly safe and comfortable.

4. **Visualise a big white screen in front of you. See yourself on the screen in this place where you were COMPLETELY RELAXED. Looking at yourself with your own eyes, SEE it as clearly as you can.**
   - Where are you? What are you doing? Are you alone? Are there other people present? Animals? Birds? Trees? Take a moment.

5. **Now, I need you to visualise yourself stepping into your body on the screen. Embody everything you were feeling, seeing, hearing, smelling and tasting.**
   - Now focus on the sounds in that place. What can you hear? Leaves? People? Water? Hear whatever sounds are there. Listen for a few moments.
   - Now imagine any tastes and smells your place has to offer. Vegetation? Food? Suntan lotion?
   - Now feel whatever you can feel in this relaxing place. The temperature, any breeze that may be present, the surface you are on…Imagine every detail of this calming place in your mind.
   - Focus again on the sights of your place – colours, shapes, objects, plants, water…all of the things that make your place enjoyable.
   - Really connect with and feel yourself IN this peaceful place. Enjoy being there, relaxed and present. I want you to experience this as if it is happening right now.
   - If you were to know, what specifically is assisting you to feel relaxed and calm in this very special place?

6. **Now feeling completely relaxed, stay there and indulge in those feelings until you are ready to step out of the experience (and your body on the screen) and bring those relaxed feelings with you back to now.**

7. **How did that feel? You can journal it out if you wish. Know that you can return to that place in your mind any time to feel that newfound sense of relaxation, whenever you need a break. What did you learn?**

PART 2. To evoke a positive state

Often we need to connect with positive past experiences so that we can move forward confidently, knowing we have the skills as we have done it before. This creates an image and impact on our mind as to where to go next.

Example 1

Follow steps 1 and 2 above, to get into a comfortable position and breathe.

3. **Ask the question. For this example I am using Motivation.**
   - When you are ready, ask your unconscious mind: If I were to know, can I remember a time when I was highly motivated?

Take a moment to see and feel everything as clearly as you can.
   - Imagine every detail of this experience in your mind. Focus again on all of the things that have brought you to this place of excitement and motivation.

4. **Visualise a big white screen in front of you. See yourself on the screen in this highly motivated state. Where are you? What are you doing?**
   - Imagine yourself IN that place, and in your mind's eye, see it as clearly as you can. Are you alone? Are there other people present?

5. **Now I need you to visualise yourself stepping into your body on the screen. Embody everything you were feeling.**
   - What can you specifically see, hear, feel, smell and taste?
   - Is there anyone else there? Are there any birds or water? Is the sun shining?
   - What is it that got you so motivated or excited?
   - I want you to experience this as if it is happening right now. Really connect to your feelings and emotions.

6. **Stay there and indulge in those feelings until you are ready to step out of the experience and bring the understandings and what you are feeling around motivation with you.**

7. **How did that feel? Journal it out. Know that you can return to that place in your mind any time you feel unmotivated, reassess and realise what you need to change to get back to that amazing feeling of being really motivated.**

Example 2: Happiness

Follow the steps of example one, except change the wording of the focus to:
- If you were to know, when was the last time you were really happy and relaxed that you laughed so much and it felt so good?

At the end, journal it out and realise what you need to change to get more happiness and fun into your life.

PART 3. Setting goals or preparing oneself for that all important job interview, and manifesting success

1. Write down your outcome and be very specific with the details: the date, the time, what you are wearing, and your whole day planned as if it was happening right now. Refer to goals to make sure it is all correct and ready to go.
2. Follow steps 1 and 2 from the relaxation exercise to begin the journey to your desired outcome.
3. When you are ready, ask your unconscious mind to take you into the future to that specific date and time on your calendar, and actively imagine you are there right now. Create a movie. Be specific, where are you? etc, etc.
4. Visualise a big white screen in front of you. See yourself on the screen, from the time you get up to the time the desired outcome has been achieved. Imagine the best scenario ever. Get excited and connect to the feelings you will feel when you have successfully achieved the desired outcome. Take a moment to see everything as clearly as you can.
5. Now I need you to visualise yourself stepping into your body on the

THE TOOLBOX

screen. Embody everything you are feeling, seeing, hearing, smelling and tasting in your movie. Feel it as if it is happening right now!
6. How do you feel? Put words to every single feeling you are experiencing around the success of your outcome.
    - Is there anyone else there? Are there any birds singing? Is the sun shining?
    - What is assisting you to feel so good?
7. Now feeling completely relaxed, stay there and indulge in those feelings until you are ready to step out of the experience and bring those feelings with you back to now.
8. How did that feel? Journal it out and know that you can return to that place in your mind any time to feel that newfound sense of confidence. It feels right, it is right and IT IS going to happen.

Just believe. Anything is possible when you believe in yourself and all the signposts are aligned with who you are and what you want.

Please note: if you want, you can record the script steps on your phone, close your eyes and go for it. It will make it easier to follow the process.

What did you learn?

4. The power of observation: A different perspective

Use your active imagination to create the scenario of your specific challenge.

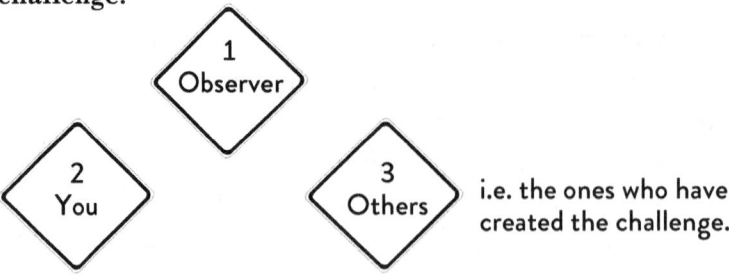

STEP 1. Now as the creator of the challenge (3.) ask yourself the following questions:
- Why did you do or say those things?
- What are you trying to gain from this situation?
- What is happening in your world at the moment? What is your reality?
- What could have triggered your words and/or behaviour? Was it stress? Was it something else?

Frequently, the ones who have created your challenge are challenged also in some way. Gather this information to give you a different perspective.

STEP 2. Now as the observer (1), ask the following questions of yourself (2):
- Do you think they created the scenario to challenge you intentionally?
- Are you potentially misreading this person's intentions?
- What if there is a misunderstanding here?
- What information will you need from the other person to clarify this situation?
- Do you need to ask them some questions? If so, what would they be?

STEP 3. Now step into your shoes (2) and ask yourself the following questions:
- What am I feeling now?
- In reality, do I need to change my thinking?
- Is what they said or did true, or is what they said or did just a trigger that set off a reaction (a negative emotion/limiting belief)?
- What did I expect to happen in this situation?
- What did I expect the other person to do?
- Were my expectations realistic? Were they helpful?
- What specifically did I learn?

Maybe your perceptions are simply clouding your judgement and subsequently triggering your hurt feelings. Let's dive a little deeper.

 THE TOOLBOX

- Do you have unmet needs?
- Do you already feel rejected?
- Do you feel betrayed, disrespected, deceived, let down, etc?
- Has what happened not lived up to your expectations?
- Has there been a misunderstanding or a lack of communication?
- Was it a direct personal attack? If so, did you take it personally because you are always feeling sorry for yourself?

STEP 4. Resolve the challenge and take responsibility for your thoughts and behaviour. The key is to be open to possibilities and willing to fully understand the other person's point of view and true intentions. A good conversation can heal your mind and make it easier to accept the outcome. As the observer what advice would you give you (2).

Use the COMMUNICATION SANDWICH in this Toolbox if you need to. Release and let go of that which does not serve you or simply forgive and make amends.

What did you learn? What do you need to do next?

5. Breathe

'Breathe' for me is an exercise to use on the spot, for the purpose of releasing tension and taking time out when challenged or triggered is interrupting my day. One just needs to get back on track and think clearly.

Breathe to release stress tension and emotion in your body

1. Breathe: Take a few deep breaths then get into the rhythm – in for six, hold for three, out for nine – to help release burgeoning tension.
2. Repeat until you feel a sense of calm come over your body. Just relax and come back to now.

Breathe to solve a challenge you may have

When you recognise negative thoughts, tension and stress in your body cropping up, take the following steps.

1. **Stop**: consciously call a mental timeout.
2. **Breathe:** take a few deep breaths then get into the rhythm – in for six, hold for three, out for nine.
3. **Repeat** until you feel a sense of calm wash over your body and you have been able to still the mind.
4. **Reflect**: ask some hard questions.
   - Am I letting negative thoughts take over my day and create tension in my body?
   - Did I jump to a conclusion?
   - Is the challenge or constraint a real one, or is it one of your mind's making?
   - What evidence do I actually have to prove that it is true?
   - Does it serve me to think this way?
   - If distortion is the root of the problem, can you recognise this and let it go?
   - Is there another way to view the situation that is triggering my negative reaction or tension in my body and thoughts?
   - What would be the worst that could happen?

   What did you learn?
5. **Choose**: Decide how to deal with the source of your stress, tension and trigger. (Use some of the exercises in the Toolbox or go to relevant section in the book and work on it.)
   - If the problem or challenge is real, are there practical steps you can take to cope with it?
   - What actions do you need to take to solve this challenge?
   - What action can you do today or right now to get you back on track?

 THE TOOLBOX

6. Communication reality check/ relationship triangle

No matter what is happening in your life at any one point in time, if we get emotional or are triggered and we can't see clearly, we need to.

Stop, Think and Flick the Switch.
and ask "What's happening/not happening."

Whatever it is, is it yours? Or is it someone else's challenge that has created the situation? Ask the question, "R U OK"? The reality of the situation might have nothing to do with you.

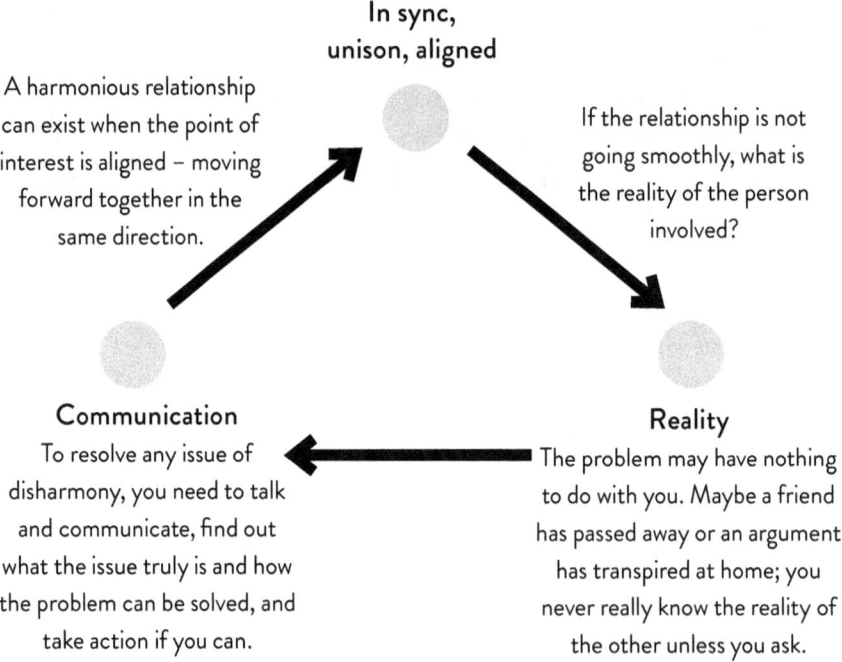

In sync, unison, aligned

A harmonious relationship can exist when the point of interest is aligned – moving forward together in the same direction.

If the relationship is not going smoothly, what is the reality of the person involved?

Communication
To resolve any issue of disharmony, you need to talk and communicate, find out what the issue truly is and how the problem can be solved, and take action if you can.

Reality
The problem may have nothing to do with you. Maybe a friend has passed away or an argument has transpired at home; you never really know the reality of the other unless you ask.

7. Communication sandwich: A handy tool for communication

To say what we have or need to say is freedom.

I totally see the communication sandwich as a freedom tool. It allows you to say what you need to say and get it out of your head, at the same time as sharing the love and keeping the energy around a situation positive.

Never assume you know someone else or how they feel, or that they even understand how you feel – they are not you and you are not them. This tool is good for any sort of relationship communication – family, personal, child related and work relationships.

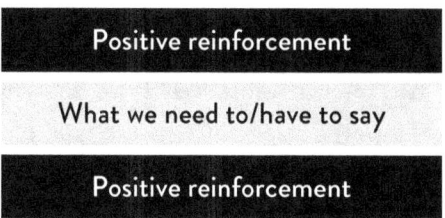

For example:

- **Personal.** Honey, I love the fact that you do the dishes every night, but it really annoys me that you don't put the dishes away in the right place. Sometimes I can't find what I need. We have been married for thirty years, so I think by now you would know where the dishes go. I am grateful and it really does help me when you wash the dishes. I feel so supported, thank you.

- **Children.** I am so impressed with your creativity and you produce some lovely work. Can you help me by packing away your tools when you are finished for the day? If you leave them on the floor they will get damaged. Maybe we can create a workstation just for you, let's think about it. And we can put your pictures on the fridge so everyone can see them.

THE TOOLBOX

- **Work.** I love the work you do in our business and you are very efficient when you are here. However, you have had a lot of days off lately and you are not getting to work on time, so I really would like to have a chat to see if we can do things a little differently as I don't want to lose you.

Tip: The responsibility is transferred to them, and the outcome might not be what you would like. As the saying goes, "You only worry about what you can change, you do NOT worry about what you can't change." And you have set the wheels in motion.

8. Monthly habit tracker

Generally, it can take anywhere between 18 to 254 days for a person to form a new habit. However, depending on the type of habit you want to achieve, the average is 66 days. Some habits are easier to form than others. Depending on your unique self, the key is never to give in, do not be hard on yourself, have patience with the process and celebrate your achievements along the way.

I personally have found that following a habit tracker makes it easier and is a positive way to reinforce what you CAN achieve. Be mindful and only work on creating one good habit at a time.

It could be as simple as drinking eight glasses of water a day, to exercising 3 times a week, or going a month without alcohol or coffee, or limiting yourself to one coffee a day. Whatever it is, mark it down so you can see your progress, have evidence that you can do it, and celebrate when your new habit has been formed.

The New Habit: ....
What do I need to do? ....
Are you going to piggyback off another habit you don't want? ....

Monday	Tuesday	Wednesday	Thursday	Friday	Saturday	Sunday

9. Journal it out: It's good for your health

Journalling does more than just help you record your memories, it's good for your health.

When you are feeling challenged around a certain scenario, asking the right questions and getting your thoughts out of your head can lead to clarity, problem solving and a way to keep moving through any challenge you may have.

Journalling helps us figure out who we are, what we need and what we want. It can help us make better decisions and focus on the very things that support us on our journey through life.

So why wouldn't you make journalling a habit?

Benefits of journalling

- Reduces stress and anxiety
- Helps you learn from your experiences
- Improves your communication skills
- Helps you sleep better
- Improves your memory
- Moves you towards your goals
- Improves your mood
- Helps you solve problems

THE TOOLBOX

- Reduces stress symptoms
- Helps you after a traumatic event
- Boosts your creativity
- Improves your sense of gratitude
- Helps you discover your voice
- Leaves a record for your future self
- Improves your mindfulness
- Boosts your self-esteem

Make time to journal and keep up your "Attitude of Gratitude" – there is always a flip side. Aim to turn your negatives into positives and enjoy the process. It's a choice.

Journalling tips for beginners

1. When adversity (a difficult or unpleasant situation) hits:
   - Write down your deepest emotions and thoughts about an emotional challenge that is affecting you at the present time.
   - Write continuously for twenty minutes.
   - Write only for yourself.
2. Write for at least four days in a row.
3. Choose a time of day that suits you. Schedule at least 20 minutes into your day.
4. Start small to get into a habit. Track your habit.
5. If you get writers' block, use the journalling prompts.
6. Try a different environment – ie coffee shops, lunch time.
7. Use different techniques on weekends, for example – get creative.
8. Make it fun, a pleasure. Write for your eyes only.
9. Don't wallow in self-blame
10. Keep your journal handy.
11. You can use anything from an old exercise book to a beautifully bound journal. Whatever you do, make it special.

Prompts to get to know yourself better
1. My favourite way to spend the day is..........

2. Describe a time when you felt fulfilled. Where were you? What were you doing? What about that moment felt so satisfying?
3. What is the thing you could do every day for a year and feel fulfilled?
4. What thoughts greet you in the morning?
5. Write about three things you'd wake up for at 5 o'clock in the morning. It could be an activity, a certain food, an adventure. Include as much detail as possible.
6. When you look in the mirror, what do you see?
7. What is your favourite thing to do when it's raining and why?
8. What is your favourite thing to do when the sun is shining and why?
9. What is your favourite smell?
10. What is your favourite sound?
11. What are your favourite songs?
12. Write a list of at least 50 things you love to do – you don't have to do this all at once, but make space for 50.
13. Write a list of at least 50 things you love about yourself – you don't have to do this all at once, but make space for 50.
14. Write a list of 50 things you know you are good at – you don't have to do this all at once, but make space for 50.
15. What do you love about life?
16. Make a list of everything that inspires you, from books to websites to quotes to people to paintings to stores to the stars.
17. Write about a time when work felt real, necessary and satisfying. This work can be paid or unpaid, professional or domestic, physical or mental.
18. I feel most energised when..........
19. What always brings tears to your eyes?
20. If my body could talk, it would say..........
21. Write a love letter to yourself.
22. The two moments I'll never forget in my life are..........Describe them in great detail, and explain what makes them so unforgettable.
23. So far, I've learnt these lessons about life..........
24. I couldn't imagine living without..........
25. Write about your favourite holiday. List three reasons why it's your favourite.

THE TOOLBOX

26. What's one topic you need to learn more about to help you live a more fulfilling life? (Then learn about it.)
27. Using 10 words, describe yourself.
28. Make a list of 30 things that make you smile.
29. Name a compassionate way you've supported a friend recently. Then write down how you can do the same for yourself.
30. What surprises you the most about your life, or life in general?
31. If your heart could talk, what would it say?
32. I feel happiest in my skin when..........

Prompts to check in with yourself when things are not quite right
1. Write about the questions swirling in your mind lately. Then answer them.
2. Write about how you're doing right now. Don't censor it. There's no need for complete sentences; just spill.
3. What do your emotions sound, look and feel like?
4. What are you feeling right now?
5. Use the Stop, Think and Flick the Switch strategy in this Toolbox.
6. When I'm in pain (physical or emotional) the kindest thing I can do for myself is..........
7. How can you heal it? What can you do better next time?
8. Write a list of questions to which you urgently need answers.
9. Make a list of everything you'd like to say 'no' to.
10. Make a list of everything you'd like to say 'yes' to.
11. Write the words you need to hear.
12. Make a list of the people in your life who genuinely support you, and who you can genuinely trust. Then make time to hang out with them.

Prompts for the future
1. If you had no limits to anything in your life, what would you like to do, see and experience? Dare to Dream!!! Write a bucket list.
2. What is something you wish to experience for the first time and why?

3. Where would you like to spend the week? This place may or may not exist yet – and it may or may not be on this planet.
4. What are the three most important things you want to achieve in your life?
5. How do you want your life to look in five years (Where are you living? What is your lifestyle? What do you see each morning when you get up?)
6. Describe a day in your life in 2 years.
7. Describe a day in your life in 5 years.
8. Describe a day in your life in 10 years.
9. Make a U CAN B SMART goal for each area of your Life Circle. (Refer to Part 3 in this book.)
10. Make a list of what works well in your life right now.
11. Make a list of what is not working well in your life right now.
12. Make a list of what you need to do to make your life better right now.
13. Make a list of the top 10 values that are guiding you through your life right now.
14. What can you learn from your biggest mistakes?

10. Stop, Think and Flick the Switch

"Stop, Think and Flick the Switch"

is my Mantra for my journey. I use it as a gentle reminder for when I feel that something is not quite right in my world, or I have been triggered and I take action before it becomes a real challenge.

Putting it simply, you need to:
- **STOP and ask,** *What's happening?*
- **THINK and ask,** *Why is it happening?*
- **FLICK THE SWITCH and ask,** *What positive actions do I need to do next?*

 THE TOOLBOX

When we get emotional or reactive, it is very hard to think clearly. If you find yourself in a real state please have a go and find your clarity. Once you get to the root cause of why you are feeling emotional or unwell, you know what you are dealing with and it's easier to get through the roadblock.

5 Steps to clarity

Self-awareness and connection with self are your keys to clarity.

STOP!

Step 1. Breathe
- Find a quiet space where you will not be disturbed.
- Breathe in for six, hold for three, and out for nine.
- Repeat at least five times or until you feel a wave of calm wash over you.

Step 2. Allow
- Allow your thoughts and feelings to bubble up.
- Recognise them.
- Sit with them.
- Ask yourself, *What specifically is happening right now?*
- *What is my reaction? Is it a thought, a feeling or a behaviour?*
- This time, take your breath down to the space in your pelvis between your hips. Take that breath all the way down. Breathe in for six, hold for three, and out for nine.
- Repeat at least three times.

THINK!

Step 3. Ask the question
1. How are you feeling now?
   I am feeling..........
2. Now ask yourself, "Why am I allowing myself to feel, react or behave this way?"

3. *I am allowing myself to..........because..........*
4. Using the answer from the last question ask again
   "Why am I allowing myself to feel, react or behave this way?"
5. *I am allowing myself to..........because..........*
   Repeat the question three more times using the answer from the previous question.
6. *The last answer of these questions is that at a deeper level, I am allowing myself to feel/react/behave this way because..........*

As we go deeper, the root cause or trigger of the feeling, emotion or behaviour becomes clearer.

Once you have exhausted the reasons above, we move onto the **5 Whys**. Ask the next question about your last answer from above.

7. Why is..........important to me? *It is important to me because..........*
8. Why is *(the answer from the previous question)* important to me? *It is important to me because..........*
9. Ask question 7 three more times.
10. *The result of these questions at a deeper level was that it is important to me because..........*

Step 4. Recognise

Recognise and take responsibility around your reality.
Recognise and ask:
- What did you learn?
- What are you feeling now?

I am feeling..........
- What specifically is your remaining challenge (if any)?

My remaining challenge is..........
You may find you have a smile on your face, because now you know that you don't need to feel this way and you know what you need to do next.

THE TOOLBOX

FLICK THE SWITCH!

Step 5. Action
- What specifically is it that you need more of in your life right now?
- What actions do you need to take? Make a list.
- What can you do differently next time?
- How can you make today better?
- Create an affirmation around the issue/challenge. Refer to the Affirmation section at the beginning of the Toolbox.
- Create an attitude of gratitude around the issue/challenge. Refer to attitude of gratitude in the Toolbox.

Today I am grateful for ....
because it makes me feel ....

If you find you have not gotten to the root cause of any issue, just remember to keep asking the question, "Why?"

MY EXAMPLE
What is happening? *I am feeling frustrated.*
A) Ask the right question
Why am I allowing myself to feel frustrated?
1. *I am feeling frustrated because I don't have enough time to get everything done.*

Take the answer above and ask the question again.

2. ***I am feeling that I don't have enough time to get everything done, because I am doing too much.***
3. *I am allowing myself to do too much because I love what I do.*
4. *I allow myself to do what I love because it makes me happy/fulfilled.*

I have gone far enough.

B) The 5 Whys
1. Why is it important for me to be happy and fulfilled?

It is important to me to be happy and fulfilled because when I am happy I can do things more easily.

Take the answer from above and ask the question again.
2. Why is it important for me to do things more easily?
It is important to me to do things more easily easier because then I can live a life I can love.
3. Why is it important for me to live a life I can love?
It is important for me to live a life I can love because then I can enjoy my life.
With this questioning I have gone far enough.

C) **Flick the switch**
Then I would ask, "What do I need to do to be able to live a life I can love and enjoy?"
And then take ACTION!

11. The power of intention

Positive Energy – Focus – Belief – I Can – I Will

Intention is defined as "a thing intended; an aim or a plan." The power of intention is the power of a focused mind, a positive energy that comes from within.

If we live with an expectation of a particular result and it does not turn out the way we expect it to, then our energy levels dive and this can lead us into a downward spiral of negativity.

But to plan and hold an intent (positive energy and focus) will lead us to success at whatever level. Experiencing the feeling of balance and achievement we can reach during the day.

We need to ask ourselves these three questions:

1. What is my intention – what do I want, value or desire today, tomorrow, next week, next year?
2. Get clear on my why – what is my why?
3. What can I do today to continue to achieve my intention?

THE TOOLBOX

Here are some examples of intent to inspire you to write your own.

> *"Our intention creates our reality."*
> **Wayne Dyer**

Life
I intend to live the most beautiful life possible, while experiencing, fun, love, creativity, connectedness, peace, safety, elegance and ease.

Daily
I intend to experience today in a positive way, with ease, confidence and good communication.

Relationships
I intend to enjoy my relationship with my partner, allowing it to unfold and deepen with elegance and ease.

Physical
I intend that my physical body is one hundred percent vital healthy and filled with energy by being focused on a balanced lifestyle: my diet, my exercise, my sleep, fun and connection.

Knowing what you want and why serves as your foundation. Visualising your intention actually happening sets up a pathway of intent and focus for you to follow to success. Maybe you could use a visualisation exercise to imprint it into your day, week or year.
Enjoy!

12. Asking the right questions

Connect, review, research and consolidate your learning – use the system. Be flexible and ask for help if you need it.

Now you've seen the signs of something being out of balance in your life, it's time to get clarity around why you feel the way you do through asking the right questions.

FOUNDATION
- Are you a VIP in your life?
- Are you in the driver's seat?
- Do you have clarity and focus about what you want? If not, why not?
- What do you want?
- Why do you want it?
- Why haven't you got it now?
- Do you feel supported? If not, why not?
- Do you live in a positive environment that supports you? If not, why not?
- Do you work in a positive environment that supports you? If not, why not?
- Do you have positive relationships around you that support you? If not, why not?
- Do you live a balanced lifestyle?
- Do you exercise regularly?
- What regular exercise have you been doing?
- Do you eat a balanced diet?
- Did you eat at least three nutritiously balanced meals today? If not, why not?
- Do you get enough sleep? If not, why not?
- Did you take time out for a break today? If not, why not?
- Did you breathe to relax today? If not, why not?
- Do you meditate to relax on a regular basis? If not, why not?
- Are you doing the things that you love to do?
- What fun things do you do on a regular basis?

What did you learn?
Make a list of challenges you have in this area.

GOALS/THE DESTINATION
- Where are you at this point in time?
- What's working?
- What's not working?

- Have you set a U CAN B SMART goal?
- Do you have a clear plan of action?
- Are you committed to the outcome, your success, your dreams? If not, why not?
- Is your why strong enough?
- Does your goal align with your values and what is important to you?
- Are you inspired, excited or stimulated to follow through on what you need to do to achieve your desired outcome? If not, why not?
- Are you committed and taking action by sticking to the habits/daily routines that support you and keep you on track?
- Have you broken up your goal into steps, creating a pathway to your desired outcome?
- Is a part of what you are doing aligned with your strengths, what you are naturally good at and what you love to do?
- Are you giving yourself space and time out to review, research, reset and become self-aware of what is and isn't working, and celebrating your achievements?
- Do you have the skills to reach your desired outcome?
- Do you know where to acquire the skills you need?

What did you learn?
Make a list of your challenges in this area.

MINDSET

- Are you maintaining a positive/growth mindset and have you made positive thinking a habit? If not, why not?
- Are you practicing an attitude of gratitude on a regular basis? If not, why not?
- Are you a good communicator? If not, why not?
- In which area of your Life Circle is communication a challenge?
- Do you find humour in bad situations?
- Do you turn failures/mistakes into lessons?
- Are you a positive thinker and do you have an emotional attitude that focuses on the bright side of life and expects positive results?

- Do you start each day with a positive affirmation or intention?
- Do you live at cause and take responsibility for your thoughts/behaviour around the choices you make every day?
- Do you flick the switch and reframe negative self-talk into positive self-talk?
- Are you mindful through focusing on the present? The past has gone and the future has not happened yet.
- Have you developed an attitude of gratitude by focusing on the good things, however small?
- Do you believe in yourself?
- Do you set boundaries to keep you safe?
- Do you let go of that which does not serve you?
- Are you aware of your negative self-talk?
- Do you love, nurture, accept and protect yourself?
- Do you take time out on a regular basis?
- Do you ask for help if you need it?
- Do you celebrate each achievement along the way?

What did you learn?
What is your biggest challenge around mindset?

ROADBLOCKS
- Do you have a challenge at the moment?
- What is working?
- What is not working?
- Are you dealing with an old roadblock/challenge, or is it something new?
- Has that challenge become a roadblock?
- If so, in which area of your Life Circle is the challenge?
- Do you notice how you react to what other people say and what triggers an uncomfortable feeling?
- Do you notice how many choices you make every day?
- Are you journalling on a regular basis? If not, why not?
- Are you asking the right questions, going within to find the answers?

- Are you meditating on a regular basis to go within and find the answers? If not, why not?
- What is triggering your roadblock right now? For example, did someone say something to stir up some negative emotions or negative self-talk?
- What specifically was the trigger?
- Do you react to the same trigger on a regular basis?
- Why were you allowing that trigger to bother you?
- When you are triggered, do you hang on to the feelings?
- If you were to know, why are you feeling this way and why are you allowing this feeling to bother you?
- Do you want to get to the root cause of your roadblock?
- Can you overcome this roadblock yourself?
- If so, what are you going to do?
- If not, do you need help and support?
- If so, what do you need help with?
- How important is the outcome to you?
- What are you focusing on?
- Is what you are focusing on now getting you any closer to where you want to be?

Check your behaviour.
- Have you used the word "try" today? If so, why?
- Have you used the excuse "I don't know" today? If so, why?
- Do you push the feelings away instead of dealing with them?
- Have you lost motivation or the inspiration to keep going?
- Are you depressed? If so, why?
- Are you stressed? If so, why?
- Are you anxious? If so, why?
- Are you overwhelmed? If so, why?
- Do you feel lost? If so, why?

What did you learn?

What actions do you need to do next?

ACTION

- Do you take the actions you need to, to be successful?
- What is stopping you from taking action?
- Are you able to recognise what is working?
- What is working?
- What is not working?
- Are you practicing an attitude of gratitude?
- Are you creating positive affirmations to support you?
- Do you find it a challenge to step out of your comfort zone?

What did you learn?

13. Lists (A - E)

The following lists have been put together to support you to find clarity around the exercises I have challenged you with.

A. Feelings list

Accepting/Open			
Calm	Fulfilled	Present	Serene
Centred	Patient	Relaxed	Trusting
Content	Peaceful		
Aliveness/Joy			
Amazed	Energised	Inspired	Refreshed
Awe	Engaged	Invigorated	Rejuvenated
Bliss	Enthusiastic	Lively	Renewed
Delighted	Excited	Passionate	Satisfied
Eager	Free	Playful	Thrilled
Ecstatic	Happy	Radiant	Vibrant
Enchanted			

THE TOOLBOX

Angry/Annoyed			
Agitated	Disgruntled	Grouchy	On edge
Aggravated	Disturbed	Hostile	Outraged
Bitter	Edgy	Impatient	Pissed
Contempt	Exasperated	Irate	Resentful
Cynical	Frustrated	Irritated	Upset
Disdain	Furious	Moody	Vindictive
Courageous/Powerful			
Adventurous	Confident	Free	Strong
Brave	Daring	Grounded	Worthy
Capable	Determined	Proud	Valiant
Connected/Loving			
Accepting	Compassion	Present	Warm
Affectionate	Empathy	Safe	Worthy
Caring	Fulfilled		
Curious			
Engaged	Fascinated	Intrigued	Stimulated
Exploring	Interested	Involved	
Despair/Sad			
Anguish	Forlorn	Lonely	Unhappy
Depressed	Gloomy	Longing	Upset
Despondent	Grief	Melancholy	Weary
Disappointed	Heartbroken	Sorrow	Yearning
Discouraged	Hopeless	Teary	
Disconnected/Numb			
Aloof	Empty	Listless	Shut down
Bored	Indifferent	Removed	Uneasy
Confused	Isolated	Resistant	Withdrawn
Distant	Lethargic		
Embarrassed/Shame			
Ashamed	Inhibited	Self-conscious	Weak
Humiliated	Mortified	Useless	Worthless

Fear

Afraid	Frightened	Panic	Terrified
Anxious	Hesitant	Paralysed	Worried
Apprehensive	Nervous	Scared	

Fragile

Helpless	Sensitive

Grateful

Appreciative	Fortunate	Lucky	Thankful
Blessed	Grace	Moved	Touched
Delighted	Humbled		

Guilt

Regret	Remorseful	Sorry	Trusting

Powerless

Impotent	Resigned	Victim
Incapable	Trapped	

Tender

Calm	Loving	Self-loving	Vulnerable
Caring	Reflective	Serene	Warm

Hopeful

Encouraged	Expectant	Optimistic

Stressed/Tense

Anxious	Edgy	Rattled	Tight
Burnout	Exhausted	Rejecting	Weary
Cranky	Frazzled	Restless	Worn out
Depleted	Overwhelm	Shaken	

Unsettled/Doubt

Apprehensive	Hesitant	Rejecting	Suspicious
Concerned	Inhibited	Reluctant	Ungrounded
Dissatisfied	Perplexed	Shocked	Unsure
Disturbed	Questioning	Sceptical	Worried
Grouchy			

THE TOOLBOX

B. Negative emotions list

List of Negative Emotional States (*I feel*..........).

When working on an issue, it is not always easy to give a name to how one feels. Having a list of emotions handy can help with pinpointing the emotions you may be feeling in a given situation. This helps you be more specific with your tapping in, and you get faster and better results.

Lost	Hurt	Sad	Disappointed
Worried	Powerless	Bored	Trapped
Unfulfilled	Uncomfortable	Anxious	Inferior
Shocked	Weak	Confused	Hate
Embarrassed	Guilty	Stupid	Miserable
Deprived	Exhausted	Lonely	Frustrated
Overwhelmed	Panicked	Jealous	Terrified
Stressed	Hopeless	Disgusted	Afraid
Angry	Ashamed	Nervous	

C. Fear list

Although it's a natural human emotion, fear can be so powerful. It can temporarily paralyse us if we let it. Instead, understand that it is a coping mechanism and understand that we can make a choice about how we react to fear.

We can realise what level of fear we are experiencing at any one point in time, and take the appropriate action to minimise our reaction to the trigger/cause. We need to allow ourselves to look at how we are coping and our reaction to what is happening or not happening, then take control and take appropriate action.

You could talk to a counsellor, learn something new, talk to a friend or that special person who is part of your support network, start a gratitude diary/practice and take time out to access clarity – whatever you do, it's a choice. You will feel so much stronger and courageous when you do.

Look out for the symptoms to help you understand where you are at. Don't let the fear take over.

Soft Fear	Mood State Fear	Intense Fear
Alert	Fearful	Terrorised
Hesitant	Afraid	Shocked
Pensive	Suspicious	Panicked
Watchful	Startled	Filled with dread
Cautious	Unnerved	Horrified
Curious	Anxious	Phobic
Leery	Nervous	Petrified
Uneasy	Worried	Paralysed
Doubtful	Alarmed	
Confused	Shaky	
Fidgety	Perturbed	
Apprehensive	Aversive	
Shy	Wary	
Concerned	Distrustful	
Disquieted	Rattled	
Timid	Unsettled	
Edgy	Jumpy	
Disconcerted		
Insecure		
Indecisive		
Disoriented		

D. Values list

VALUES

Values are the guiding principles that dictate our behaviour and help people understand the difference between right and wrong. They help you determine if you are on the right path to fulfilling your desires and dreams. They create a guide for you to follow and become an important part of your personal foundation that you can build on.

This list can be used to support you to find clarity around who you are, what you want and can support you to be who you want to be. The values elicitation tool is a tool of awareness.

When you go through the process of recognising the values that are most important to you in the area of your life that you are working on you

THE TOOLBOX

generally find clarity on why you do the things you do, and what you might need to change if things are not working out the way you expect them to or want them to.

VALUES ELICITATION TOOL

1. Go through the Values list and write down all of the ones that you connect with. Make a list.
2. Now choose the values that are important to you in the area you have chosen to work on and make a list.
3. Choose the top five.
4. Put them in order from most important to least important.
5. What did you learn?

    For example:

    Your business may not be making the profit you desire; if you do not have money and success in your business values list, then you know you have to change something.

    If your relationships are not working out for you, then you may not have communication or respect in your top five values in the area of relationships.
6. Have fun; remember it is just an exercise to find some clarity and become aware.

WHAT DID YOU LEARN?

If you want to know more about Values Elicitation, join my program. **Go to www.deanpublishing.com/gilliangorrie for details.**

A			
Authority	Activity	Altruism	Assertive
Autonomy	Adaptability	Ambition	Attentive
Acceptance	Adventure	Amusement	Authenticity
Accomplishment	Affection	Anticipation	Availability
Accountability	Affective	Appreciation	Awareness
Accuracy	Aggressive	Approachability	
Achievement	Alert	Approachable	

THE TOOLBOX

B			
Balance	Boldness	Bold	Brilliant
Beauty	Being the best	Brave	

C			
Compassion	Caring	Communication	Consistency
Challenge	Certainty	Compassion	Contentment
Citizenship	Challenge	Commitment	Control
Community	Change	Competence	Contribution
Competency	Charity	Competitive	Conviction
Contribution	Character	Completion	Cooperation
Creativity	Clean	Concentration	Coordination
Curiosity	Cheerful	Confidence	Courage
Calm	Collaboration	Confidentiality	Creativity
Candour	Clever	Connection	Credibility
Capable	Clear	Conformity	Curiosity
Careful	Comfort	Consciousness	

D			
Determination	Duty	Determination	Direct
Daring	Drive	Different	Discover
Decisive	Dedication	Dignity	Diversity
Down-to-earth	Dependability	Discipline	Dominance
To dream			

E			
Effective	Encouragement	Enthusiasm	Experience
Ecological	Endurance	Environment	Expertise
Elegance	Energy	Equality	Exploration
Education	Engagement	Ethical	Expressive
Efficiency	Enjoyment	Expectations	Explore
Empathy	Entertainment	Excellence	Extrovert
Empowerment	Entertaining	Excitement	

F			
Fairness	Family	Fluent	Fresh
Faith	Fearless	Focus	Friendly
Fame	Firm	Foresight	Friendship
Friendships	Fitness	Formal	Frugality
Fun	Flair	Freedom	Fun
Famous	Flexible		

THE TOOLBOX

G			
Growth	Generosity		
H			
Happiness	Harmony	Helpful	Humble
Honesty	Health	Hope	Hygiene
Humour			
I			
Influence	Improvement	Inquisitive	Inspiration
Inner harmony	Independence	Innovative	Intelligence
Imagination	Influence	Insight	Intuitive
Impartial	Individuality	Integrity	Inventive
Impact	Informal		
J			
Justice	Joy		
K			
Kindness	Knowledge		
L			
Leadership	Love	Listening	
Learning	Loyalty	Lively	
M			
Meaningful Work	Meaning	Modesty	Moderation
Maturity	Mindful	Motivation	Mystery
Mastery			
N			
Neatness			
O			
Openness	Optimism	Organisation	Originality
Obedience	Outrageous	Order	

P

Peace	Perfection	Popularity	Private
Pleasure	Perception	Positive	Proactive
Poise	Performance	Potential	Productive
Popularity	Persistence	Powerful	Professional
Partnership	Personal	Practical	Profitable
Passion	Perseverance	Prepared	Progress
Patience	Playfulness	Preservation	Punctuality
People	Poise	Pride	

Q

Quality

R

Recognition	Relationships	Respect	Realistic
Religion	Reflection	Resilience	Results
Relaxation	Reputation	Responsibility	Risk
Reliable	Recreation	Rational	Rules

S

Security	Satisfaction	Silliness	Structure
Self-respect	Secure	Simplicity	Strength
Service	Selfless	Sincerity	Success
Spirituality	Sensitivity	Skilfulness	Support
Stability	Serious	Smart	Surprise
Success	Service	Spirituality	Sustainability
Status	Sharing	Spontaneous	Sympathy
Sacrifice	Significance	Status	Synergy
Safe	Silence	Stability	

T

Trustworthiness	Teamwork	Timely	Training
Talent	Thoughtful	Tough	Trust
Thankful	Tolerance	Traditional	Truth
Thorough			

U

Understanding	Universal	Useful	Unity
Unique			

THE TOOLBOX

V			
Value	Victory	Virtue	Vitality
Variety	Vigour	Vision	

W			
Wealth	Watchful	Wilfulness	Wonder
Wisdom	Warmth	Winning	Welcoming

E. Body sensations list

Achy	Dull	Itchy	Releasing	Still
Airy	Electric	Jumpy	Rigid	Suffocated
Blocked	Empty	Knotted	Sensitive	Sweaty
Breathless	Expanded	Light	Settled	Tender
Bruised	Flowing	Loose	Shaky	Tense
Burning	Fluid	Nauseous	Shivery	Throbbing
Buzzy	Fluttery	Numb	Slow	Tight
Clammy	Frozen	Pain	Smooth	Tingling
Clenched	Full	Pounding	Soft	Trembly
Cold	Gentle	Prickly	Sore	Twitchy
Constricted	Hard	Pulsing	Spacey	Vibrating
Contained	Heavy	Queasy	Spacious	Warm
Contracted	Hollow	Radiating	Sparkly	Wobbly
Dizzy	Hot	Relaxed	Stiff	Wooden
Drained	Icy			

ABOUT THE AUTHOR

The Journey: Gillian grew up as an only child on an isolated dairy farm until she started school. She was bullied at school, lacked self-confidence and self-esteem, and was burdened by a deep desire to belong and please others. This unravelled into depression in her later years and resulted in a life of medication and unhappiness. That is, until one day, Gillian decided there must be more to life than antidepressants and misery. She made a decision that would ultimately transform her life.

The Decision: Gillian began a journey of self-development, starting with education, training, and research. Her insatiable curiosity about human potential soared and Gillian became equipped with a myriad of tools, passion, and life experiences that changed her life, and ultimately helped others transform theirs too.

The success: Gillian is a Stress Management Specialist, Master Practitioner in NLP, TimeLine Therapy and Hypnotherapy, a teacher, life coach, counsellor, artist, and author. Today, Gillian's life has become an amazing adventure, she remains driven to empower others with the right tools and strategies so they too can live their best life.

www.gilliangorrie.com

ACKNOWLEDGEMENTS

Firstly, while writing this book has been an amazing opportunity, the experience itself and my belief that anything is possible has been a challenge. Therefore, I acknowledge myself, my journey, my experience, my words, my learnings and finding the courage to put them into a book to send out into the world to help and support others.

I am also grateful for all those who supported me along the way and the fact that I never gave up.

I acknowledge my husband and family for their patience and understanding seeing me through the highs and lows of depression and my journey to change from depression to self-empowerment and happiness.

Thank you to my parents who always supported and encouraged me to follow my interests and find my passion.

To all my trainers and teachers for their knowledge and guidance to be the best I can be, who had faith in me and encouraged me to never give up. The team at Success and You, Matt Catling, Ben Harvey from Authentic Education, Tad and Adriana James and Conor Healy from The Tad James Company, Rachel Jayne Groover from The Art of Feminine Presence® – thank you all.

To Susan Dean and the Dream Team of editors and designers at Dean Publishing for making this book come to life and encouraging me throughout the process to get my teachings out into the world. I am now a published author, thank you!

And a special thank you goes to Imran Abul Kashem from Westend Photography who created the image of my dream for the cover of my book.

TESTIMONIALS

"I was suffering deep depression and anxiety due to many situations in my life and I was struggling to comprehend what was going on. Gillian had just completed some studies around life coaching, and thought she could help me. I attended around a dozen sessions and we were able to unlock the puzzle. I am now in a much clearer headspace without any depression or anxiety. I would recommend Gillian to anybody – she was simply wonderful. Great work Gillian, thanks for your caring and patient attitude."

– Bill, coaching client

"I was frustrated, disappointed and often angry. I had failed to achieve my goal to publish my book and it wasn't my fault – or so I thought. Gillian and her wonderful coaching techniques made me confront the real issues: why I felt like a failure and why finding a publisher was so important. Gillian and her tools helped me face my insecurities and reprogram my brain to dispel my limiting beliefs and see things clearly. Having eliminated limiting beliefs regarding my career and other areas in my life, I discovered the confidence I needed and gained control of my life. You see, I am worthy and I deserve to be happy and now I am. If you need help in any area of your life (personal, career, health, financial, spiritual, or anything else), I highly recommend Gillian."

– Amy, coaching client

SUGGESTED READING

Real Talk, Real Change: Life Strategies from a Psychologist and Life Coach – Dr Natasha Davidson

My Bucketlist Blueprint: The 12 Steps to #tickitB4Ukickit – Travis Bell

When the Body Says No: The Cost of Hidden Stress – Gabor Maté

Wear Your Warrior: The Evolution of the Stress-Free Super Mum – Katrina Wurm

Standing Tall from the Inside – Angie Clucas

Powerful and Feminine: How to Increase Your Magnetic Presence and Attract the Attention You Want – Rachael Jayne Groover

The Five Love Languages: How to Express Heartfelt Commitment to Your Mate – Gary Chapman

You Can Heal Your Life – Louise L. Hay

The Power Is Within You – Louise L. Hay

Empowering Women: Every Woman's Guide to Successful Living – Louise L. Hay

Ask and It Is Given: Learning to Manifest Your Desires – Esther and Jerry Hicks

Mindfulness for Life – Dr Stephen McKenzie and Dr Craig Hassed

The Art of Happiness: A Handbook for Living – The Dalai Lama XIV

Change Your Thoughts – Change Your Life: Living the Wisdom of the Tao – Dr Wayne W. Dyer

The Power of Intention: Learning to Co-create Your World Your Way – Dr Wayne W. Dyer

The Shift: Taking Your Life from Ambition to Meaning – Dr Wayne W. Dyer

The Healing Power of the Mind: Practical Techniques for Health and Empowerment – Rolf Alexander

Having It All: Achieving Your Life's Goals and Dreams – John Assaraf

Self Power: Spiritual Solutions to Life's Greatest Challenges – Deepak Chopra

The Breakthrough Experience: A New Perspective on Life – Dr John Demartini

Changing Habits, Changing Lives – Cyndi O'Meara

Meditation: Pure and Simple – Ian Gawler

21 Days to a Happier Family – Dr Justin Coulson

ENDNOTES

1. Published on Andrew's Facebook page and used with permission from the author.

2. Ware, B, 2012, *The Top Five Regrets of the Dying: A Life Transformed by the Dearly Departing*, Hay House Inc, Carlsbad.

3. Maslow, A 1954, *Motivation and Personality*, Harper & Row Publishers, New York.

4. Williamson, N 2018, '4 ways to grow your self-awareness', online article, *WellBeing Magazine*, North Ryde, viewed November 22, 2022, https://www.wellbeing.com.au/mind-spirit/mind/4-ways-to-grow-your-self-awareness.html.

5. Byrski, L 2014, *Food, Sex and Money*, Pan Australia, Sydney.

6. Spring, C 2019, *Unshame: Healing Trauma-Based Shame Through Psychotherapy*, Carolyn Spring Publishing, Peterborough.

7. Extract from speech by Pamela Edwards at the Women's Health Conference in Portland, Oregon. Edwards is a psychiatrist and director of the adult psychiatry clinic at Oregon Health Sciences University (OHSU).
Vogin, GD n.d., *Stress, Coping and Balance*, online article, WebMD, viewed November 22, 2022, https://www.webmd.com/balance/features/stress-coping-balance.

8. Henry, M 1853, *An Exposition of the Old and New Testament*, 3rd edn, Haswell, Barrington & Haswell, Philadelphia.

www.ingramcontent.com/pod-product-compliance
Lightning Source LLC
Chambersburg PA
CBHW070456120526
44590CB00013B/662